PRAISE FOR

THE LAZY PERSON'S GUIDE TO INVESTING

"Thoroughly enjoyable and straightforward . . . Packed with clear examples of how regular people can easily handle their own investments."

—*Publishers Weekly*

"A book I recommend to everyone . . . Farrell does the best job I've seen of presenting the material in an entertaining style that keeps the reader turning pages and, perhaps without realizing it, learning important investment principles and concepts."

—*Sun-Sentinel* (**FL**)

"An investing book for people who want their money to work hard for them, not the other way around. Farrell shows that the best investment strategies are often the easiest ones!"

—**John Nofsinger, author of** *Investment Madness* **and coauthor of** *Infectious Greed*

"Startling . . . It's among the best on the subject that I've read in recent years."

—**RetireEarlyHomePage.com**

more . . .

"In the field of personal finance writing, Paul Farrell is one of the good guys."

> —Ric Edelman, author of *Ordinary People, Extraordinary Wealth*

"A good introduction to a safe and easy approach to investing, that anyone can apply."

> —BookLoons.com

"Clear and straightforward."

> —*Library Journal*

"Enlightening, entertaining."

> —*Power HomeBiz Guides*

"I couldn't agree more with Farrell's message . . . Sound advice for any investor."

> —Charles B. Carlson, author of *Eight Steps to Seven Figures*

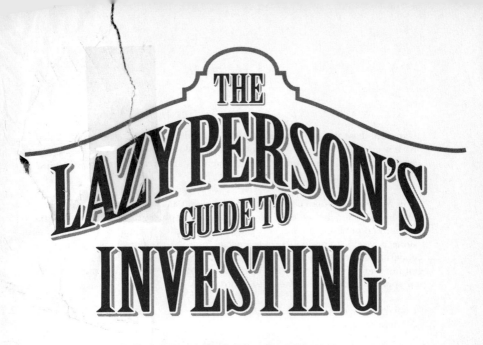

THE LAZY PERSON'S GUIDE TO INVESTING

A BOOK FOR PROCRASTINATORS, THE
FINANCIALLY CHALLENGED, AND EVERYONE WHO
WORRIES ABOUT DEALING WITH THEIR MONEY

PAUL B. FARRELL, J.D., PH.D.

COLUMNIST, CBS MARKETWATCH

WARNER
BUSINESS
BOOKS

NEW YORK   BOSTON

This publication is designed to provide competent and reliable information regarding the subject matter covered. However, it is sold with the understanding that the author and publisher are not engaged in rendering legal, financial, or other professional advice. Laws and practices often vary from state to state and if legal or other expert assistance is required, the services of a professional should be sought. The author and publisher specifically disclaim any liability that is incurred from the use or application of the contents of this book.

Warner Business Books
Warner Books

Time Warner Book Group
1271 Avenue of the Americas
New York, NY 10020
Visit our Web site at www.twbookmark.com.

The Warner Business Books logo is a trademark of Warner Books

Printed in the United States of America
Originally published in hardcover by Warner Books
First Trade Edition: April 2006
10 9 8 7 6 5 4 3 2 1

The Library of Congress has cataloged the hardcover edition as follows:
Farrell, Paul B.
    The lazy person's guide to investing : a book for procrastinators, the financially challenged, and everyone who worries about dealing with their money / Paul B. Farrell
        p. cm.
    Includes index.
    ISBN 0-446-53168-5
      1. Investments.   2. Finance, Personal.   I. Title.

HG4521.F3438 2004
332.6—dc21

                                                              2003053514

Book design by H. Roberts Design

ISBN-13: 978-0-446-69387-5 (pbk.)
ISBN-10: 0-446-69387-1 (pbk.)

To
Dorothy,
the love of my life.
The best is yet to come!

Acknowledgments

WHEN YOU LOVE WRITING AS MUCH AS I DO AND YOU HAVE A COU-
ple of guys like Gene Brissie, my literary agent, and Rick
Wolff, my editor at Warner Books, who believe in you and
encourage you as much as they do, you know deep in your
heart there's a God in heaven and a whole bunch of his angels
down here guiding every line you write. I can never thank you
two guys enough: "May the road rise to meet you. May the
wind be always at your back. May the sun shine warm upon
your face. May the rains fall gently upon your fields. And may
you always enjoy a life filled with love and grace and prosperity." All blessings to you and the incredible Warner staff, especially Penina Sacks and Dan Ambrosio, who helped make this
work soar.

Also, a warm round of thanks to each and every one of the
wonderfully creative men and women at CBS MarketWatch
who have been my family for many years, giving me endless

opportunities to stretch my wings as a journalist, especially: David Callaway, Thom Calandra, Chris Pummer, Alec Davis, Anne Stanley, Tom Bemis, Barb Kollmeyer, Deborah Adamson, Barbara Costanza, Jeanne Stewart, Craig Tolliver, Chuck Jaffe, Jonathan Burton, Paul Merriman, Paul Erdman, Marshall Loeb, Irwin Kellner, and, of course, Larry Kramer, whose vision and leadership turned our little on-line financial news service into a broad-based media powerhouse. Thanks for the memories!

And as always, a special thanks to five incredible mentors who encouraged me to take the road less traveled: Joseph Campbell, an extraordinary man who taught me about *The Hero of a Thousand Faces* and the *Power of Myth;* Carl G. Jung, the mystical grandfather who spoke to me across time in his *Memories, Dreams, Reflections;* Bill Wilson, who taught so many of us in The Program how to live the impossible dream one day at a time; my dear friend Calvin Holt, whose serendipity was so much more than a classy restaurant in Manhattan and a magical dance meditation class in Soho; and most of all, my wonderful wife, Dorothy Boyce, a brilliant psychotherapist, who is my best friend, soul mate, companion, confidante, teacher, and cheerleader—nothing would be possible without her love.

Contents

INTRODUCTION

AMERICA'S
LAZIEST PORTFOLIOS

For People Who Have More
Important Things to Do Today
Than Worry About Their
Investments

Investing should be dull. It shouldn't be exciting.

Investing should be more like

watching paint dry or watching grass grow.

If you want excitement, take $800 and go to

Las Vegas . . . it is not easy to

get rich in Las Vegas, at Churchill Downs,

or at the local Merrill Lynch office.

—Paul A. Samuelson,

Nobel economist

R elax. Sit back in your chair. Enjoy a cup of your favorite coffee and a bagel. Maybe tea and a muffin. And I hope you can occasionally glance out a window at some quiet trees, birds flying overhead. Get comfortable, and take a deep breath.

I'm going to tell everything you'll ever need to know about successful investing. Simple, no-hassle, low-stress, time-saving stuff about America's laziest portfolios.

Why "lazy"? I started calling them lazy because that seemed like the best way to describe the kind of low-maintenance portfolios most Main Street investors really want. It took me a while to get the simplicity of this message, and now I'd like to pass it along.

LAZY INVESTING IS A FAMILY AFFAIR!

This book came about in an interesting way. My wife—*a family therapist whose eyes usually glaze over when I start talking about investing*—convinced me to write it. Seriously, I remember showing her one of my columns on the "Laziest Portfolio Oscar Contest" a while back, a summary of three simple, successful, long-term winners.

I felt rather complimented when she actually read it. I was hoping the piece might at least amuse her—*I discovered long ago that investing, especially with mutual funds, is incredibly boring to most people, including my wife, so I try to write in an engaging, lighthearted style to keep people from falling asleep or quickly turning to the sports pages or comics.*

When she finished reading the article about lazy portfolios, she became uncharacteristically animated: "Now, that's a book! Anyone could read it! Simple, easy-to-read stuff anyone can understand—stuff that'll make their lives work better." That was all I needed—the spark! I had my first lazy investor! She was absolutely right. So that's been my goal: simple lazy portfolios that'll work for anyone and are easy to understand.

LAZY WINNERS FOR PEOPLE WITH MORE IMPORTANT THINGS TO DO

Most people really do want a portfolio that's like a lazy day in the sun, stuff to reduce anxiety, increase peace of mind, and help you feel confident about the future so you can live like a millionaire today, whether you have your million already or are slowly inching your way toward it.

You want a lazy portfolio that works "in the background," so to speak, while you go about your daily life doing what's really important to you—holding hands with someone you love, playing with your kids, cheering at a ball game, running on the beach, hiking the trails, working at your favorite hobby, finishing a project around the house, or going to a job that you enjoy, that even has you feeling like you're making the world a better place.

Let's face it, there really are so many more important things in life than worrying about your investments every day. So you need a lazy portfolio that works on autopilot—*so you can get on with living your daily life!*

YOU CAN "DO-IT-YOURSELF"—YOU DON'T NEED "THEM"

So first, forget everything you've ever read about how darn complicated investing is. About why you should leave all your investing up to some so-called experts, gurus, and pundits who are telling you that they know tons more than you know—in fact, far more than anybody on Main Street America.

Unfortunately, they don't. Wall Street's financial geniuses also lost huge sums during the recent bear market, a lot more than you. And just like you, they watched helplessly, unable to do much about the collapse. You'd never know it from their advertising hype, however, because they continue talking as if they know what they're doing—*even though they're faking it.*

HELP . . . TURN OFF THE HYPE MACHINE!

Wall Street's $15-billion-a-year "Hype Machine," as *BusinessWeek* calls it, is a relentless machine created to make you believe Wall Street has some kind of mystical pipeline to the Gods of Money, a secret connection you will never have—in other words, they know something about successful investing that you can never know. So you need them. You can't possibly do it yourself.

That message comes through all their newspaper ads. They blast it at you in every financial periodical. Columns.

Newsletters. Brokers' tips. Planners' recommendations. Financial calculators. A steady stream of how-to-get-rich-quick books. And the endless talking heads on cable news channels, loaded with Wall Street gurus pontificating, predicting, and pitching their message.

Somewhere in your gut all this hype is calculated to make you feel inadequate; to convince you they really do have some inside information from the Money Gods that you'll never grasp. They want you to feel embarrassed and insecure, questioning your abilities and judgment as an investor, even agreeing with them, afraid that maybe you can't go it alone.

CURE FOR THE INFORMATION OVERLOAD HEADACHE

On top of that I'll bet your library, your mailbox, and your brain are stuffed to the limit with fancy theories, diversification strategies, formulas, quotes, company profiles, model portfolios, calculators, spreadsheets, tips, tools, and links to all kinds of Web sites with tons of data on thousands of stocks, funds, and bonds—you name it, it's called information overload.

And I'll bet all the stuff is giving you one big fat headache, making you feel kinda dumb about investing, with a very cloudy view of the financial world, like you're lost in a huge coliseum with a hundred thousand other spectators and you can't see much of the game from the top bleachers.

GLOBAL TURMOIL ALSO CHURNING UP THE OL' ANXIETIES

Plus we both know there's an even bigger reason why you and I and everybody on Main Street America need to find a newer, easier, more relaxing way of investing—because on top of today's mountain of information about how to invest, we are now living in an ever-more-frightening world that's added a new layer of unpredictability, filled with real bad guys, evildoers, and lots of shady characters.

Think about it. You don't have to go back more than a few years to see where all the outside anxiety's coming from: Every day the media overwhelms us with news of catastrophes, nuclear threats, terrorism, wars, budget deficits, economic problems, corporate chicanery, and a confusing, roller-coaster stock market that goes triple digits up and down in a heartbeat. We've got a market nobody understands, least of all Wall Street's so-called experts.

Yes, today we live in a scary world that feeds into our doubts and fears and worries about today, tomorrow, and virtually everything else, and not just about how to play the markets successfully.

YOU CAN'T BEAT THE MARKET—DON'T EVEN TRY GUESSING

I know how you feel. I've been wrestling with all this insanity—*the hype, the information overload, the chaotic world*—for a long time, researching and writing about all aspects of investing in four previous books on investing and a thousand personal finance columns on CBS MarketWatch the past seven years. And before that, publishing a newsletter for market timers and day traders.

And I have to confess, I'm far more baffled today, because I see how much the people who should know, really don't. The best and the brightest are guessing, too—*and they're wrong more often than you and me.*

I mean it. I've logged well over two million words while researching, interviewing, and trying to figure out and explain where the market's headed, how it twists and turns, when to buy and sell, why and when and how much you can make. And the more I know, the more I know I just don't know, and neither does anyone else.

Yes, it can make you feel pretty dumb not to know, worse to admit it. But the truth is, nobody really knows—the market is totally unpredictable. And it loves to humble the mighty.

THE FUTURE IS RANDOM AND UNPREDICTABLE—STOP GUESSING

Even scarier, you see how much the experts don't know—that is, all the guys who sound like they do know when they don't. Seriously, when you look closely day after day, you discover that the so-called gurus of Wall Street and the fund industry who show up regularly in places like CNBC, Fox, and CNN, *Kiplinger's, Barron's,* and *The Journal,* are so consistently wrong so much of the time that you lose faith in all market predictions.

So finally I gave up on timing the market—all I know now is that the market truly is random and unpredictable. In fact, only a damn fool would try to outguess it. Flow with it, maybe. But you'll never beat it. At least the average Main Street investor won't. Wall Street never does.

LOOKING FOR A NEEDLE IN THE HAYSTACK

For example, Wharton economics professor Jeremy Siegel did a research project that best summarizes the impossibility of beating the market. Siegel researched *120 of the "biggest-move" days in market history since 1802*—moves both up and down.

Guess what he discovered? In the final analysis, Siegel could find specific reasons for the moves in only thirty of these 120 big-move days. What that means is: *The markets were totally irrational and unpredictable the other 75 percent of the time.* "There's no real reason for the market to move . . . and that is unsettling," he told *Forbes ASAP.*

Now add this into the equation: In another study, it turned out that over a ten-year period 88 percent of the stock market's returns were concentrated in just forty days. But those forty days weren't bunched together. Instead, they were randomly spread out over the ten years, averaging just four a year, and unpredictable.

So how good are you at market timing? Can you pick the best forty days out of twenty-five hundred possible trading days over a ten-year period? I stopped trying. And you should, too. It's one bet you're guaranteed to lose, because it's a crapshoot. The only solution is to be in the market all the time, and stop jumping in and out.

THE MORE YOU TRADE, THE LESS YOU EARN

Here's another bunch of interesting facts to chew on: In a study of 66,400 Merrill Lynch investors, professors Terry Odean and Brad Barber of the University of California at Davis discovered that the more passive buy'n'hold investors (2 percent annual turnover) actually beat the more active investors (258 percent annual turnover) by a fairly sizable margin, 18.5 to 11.4 percent over a six-year period.

Here's how the good professors summarized active trading: "The more you trade the less you earn." And their research turned up a few very simple reasons. Bad stock picking was one. But the biggest factor was the added transaction costs from all the buying and selling. Extra taxes was another big problem. Altogether more than a third of the returns were erased, most of it paid to brokers. Another vote for passive lazy investing.

LAZIEST WAY IS THE BEST WAY FOR 99% OF INVESTORS

So relax, take off your shoes, and sit back in a comfortable chair. Forget all the challenges and let all your troubles go—

because I'm going to show you the simplest and laziest ways to invest, so you can enjoy life and live like a millionaire.

The laziest portfolios are the future of investing, the cutting edge in financial technology, the way to go! They work like tranquilizers, calming the anxieties triggered by the Wall Street Hype Machine, information overload, unpredictable markets, and international chaos.

In this book is the best and only investment strategy you will ever need to cope with your investments. Moreover, you will be on the ground floor of a quiet revolution. How so? Because less than 5 percent of all American investors know this secret. You will be one of a unique and very special breed. And you can kiss Wall Street good-bye.

REPEAT AFTER ME—INVESTING IS VERY, VERY SIMPLE!

Seriously, investing is not really very complicated. Here's an affirmation to remind you. Write this down and tape it to your bathroom mirror and the refrigerator door: INVESTING IS VERY, VERY SIMPLE. YOU CAN DO IT ALL BY YOURSELF.

This is the only book you'll ever need. You'll get a simple overview of America's laziest do-it-yourself method of building a winning portfolio—a simple strategy that anyone can follow with little talent, little effort, and even with no interest at all in tracking your investments, your portfolio, or the markets.

In fact, it's so simple that once the portfolio's up and running, you can forget about it and go about making your dreams come true. The laziest portfolios are truly the best portfolios for procrastinators, the financially challenged, and everyone who worries about dealing with their money— because they work.

NO COMMISSIONS, LOWER TAXES, LOW-LOW EXPENSES

Not only can you avoid tinkering with your portfolio, you'll never again have to pay a sales commission in your life. Never? That's right, you heard me—you will never again pay a salesperson to sell you something you can buy all by yourself, at no cost. You can stop helping your broker make payments on her Mercedes.

Pocket the money you save from not paying commissions and watch your portfolio grow faster as you buy some of the more than two thousand no-load funds just waiting patiently for you to see the light.

And in addition to not paying any commissions, you'll save even more money thanks to lower expense ratios and lower capital gains taxes with most index funds in the laziest portfolios.

BEING AVERAGE BEATS THE ODDS—BUY INDEXES AND HOLD FOREVER

So now you're getting a handle on what I mean by "laziest" portfolios. They require no special talent and no effort, thanks to indexing. They'll make you more money with less hassle. And they run on autopilot once set up—because they fit Warren Buffett's prescription for a true buy'n'hold portfolio: Buy quality, and hold, and hold, and hold, forever!

Yes, I know, all this sounds too good to be true—but fortunately, it is true. Millions of investors have already found the secret of lazy portfolios. Nobel Prize winners use this simple method. This is where active managers secretly stash their own money. And this strategy is so darn easy to grasp, a sixth-grader could master it during recess.

SOLID 10% OVER LONG-TERM BULL–BEAR CYCLES

The great beauty of the laziest portfolios is that they work in both bear and bull markets. For example, you know that the stock market lost $8 trillion at the bottom of the recent bear market. Trillions of your dollars flushed down the drain in a few short years, wiping out much of the future.

And I'll bet you or your funds probably owned a few of those so-called rock-solid Dow 30 and S&P 500 blue-chip companies that lost 40 percent or more during the recent bear market. You may even have been one of the unlucky ones owning a few of those unfortunate dot.coms and tech funds, where 80 percent losses and bankruptcies were suddenly commonplace.

Compare that to the average annual returns of our laziest portfolios. They were in the 10 percent range the past ten years. More important, the laziest portfolios did remarkably well during the bearish years following the tech collapse.

In fact, during the bear market one of the laziest portfolios beat the Dow Jones Industrials by 17 percent, the S&P 500 by 25 percent, and the Nasdaq by an embarrassingly huge ratio of well over 50 percent—and the portfolio did it in a financial world where more than 80 percent of the so-called hotshot stock-picking fund managers regularly fail to beat their indexes.

THE REST OF THE BOOK—EVERYTHING YOU'LL EVER NEED TO KNOW ABOUT LAZY DO-IT-YOURSELF INVESTING

So again I invite you to sit back, relax, and enjoy the read, whether you're at home, at a coffee shop, on the beach, or jetting back from a business trip. Take a deep breath and find out how you, too, can easily build the laziest portfolio you'll ever need to retire a millionaire. Here's an overview:

1. **Three of the laziest contest winners.** Here are the results of our contest between America's three laziest portfolios, all of which you can track in the future on the Web. The voting was surprisingly close, with the Couch Potato Portfolio edging out the No-Brainer and the Coffeehouse Portfolios. More important, all three scored with long-term annual returns averaging 11 percent at that time, well over the market.

2. **Testing your six laziest strategies.** Here's a simple little summary of the six key strategies that make the laziest portfolios the success they are. More really simple stuff that any grade school kid can understand: Compounding. Autopilot savings. Diversification. Asset allocation. Being average, and swinging for singles. Buying quality and holding forever. And finally, a short tale about why the tortoise always beats the hare—while running in the race no more than six minutes a day.

3. **Six more of the top ten laziest portfolios.** Yes, there are more, straight out of the Motley Fools, Idiots, and Dummies books, one from Dilbert's great Weasel collection, plus lazy portfolios favored by Nobel laureates and the guys who run actively managed funds. All these variations on the theme serve to reinforce the awesome power of the lazy portfolio investment strategy for anybody, anywhere.

4. **Seven "outside the (Vanguard) box" solutions.** Vanguard funds are the big favorite among the lazy investors because of their low cost. But what do you do if, for example, you don't have access to Vanguard funds? After all, Vanguard manages less than 10 percent of all funds, and may not be available in your 401(k). Solution: You go searching for other no-load low-cost funds at some of America's other respected fund families. You can also build your portfolio with

exchange-traded funds (ETFs), corporate DRIP programs, folios, and one-fund hybrids. There's even a zero-fund option and one for "not-so-lazy" kids.

5. **When laziness fails and you're itchin' for action.** The hype is very enticing—and very dangerous. We all face this relentless temptation on a daily basis. The Wall Street Hype Machine is going to come at you full blast every single day, working hard to push some hot button in you, doing everything in its power to entice you into the action—into buying, selling, trading, and worrying. It acts like a drug on your brain. I'll show you how to cope.

6. **A lazy library for millionaires-in-training.** Finally, there's a library for America's laziest (and savviest) investors in the back of the book. In it you'll find suggestions for further reading, books I've found helpful over the years, some of the more practical books ever written about personal finance, investing, and behavioral economics, as well as some thought-provoking books on the ethics and metaphysics of money, many of which will be discussed throughout this book.

So sit back and relax in a comfortable chair, with a latte and muffin, and enjoy the book. I'll do my best to make the laziest portfolios as simple, informative, and entertaining as possible—because this is the single best way to invest for Americans who have a lot more important things to do today!

The Lazy Person's Guide to Investing

PART ONE

THE CONTEST WINNERS

America's
Three Laziest
Portfolios

I am really no different from any of you.
I may have more money than you,
but money doesn't make the difference. . . .
If there is any difference between you and me
it may simply be that I get up every day
and have a chance to
do what I love to do, every day.
If you learn anything from me,
this is the best advice I can give you.

—Warren Buffett

Over the years I kept running across three of America's laziest portfolios. What's so impressive about them is that these three consistently beat the market just sitting there doing nothing but making money for investors—the Couch Potato Portfolio, the Coffeehouse Portfolio, and the No-Brainer Portfolio. You can find all three on the Web like I did, so check them out for yourself.

The creators of these three portfolios are professionals with exceptional credentials and the highest integrity. One's a nationally known financial journalist. Another a money manager who earlier spent years as a Wall Street stockbroker. The third is a neurologist who now manages money for high-net-worth individuals and writes some of the world's most intelligent books on investing.

TOO GOOD—OR TOO GOOD TO BE TRUE?

What impresses me most is that all three portfolios are based on rock-solid, easy-to-understand asset allocations using no-load index funds. You don't have to suffer through any big theoretical explanations. Plus you don't have to waste a lot of time trading stocks, while enjoying low expenses and saving huge sums on commissions and taxes. They seem perfectly designed to deal with the inherent natural laziness of us investors.

When I first saw these portfolios, I was skeptical. They were so darn simple, they just seemed too good to be true. So naturally, like anybody with a lick of common sense, I thought: *You get what you pay for.*

At this point—if you're anybody with a lick of common sense—comes the nagging feeling: Should you go pay someone for a second opinion, a real "professional" opinion? Meanwhile, I was wondering: *What's the hook? There's gotta be a gimmick, something must be wrong here.*

AND THE WINNER IS . . . AMERICA'S THREE LAZIEST PORTFOLIOS!

So one day I noticed all those *USA Today* and CNN viewer polls and decided to ask my readers to vote for the "Laziest Portfolio Oscar." Then the big moment arrived. All those Main Street "Academy" members had cast their ballots in a great turnout. And we had a lucky winner of the Laziest Portfolio Oscar.

The big surprise to me was not the individual winner. More important was the huge margin readers gave the laziest portfolios *as a category*—Americans agreed overwhelmingly that they were the big winner by a huge 98 percent margin. Savvy investors obviously do not believe that investing is as complicated as Wall Street wants people to believe.

Only 2 percent of the votes were cast in favor of actively managed portfolios. To me that's obvious proof that the best strategy for American investors building a portfolio is being as lazy as possible. So let's take a close look at the three Laziest Portfolios in America.

Think like an amateur.
If you invest like an institution, you're doomed to
perform like one, which in most cases isn't very well.
If you're a surfer, a truck driver, a high school dropout,
or an eccentric retiree, then you've got an edge already.

—Peter Lynch, One Up on Wall Street

ONE

The Couch Potato Portfolio Is Microwavable

Scientific Evidence That Sloth Always Beats Greed

SCOTT BURNS IS A SYNDICATED FINANCIAL COLUMNIST WITH THE *Dallas Morning News*. His lighthearted, impish sense of humor makes him a big favorite among Texans, not to mention a growing audience throughout the country.

And it's easy to understand why he's so popular once you read any of Scott's columns or visit his Web site. His casual, keep-it-simple style takes the edge off the all-too-often serious world of finance, making readers smile and come back for more.

Scott launched the Couch Potato Portfolio back in 1991. You can track the glacial no-news-is-good-news progress of the portfolio on Burns's Web site, where he updates its performance once a year in feature columns that are as eagerly anticipated as Warren Buffett's annual barbecue in Omaha.

A BIG WINNER IN THE PRETRIAL RUN, BEFORE TAKING OFF

Before Scott introduced his portfolio in 1991, he back-checked the data from 1973 through 1991.

How did it perform? Absolutely super, with an incredible 10.29 percent average annual return for that eighteen-year period. Incredible because, as you recall, those numbers carry through the 1982 bear market and the crash of '87. Hot stuff, I'd say. Moreover, as Scott puts it, the Couch Potato Portfolio achieved these results with:

- No complicated accounts.
- No diligent reading of the financial press.
- No phone calls from brokers with "opportunities."
- No meetings with investment advisers demonstrating their constant supervision of accounts.
- Very simple tax returns.

So the Couch Potato is the perfect candidate for laziest portfolio. The Couch Potato Portfolio is so simple it's an embarrassment to Wall Street's army of brokers, analysts, and money managers who labor so long and so hard to build their supersophisticated portfolios of handpicked stocks that generate commissions for them.

THE BIG SECRET TO CREATING A COUCH POTATO PORTFOLIO

Here's the keep-it-simple trick to building your own Couch Potato Portfolio: You need only two funds in a 50-50 asset allocation. That mix will give you all the diversification you'll ever need for your natural life, through bear markets and bull markets. This is it:

1. **(50%) Vanguard 500 Index (VFINX).** The Vanguard 500 Index is a $75 billion no-load fund that tracks the Standard & Poor 500. The S&P 500 includes America's five hundred largest companies. The market capitalization of the index includes roughly 80 percent of all American companies. And the fund's expense ratio is only 0.18, substantially less than the average 1.30 expense ratio for large-cap funds.

2. **(50%) Vanguard Total Bond Market Index Fund (VBMFX).** This $15 billion bond fund matches the performance of the Lehman Brothers Aggregate Bond Index and has an expense ratio of just 0.22. Both the stock and the bond funds require a minimum investment of $3,000. So you need at least $6,000 to start your own Couch Potato Portfolio.

That's all? Yes, that's it. You heard me: All you need to do here is take $6,000, for example, and put $3,000 in the stock fund and the other $3,000 in the bond fund. Then grab the remote, lie down on the couch, enjoy your favorite programs, and forget about your portfolio till next year, when you'll need to do about ten minutes of rebalancing (that's right, just ten minutes a year!).

PERFECT GIFT FOR THE INVESTOR WHO HAS EVERYTHING

There's more: For the aggressive couch-bound investor who invariably believes you can always add some bells and whistles and improve on virtually anything, Scott also offers the "Sophisticated Couch Potato Portfolio."

How "sophisticated"? This much: Instead of a 50-50 split between stocks and bonds, the allocation is 75-25. But not to complicate things any more than necessary, you get to use the same two funds.

Put 75 percent of your money in the Vanguard 500 Index and 25 percent of the portfolio in the Vanguard Total Bond Index Fund. That means if you have $10,000 cash to start, you put $7,500 in the stock fund and $2,500 in the bond fund.

YES, IT REALLY IS THAT SIMPLE—AND THAT GOOD

You think it's too simple? Too good to be true? That there's gotta be a gimmick? Sorry folks, no tricks. It *is* that simple. Because it works. Here's how. In his 2001 annual update Scott reports:

1. **Short-term performance.** "The Traditional 50/50 Couch Potato lost only 1.80 percent compared to the 11.32 percent loss suffered by the average domestic equity fund." In other words, the Couch Potato Portfolio beat the stock market by about 10 percent during the very bearish 2001.
2. **Ten-year pretrial run.** Remember, Scott back-checked performance for the ten-year period prior to the fund's launch in 1991. Again, very credible results, with a 14.18 percent average annual return. And get this: That outperforms more than 60 percent of all funds with ten-year records. Superior performance with less risk, less volatility, and no tinkering.
3. **Recent performance.** Scott also points out that "over the last fifteen years the 50-50 Couch Potato provided an annualized compound return of 10.96%. The 75-25 Sophisticated Couch Potato provided a compound return of 12.30%." Meanwhile, the average balanced fund returned only 9.45 percent, and domestic equity funds returned 11.85 percent.

Once again, folks, dazzling proof positive that pure unadulterated laziness wins in both the short run and the long run.

REBALANCE JUST ONCE A YEAR . . . TAKES TEN MINUTES!

Okay, I know I said no tinkering. So I told a little white lie. But just a little one. Scott says you gotta get up off the couch and away from the tube for maybe ten minutes a year. Here's how the impish genius puts it:

> Try this: Once a year—like when you add new money—you take the total value of your investment and divide by two. That tells you how much you need in stocks. And in bonds. So you move some money, as necessary, from stocks to bonds. Or vice versa.

Actually, you may even be able to work it out so you tinker with only one fund. Simply add *new* money to the fund that's now underallocated—just enough to bring both back in line with the recommended 50-50 or 75-25 model asset allocations. Keep it real simple!

YES, YOU CAN MAKE A GOOD THING . . . MUCH BETTER

Scott then adds this amusing tidbit: "With telephone exchange privileges at most mutual fund families, you can do this in less time than it takes to go to the refrigerator. Indeed, as a timing exercise, I suggest you put a medium sized potato in your microwave: Your annual portfolio management will be done in less than the ten minutes it takes to cook the potato." Then back to the tube.

Before you forget it, make a note to check out Scott's Web site, especially his columns on Couch Potato Portfolios. He does have some interesting suggestions on possible refinements, including situations when a tax-free bond fund makes sense, exchange-traded funds, and how to eliminate all bond fees by buying Treasury securities direct rather than in a fund.

But as Scott tells us, none of those refinements is required in order to retire a millionaire. You don't need to complicate your life—just stick to the basic Couch Potato Portfolio with no stress, except your little ten-minute annual rebalancing efforts.

WALL STREET HYPE MACHINE—WHERE SILENCE IS GOLDEN

The Couch Potato Portfolio is definitely not going to win any applause from Wall Street's commissioned brokers, nor from America's day traders, nor even from fee-based professional financial advisers.

Yes, they'll put down this oversimplified no-stress portfolio strategy. But secretly, they all know it's virtually impossible for them to beat the Couch Potato Portfolio. Since none of them can make any money recommending no-load index funds, however, they'll stay noticeably silent, because they know in their hearts that indexing is the best and safest solution for most Americans.

ACCEPTANCE SPEECH—SLOTH BEATS GREED!

When I informed Scott that his Couch Potato Portfolios were getting the most votes in the laziest portfolio contest, Scott offered this brief acceptance speech: "Let's hope sloth becomes a universal virtue for investors."

If you want more of Scott's straight shooting and light-hearted insights into the Byzantine world of personal finance and investing, have the *Dallas Morning News* delivered to your doorstep along with your local paper. Well, at least your on-line doorstep, by linking to Scott's "It's Only Money" column and his rather extensive archive at DallasNews.com.

*Instead of focusing almost exclusively on our finances,
we should be thinking about the things that truly
make a difference in our later years: our health,
spiritual life, relationships with family and friends,
and having a plate full of interesting things to do.*

—Ralph Warner, Get a Life: You Don't Need a Million to Retire Well

TWO

The World-Famous Coffeehouse Portfolio
Latte, Lite Lyrics, and a Little Laziness

STARBUCKS IS AN AMERICAN CULTURAL INSTITUTION, LIKE IRISH pubs. It's more than a place to grab your daily caffeine fix; it's a place to relax and meet old friends—even virtual old friends like Bill Schultheis. It happens to me.

Back in late 1998, Bill, a former Salomon Smith Barney broker turned financial adviser, published *The Coffeehouse Investor,* an easy-to-read little book outlining the basics of successful investing. Bill narrows investing down to just three keep-it-simple principles. Follow these if you want to build a successful portfolio:

1. **Save.** Start early, save regularly, trust compounding to do the rest.
2. **Diversify.** Spread your risks across funds moving on different cycles.

3. Index. All you need to do is be average, and you'll come out a winner.

Almost too simple. When I run across Bill's book in my library today, I automatically think of Starbucks and Schultheis. And when I stop by the local Starbucks, I can actually feel Bill's presence, although he's way up in Seattle and I'm on the Central Coast of California.

GOOD NEWS FROM A SEATTLE COFFEEHOUSE

The Coffeehouse Investor's Web site is loaded with information about Bill's simple philosophy of investing. He's got some great stuff there, in a relaxed virtual coffeehouse atmosphere. And if you're really lazy or can't make it to the coffeehouse, he'll send you a copy of his newsletter.

When his latest e-mail newsletter arrived, it wasn't just Starbucks, coffee, and camaraderie that came to mind, it was Bill's steady message: once again, proof positive that a passive indexed portfolio was the best strategy for the average Main Street investor, especially in a tough bear market.

ENJOY THIS TASTY LAZY PORTFOLIO

Bill's simple Coffeehouse Portfolio "consists of a 60/40 stock-bond split, with the bond portion reflecting an intermediate-term corporate bond index and the equity portion equally divided between the S&P 500 Index, Large Value Index, Small Index, Small-Cap Value Index, MSCI EAFE International Index, and a REIT index."

When Bill sent his fans an e-mail update of the Coffeehouse Portfolio for the bear-market years of 2000 and 2001, it made us drool. Remember, the Dow was down about 12 percent; the S&P 500, more than 20 percent. And the Nasdaq was down well over 50 percent. Plus dot.coms were going bankrupt by the hundreds. And yet—the Coffeehouse Portfolio was in positive territory, averaging 5.3 percent for the two years.

Here are the individual performance numbers for the seven Vanguard index funds in Bill's Coffeehouse Portfolio. In this example he allocated $10,000 to each of the six stock funds, for a total of $60,000. And $40,000 in the bond fund. Returns are for the two years through 2000 and 2001.

AMERICA'S FUNNIEST (AND BEST) PORTFOLIO OF 1999

The boldness of Bill's portfolio is worth emphasizing. Remember the insanity of the 1990s with all the dot.coms? When the Coffeehouse Portfolio was created in 1999, the online and tech mania was at a peak.

Back then Bill's diversified asset allocations were like ordering a mild decaf in a culture addicted to hot triple espressos. Back then many investors were chasing tech funds returning 100 percent or more a year and laughing at the old-fashioned conservatism of this Coffeehouse Portfolio. Yet Bill was a visionary.

Here are the seven Vanguard index funds in the Coffeehouse Portfolio, along with their performances during the bear market of 2000 and 2001 when most other portfolios were in negative territory:

1. **Vanguard S&P 500 (VFINX).** This index fund tracks Standard & Poor's five hundred largest companies. It was down 9.0 percent in 2000 and 12.0 percent in 2001. So the original $10,000 investment was worth $8,001 by the end of 2001.
2. **Vanguard Large-Cap Value (VIVAX).** If you had invested

$10,000 in the Vanguard large-cap value fund in January 2000, it would have dropped a bit to $9,337 by the end of 2001. Back then, the fund matched the returns of the S&P/BARRA Value Index, which includes S&P 500 companies with lower-than-average price-to-book-value ratios.

3. **Vanguard Small-Cap Index (NAESX).** Your 10 percent allocation in the small-cap growth index fund would have just about broken even. So your investment here would have been worth $10,035 after two years. At the time, this fund tracked the Russell 2000 small-cap index.

4. **Vanguard Small-Cap Value (VISVX).** This index was a great performer and a big favorite with investors during the bear years. And no wonder: $10,000 invested back in January 2000 (just before the market collapsed, when small-caps were not hot) would have grown to $13,839 by the end of 2001. At the time, the fund mimicked the S&P Small-Cap 600 Index, which includes companies with below-average price/earnings and price/book ratios.

5. **Vanguard International (VGTSX).** This was the biggest drop in the portfolio. Your $10,000 allocation in an MCSI-EAFE international index fund would have dropped to $6,739. Who would have guessed in 1999? Back then, just before the 2000 crash, many of the international stock indexes were returning more than 30 percent annually. Again, proving how tough it is to predict the future performance of any one category.

6. **Vanguard REIT Stock Index (VGSIX).** The REIT index was red-hot during the bear years of 2000 and 2001. In fact, your $10,000 here would have grown to $14,643 in two short years while the bear was ripping apart huge chunks of the rest of the stock market. The fund invests 98 percent of your money in the stocks included in the Morgan Stanley REIT Index.

7. **Vanguard Total Bond Market Index (VBMFX).** A bond index
fund offers safety, capital preservation, and a nice
return in a bear market. Laughably low returns in the
late 1990s, but really huggable during the bear
market, as your $40,000 grew to $48,312. Fund
holdings include government, corporate, mortgage-
backed, and international dollar-denominated bonds
with maturities of one year or more.

When comparing the Coffeehouse Portfolio to the other laziest portfolios, readers especially liked the fact that the REIT
index fund was included (absent in the Couch Potato). It was
the portfolio's top performer, even beating the small-cap
index that did so well during the bear market.

Also keep in mind that an older retiree might increase the
bond funds portion above 40 percent relative to the total of
the six stock funds. And a younger investor might want less
than 40 percent.

COFFEEHOUSE—A BIG WINNER IN A BEAR MARKET

Once again, remember that Bill developed this portfolio's
allocations back in 1999 when the go-go era of triple-digit
dot.coms was at its insane peak. So you know the portfolio was
laughed out of the coffeehouse back then—or more likely,
investors just snickered and ignored it. Nevertheless, the Coffeehouse Portfolio would have been one of the best possible
moves any investor could have made at the time.

What's the bottom line here? Simply this: If you had
invested $100,000 in the Coffeehouse Portfolio's index funds
beginning in 2000, your money would have grown to $110,905
at the end of 2001.

That's an average of 5.3 percent annually for those two
years. And that was in a bear market—when the Dow Industrials

were down more than 12 percent, the S&P 500 was down more than 20 percent, and the Nasdaq was down more than 50 percent.

WORKS EVEN BETTER IF YOU DON'T REBALANCE!

After I reviewed the Coffeehouse Portfolio's 2000–2001 results, several readers said they were doing great with it in the bear market, but wanted to know how it performed over the long haul. So I scooted back to Bill's virtual coffeehouse and asked for long-term data.

And back came some detailed Excel spreadsheets at cyberspeed. Bill used the actual indexes for some of the longer-term data where funds had less than a ten-year track record. The results are also posted on his Web site.

As it turns out, with annual rebalancing, a $100,000 investment allocated in the Coffeehouse Portfolio back in 1991 would have grown to $328,590 by year-end 2001. That's an average return of 11.42 percent annually, easily beating the market.

But get this: The Coffeehouse Portfolio's annual average was even higher—11.79 percent—if you were really, really lazy and *didn't rebalance at all!*

That's right: With annual rebalancing, the seven-fund Coffeehouse Portfolio averaged 11.42 percent annual return. And if you're one of the laziest investors in America, and never rebalanced your portfolio for the entire decade, your returns would have actually increased to 11.79 percent.

COFFEEHOUSE SERENITY BEATS WALL STREET'S ANXIETY

What a record: Just by hanging around Starbucks, sitting quietly, drinking coffee, and reading the sports pages (instead of frantically watching the market on CNBC), your Coffeehouse Passive Index Portfolio would have beaten the Dow by 17 percent, the S&P 500 by 25 percent, and the Nasdaq by a humongous margin—which has gotta be one big egg-on-your-face embarrassment to Wall Street's hyperactive stock-picking gurus.

Moreover, this neat little index portfolio not only beat the S&P 500 but also beat the average U.S. hedge fund that the Wall Street hotshot stock-picking firms were offering to their high-net-worth clients.

That's right: In early 2002 *BusinessWeek* reported that: "Hedge funds have beaten the major market indices during the bear market, though they barely edged out Treasuries. The average U.S. hedge fund earned 5.6 percent last year, not including fees." And after deducting their fees, hedge funds would be lucky to beat Treasuries, the Coffeehouse Portfolio, or any of the other of the laziest portfolios.

Amusing, isn't it? The hotshot Wall Street giants aim their big sales pitches at the super-rich, touting their super stock-picking prowess—and it turns out that you can do just as well or better making passive investments in one of these laziest index portfolios.

WINNING STRATEGY: LATTE AND BLISSFUL IGNORANCE

Whenever I have to leave Starbucks, I imagine my friend Bill Schultheis still sitting there, sipping his latte—he waves, asking rhetorically about the first couple of years of the bear market:

"Does the Coffeehouse philosophy work? While most major indices (and maybe a few of your neighbors' portfolios) are trying to recover from double-digit losses of the past two years, this simple portfolio has captured double-digit gains, generating a total return of 11 percent (5.3 percent annualized)."

Then Bill pauses and adds with a wry smile: "Not bad for someone who completely ignored the financial markets the past two years amid the worst investing period in the last quarter century." Eat your heart out, Wall Street!

Most of us don't need professional planners.
We don't even need a full-scale plan.
Conservative money management isn't hard.
To be your own guru, you need only a list of objectives,
a few simple financial products,
realistic investment expectations,
a time frame that gives your investments time to work out,
and a well-tempered humbug detector,
to keep you from falling for rascally sales pitches.

—Jane Bryant Quinn, Making the Most of Your Money

THREE

Dr. Bernstein's No-Brainer Portfolio

And No Neurosurgery Is Required to Win

THE NO-BRAINER PORTFOLIO IS THE BRAINCHILD OF WILLIAM Bernstein, financial adviser to high-net-worth individuals, *SmartMoney* columnist, and author of two highly regarded books, *The Intelligent Asset Allocator* and *The Four Pillars of Investing*—in short, a well-regarded Renaissance man.

The *No-Brainer* moniker seems perfect for this winning portfolio because Bill is also a physician and practicing neurologist with a unique perspective on the workings of the human brain. He lives far away from Wall Street—in North Bend, Oregon—and can be reached through his popular EfficientFrontier.com Web site.

THE BASIC NO-BRAINER PORTFOLIO—JUST FOUR FUNDS

When it comes to investing, Dr. Bill is actually a rather uncomplicated, no-nonsense kind of strategist.

Listen to his description of a No-Brainer Portfolio: "If over the past ten or twenty years you had simply held a portfolio consisting of one quarter each of indexes of large U.S. stocks, small U.S. stocks, foreign stocks and high quality U.S. bonds, you would have beaten over 90 percent of all professional money managers and with considerably less risk."

You heard the doctor's prescription. It's very simple, folks—split your money equally among just four funds and you're way ahead in the race to a million-dollar retirement, ahead of 90 percent of the stock-picking geniuses on Wall Street.

Bernstein's Basic No-Brainer Portfolio averaged 10.8 percent over the past ten years, from 1991 to 2001, and again, while he works independently of the other two laziest portfolios, he also built his portfolio with Vanguard funds because they are no-loads with low expense ratios, well diversified across thousands of stocks and fixed-income securities:

1. **Vanguard 500 Index (VFINX).** This $75 billion S&P 500 index fund has a portfolio of five hundred stocks, and while it lost during the bear years, it is averaging 13.2 percent annually over ten years.
2. **Vanguard Small-Cap Index (NAESX).** This $3.4 billion fund tracked the Russell 2000 small-cap index at the time, with a portfolio of 1,892 stocks, averaging 11.5 percent at the time of this report.
3. **Vanguard European Stock Index (VEURX).** This $4.2 billion fund tracks the Morgan Stanley Europe Index and includes a portfolio holding 535 stocks. It has averaged 10.4 percent over ten years.
4. **Vanguard Total Bond Market Index (VBMFX).** And here's this

$15 billion giant again, with almost fourteen hundred fixed-income securities in its portfolio and averaging 7.3 percent annually over the past decade. Keep in mind that investors with a short-term horizon seeking more safety and less risk might increase their fixed-income allocation.

Get it? You don't need the sophisticated skills of a Wall Street analyst or a neurologist to build a lazy No-Brainer Portfolio. You sure don't need to make a trip to Dr. Bill's offices in Oregon. You can get the doctor's advice without even consulting EfficientFrontier.com. You've got it right here. It's that simple. Advice any sixth-grader can easily grasp—and you can, too.

THE ODD COUPLE—ROCKET-SCIENCE MATHEMATICS VERSUS LAZINESS

When my readers voted on the Laziest Portfolio Oscar, the one thing many commented on was the similarity among the three portfolios. As a result, the tie-breaker for them boiled down to the portfolio with the highest long-term returns. So while the No-Brainer Portfolio beats the historic market average, slightly higher returns gave the Couch Potato and the Coffeehouse Portfolios a slight edge over the No-Brainer.

The No-Brainer was also handicapped in the eyes of some truly lazy investors. Why? Because it relies quite a bit on mathematics. As I said, Bernstein is a brilliant analyst and loves numbers, but still, I think all his math is quite easy to follow in his *Four Pillars of Investing* book.

Trouble is, math, even a hint of it, confuses the laziest investors. Any extra thinking is taxing on the brain, causing serious headaches. And avoided at all costs. So I have to confess, even light use of mathematics is considered by many investors to be a contradiction in terms as part of one of the laziest portfolios.

But I definitely understand the problem. Some investors are natural-born couch potatoes who instinctively know all they need to know—namely, that their portfolio is working just fine, automatically, without a lot of additional numbers and theories. They'd rather head for the coffeehouse and ignore all strategies that require sophisticated math.

DO LAZIER FUNDS MAKE YOU AN INVESTING COWARD?

American investors have a hard time believing anything this simple can work. As a result, many insist on seeing what else is available, even if just to confirm that an unsophisticated two-fund or four-fund portfolio is enough. So here's one version of Bernstein's No-Brainer "Coward's Portfolio"—one he uses, with modifications, for high-net-worth clients in his money management business.

You'll notice that several of the same funds in this No-Brainer Coward's Portfolio are also featured in the seven-fund Coffeehouse Portfolio. They deserve to be repeated, because for one thing, most people learn by repetition—especially the best, the brightest, *and the laziest!*

And second, you can see with your own eyes that some of America's leading experts, each with a quite different background, are coming up with some very similar conclusions.

THE NO-BRAINER COWARD'S PORTFOLIO ALTERNATIVE

So here's the Coward's Portfolio. Notice that he, too, used all Vanguard index funds in developing the portfolio, which I first saw outlined in a December 2000 *SmartMoney* magazine article about Dr. Bernstein's work. Recently he told me that these asset allocations remain his core portfolio today:

1. (40%) Short-Term Corporate Bond Index (VFSTX).
2. (15%) Total Stock Market (VTSMX).
3. (10%) Small-Cap Value (VISVX).
4. (10%) Large-Cap Value Index (VIVAX).
5. (5%) European Stock Index (VEURX).
6. (5%) Pacific Stock Index (VPACX).
7. (5%) REIT Stock Index (VGSIX).
8. (5%) Small-Cap Index (NAESX).
9. (5%) Emerging Markets Index (VEIEX).

Actually, Dr. Bernstein's portfolio really isn't as different as it might at first appear. Yes, he substitutes a short-term corporate bond index for the total market. Short-term would be a more conservative choice.

Also, while the Coffeehouse Portfolio uses a broad international stock index, Bernstein splits his allocation into three parts: European, Pacific, and emerging markets. And he prefers the Total Stock Market Index to the S&P 500. But otherwise, there are many similarities with the Coffeehouse Portfolio.

In the final analysis, with the Sophisticated No-Brainer Portfolio reporting five-year returns at an annual average of 11 percent, it looks as if all three of our laziest contestants are pretty much in line. Bernstein has many more variations on his portfolios in his incredible book *The Four Pillars of Investing*, which Jack Bogle called his "candidate for the best investment book of 2002."

IN THE LONG RUN, DIVERSIFICATION ALWAYS WINS

The fact that the long-term returns of all three of the laziest portfolios were quite close is reinforced by some earlier studies of mine comparing the long-term returns of the nine major categories in the Morningstar database during 2001, covering more than fourteen thousand funds. This information illustrates why diversification is so critical in developing any portfolio, and why the laziest portfolios work.

If you compare the average annual returns of *all nine* of Morningstar's major equity categories over the past fifteen years, from October 1986 to October 2001, you'll see that the returns are in a very tight range: from 10.9 to 11.7 percent, despite the huge and unpredictable short-term variations. That includes all nine combinations of large-cap, mid-cap, and small-cap, in the various styles for each—growth, blend, and value.

Bottom line? The long-term performance of these nine mutual fund categories proves that the only rational strategy for the vast majority of America's ninety-four million mutual fund investors is a simple buy'n'hold strategy that diversifies portfolio assets across multiple categories of funds.

There is no such thing as stock picking skill. It's human nature to find patterns where there are none and to find skill where luck is a more likely explanation (particularly if you're the lucky manager). . . . We are looking at the proverbial bunch of chimpanzees throwing darts at the stock page. Their "success" or "failure" is a purely random affair. . . . Ninety-nine percent of fund managers demonstrate no evidence of skill whatsoever.

—William Bernstein, The Intelligent Asset Allocator

FOUR

A Challenger Jumps in Ring!
Scores on Points

"Never Buy a Load Fund, Always Buy No-Loads!"

THE TRUTH IS THAT THE VAST MAJORITY OF INVESTORS STILL FIND it impossible to believe that investing is as simple as these laziest portfolios. Consider the facts: Index funds account for only 5 percent of *all* funds. And Vanguard's fourteen million shareholders own 70 percent of all index mutual funds. In other words, index funds in general and Vanguard in particular are in the minority—yes, a powerful, vocal minority, but nevertheless a minority.

The other 95 percent of America's investors believe that "lazy investing" is for wimps who can't beat the market. That message is beamed at individual investors by Wall Street's relentless $15-billion-a-year "Hype Machine," as *BusinessWeek* calls it. Every single day the Machine bombards the little guy with thousands of ads on CNBC, in the *Wall Street Journal, Kiplinger's, Money* magazine, and in many other advertising outlets everywhere in the American media. It's a subtle and effective form of brainwashing.

And Wall Street's message is quite simple: "Wall Street has the secret to beating market averages, and you don't, so you need us." Unfortunately, too many Main Street investors are buying the hype. The truth is—*Wall Street can't beat the averages.* But thanks to their Hype Machine, Wall Street has multiple ways to manipulate the media and cover up the facts.

CHALLENGER: HOW MANY FUNDS? AND WHY PAY COMMISSIONS?

I'm reviewing this challenge here because it raises some important questions about how many funds are enough. But even more important, the challenge underscores a fundamental point that mutual fund guru Sheldon Jacobs has been pounding home for a long time: "Load funds, by whatever name, are more costly, and thus inferior to no-loads."

Why? Because sales commissions, hidden transaction costs, high turnover, higher operating expenses, and taxes combine to severely handicap Wall Street. As a result Wall Street, and in fact all actively managed funds in America, is forced to use the Hype Machine to distract investors from this harsh reality—*that load funds are inherently "inferior to no-loads."*

As a result, investors can and should totally avoid buying load funds. You're simply throwing away your money by paying brokers' commissions—and this is true whether you buy index funds or choose actively managed funds. Do a little research, get the facts, and you'll find that *there's always a better no-load fund. And you never have to buy a load fund, never, never . . . never!*

This issue came into my radar after I had run an update of Bernstein's No-Brainer Portfolio. I was marveling at the simple beauty—and profitability—of these lazy portfolios with just a few funds when suddenly, in shot a challenging e-mail . . . but I'm getting a little ahead of myself.

FOUR FUNDS ARE ENOUGH . . . TWELVE TOO MANY . . . 9,111 ABSURD

First, let me give you a bit of history, a little background. And I'd like to begin with the same ol' boring point I've been making ad nauseam: Keep it simple with one of the barebones laziest portfolios. I can point to any number of respected authorities who speak the same keep-it-simple language, including *Kiplinger's* magazine, Vanguard's Jack Bogle, and Princeton's Burton Malkiel, who wrote the classic *A Random Walk Down Wall Street*.

The whole idea of a simple four-fund portfolio first hit me like a left hook out of nowhere while reading a feature article, "9,111 Funds You'll Never Have to Own," in the *Kiplinger's 1997 Mutual Fund Annual*—certainly a catchy title that nobody could possibly pass up!

What chutzpah! I thought while staring at the four-fund indexed portfolio. *Now that portfolio's about as simple as you can get.* Here's how *Kiplinger's* described this incredibly keep-it-simple strategy:

> Organizing your investments into a coherent portfolio of funds is easier than you think. Actually, as we'll demonstrate, a sensible solution for many investors requires as few as three mutual funds. And the other 9,111 funds? You can soon forget they ever existed. . . .
>
> So just three funds—four if you want a bond fund to smooth out the volatility—are all you really need to include in a good long-term portfolio.

And that's the conclusion of one of the most reputable conservative voices in American finance, which has been advising investors since 1923. So for *Kiplinger's,* investing really is very simple.

A portfolio of three or four funds also makes a lot of sense from a practical point of view. For one thing, a new investor has to start somewhere—and buying three or four funds is an obvious first step. Moreover, research studies tell us that this is in fact what average investors have in their portfolios, although more seasoned investors usually have between six and eleven.

KIPLINGER'S KEEP-IT-SIMPLE VERSION OF THE LAZIEST PORTFOLIO

The *Kiplinger's* concept is simple: A portfolio of four index mutual funds gives you all the diversification you need. Yes, the magazine offers some more complicated alternatives, but when push comes to shove *Kiplinger's* point is quite clear—all you need is four funds, in these four asset classes:

1. **(25%) Large-Cap Stock Funds.** Either the Vanguard S&P 500 Index Fund or the Vanguard Total Stock Market Index Fund, which tracks the Wilshire 5000.
2. **(25%) Foreign Stock Funds.** In particular, the Vanguard European Stock Market Index, which tracks the MSCI European Stock Index, a market-cap weighted index of some 550 companies in fifteen European nations. Or the Vanguard Total International Stock Market Index.
3. **(25%) Small-Cap Stock Funds.** Either the Vanguard Small-Cap Index, which tracks the Russell 2000 small-cap index, or (in retrospect) possibly the Vanguard Small-Cap Value Index Fund, which originally tracked the S&P 600/BARRA Small-Cap Value Index.

4. **(25%) Domestic Bond Funds.** The Vanguard Total Bond Market Index Fund, which tracks the Lehman Brothers Aggregate Bond Index, or (for the more conservative) the Vanguard Short-Term Bond Index Fund, which tracks the Lehman Brothers 1–5 Year Government/Corporate Bond Index.

As time went on, I noticed—*and by now I'm sure you do, too*—a basic similarity between the Kiplinger's keep-it-simple portfolio and other simple portfolios, most notably William Bernstein's four-fund No-Brainer Portfolio.

FOUR-FUND INDEX PORTFOLIO CHALLENGED BY TEN-FUND VERSION

After I mentioned Kiplinger's portfolio along with Bernstein's four-fund No-Brainer Portfolio in one of my columns, I received that e-mail challenging a simple four-fund portfolio: "That's okay, but you can do a lot better," said money manager and financial adviser Paul Merriman, the publisher of FundAdvice.com. His point was simple—a portfolio of four funds isn't diversified enough. Let's see.

This was a particularly interesting challenge, since Merriman's award-winning Web site also has a section called "Explode Funds—The 100 Largest Load Funds and Their No-Load Alternatives." Explode Funds are the investor's perfect solution to avoiding brokers' commissions.

First, let's look at Merriman's rationale for challenging the four-fund portfolio and suggesting a ten-fund portfolio. Here he offers some important lessons for lazy investors: His research shows that owning ten asset classes increases your overall return and decreases your risks much better than does a four-fund portfolio.

NOW COMPARE A FOUR-FUND PORTFOLIO TO A TEN-FUNDER

Merriman's challenge got me thinking: The fact is, research studies do show that while you get 75 percent of your diversification with four funds, you gotta ask about the other 25 percent. The studies also indicate that having eight to ten funds is about right. After eleven, you've pretty much gotten all the diversification you're going to get. Any additional funds are probably duplications and overlaps, adding unnecessary costs and accounting headaches.

Second, Merriman says that if you look at longer-term statistics—twenty years or more—you'll understand why owning four asset classes doesn't provide enough diversification.

He does acknowledge that a simple four-fund strategy has its place: "The four-funds-is-enough argument is compelling for the many people who like to keep things simple and easy to understand." And it is definitely better than the ragtag collection of funds most investors put together with no real planning.

He adds, however, that "the very wide asset diversification available from ten funds is likely to give investors a significant extra edge over four funds"—sometimes with higher returns, other times with less volatility and less risk.

THE EXTRA EDGE OF A DIVERSIFIED TEN-FUND PORTFOLIO

Merriman offers the following statistical support for a ten-fund or ten-asset-class strategy, using the Dimensional Fund Advisors (DFA) database. Here are the ten categories, including the six he added to the basic four-fund portfolio above. Their twenty-year (1981–2000) average annual returns are included for eight classes (there were no twenty-year data for the international small-cap value and emerging market stocks).

20-Year Fund Performance

Asset Class	Returns
U.S. large-cap stocks	15.7%
U.S. large-cap value stocks	16.6%
U.S. small-cap stocks	13.1%
U.S. small-cap value stocks	17.6%
International large-cap stocks	13.7%
International large-cap value stocks	17.1%
International small-cap stocks	12.0%
International small-cap value stocks	N/A
Emerging market stocks	N/A
Long-term corporate bonds	11.4%

Next, he points out that the *Kiplinger's*/Bernstein four-fund portfolio had returns of a solid 13.5 percent over this same twenty-year period. And as a result, $10,000 invested in that portfolio would have appreciated to $125,315 over that period.

In contrast, the four omitted categories with twenty-year data had average returns of 15.8 percent. As a result, $10,000 invested in these four new categories would have been worth $188,819 over twenty years—considerably higher than the basic four-funds portfolio.

SURE, TEN FUNDS BEAT FOUR FUNDS OVER THE LONG HAUL— BUT CAN YOU WAIT?

Merriman is emphatic about investors using longer-term performance numbers in order to adequately diversify their portfolios: "The longer the period of past returns that you examine, the more valid they are, and the less likely they are to result from random market patterns."

Again he turns to annualized statistics from the DFA database, going back historically as far as possible—in some cases to 1926–1927, in others back to 1970–1975, as you'll see:

Long-Term Fund Performance

ASSET CLASS	RETURNS
U.S. large-cap stocks, 1926–2000	11.0%
U.S. large-cap value stocks, 1927–2000	12.9%
U.S. small-cap stocks, 1926–2000	12.7%
U.S. small-cap value stocks, 1927–2000	14.8%
International large-cap stocks, 1970–2000	14.6%
International value stocks, 1975–2000	18.7%
International small-cap stocks, 1970–2000	16.3%
Long-term corporate bonds, 1926–2000	5.7%

Here again, Merriman notes that the asset classes in the Bernstein/*Kiplinger's* four-fund portfolio averaged 11.0 percent using this longer-term data. In contrast, the asset classes added to create the ten-class portfolio averaged 15.7 percent. In short, the long-term statistics confirm that you can improve your returns and reduce your risks by using ten asset classes rather than four.

REBUTTAL: FOUR FUNDS WORK JUST FINE FOR THE LAZIEST INVESTORS

So I went back and asked Bernstein if he thought that a ten-asset-class portfolio *really* would be better than the basic four-fund portfolio, assuming DFA's long-term statistics. His answer was rather blunt: "It's an unanswerable question." Still, he added some observations.

Bernstein agrees with Merriman on core issues: A four-fund strategy "is reasonable if you don't want to put a lot of time and effort into your portfolio." He also acknowledges that a simple four-fund portfolio has "no value exposure, no exposure to REITs, no precious metals, and none of the other more exotic assets."

TAXES, TIME, AND PSYCHOLOGY FAVOR THE LAZIEST PORTFOLIOS

But while Bernstein agrees that "the odds favor a more complex portfolio and also favor value weighting," *many investors simply lack the time, motivation, or sophistication to handle a more complex portfolio.* And time and complexity can create problems—plus "the tax issues alone are staggering."

In fact, tax efficiency is probably the biggest planning issue for leading financial advisers such as Bernstein and Merriman. So Bernstein concludes that "the average investor may find a four-asset portfolio easier to implement and follow"— at least the do-it-yourself investor.

In short, basic human psychology beats hard statistics. That is, while a four-fund strategy may not have the best returns, it's good enough for most American investors—good enough for the classic laziest investor who, as Edelman says, is averaging no more than six minutes a day on investing and personal finance.

YES, IT'S PERSONAL—WHATEVER STRATEGY GIVES *YOU* THE EDGE

Two strategies emerge from these discussions. First, if you're an investor who wants to control your own destiny but are also a relative newcomer in the game, or you're someone who doesn't have much time or is relatively unsophisticated, or if you just aren't interested in following the market closely—then the basic four-fund portfolio is probably your best strategy.

But as your wealth increases, you may have no choice but

to become a street-smart do-it-yourself investor who knows how to diversify with ten funds (more if you and your spouse each have multiple IRAs, Roths, 401(k)s, Keoghs, and so forth). Alternatively, you can just hire a financial adviser like Merriman or Bernstein to do it for you.

But hey, these guys are giving you all the information right here—for free! So what's the big deal? Why not do it yourself—ten funds, Vanguard, Schwab, or Fidelity? They're really no tougher to pick than four. Get it? It's that simple!

EXPLODE FUNDS—THERE IS ALWAYS A BETTER NO-LOAD, *ALWAYS!*

Here's the big bonus for all you investors who still believe there's got to be a more complicated solution to investing . . . and still worry that maybe investing really is as simple as I'm telling you. Here's a chance to explore the no-load issue for yourself on-line.

Merriman's FundAdvice Web site has a huge library of investment information worth a close second look by investors who like the idea of doing it themselves and hate the idea of being hustled. Two of the features on FundAdvice that are most interesting for the do-it-yourselfer are the "Four No-Load Buy-and-Hold Portfolios" and the "Explode Funds."

Merriman's attitude is quite simple and refreshing in an industry known for high pressure. He tells investors: "I'll show you exactly how to do it yourself as an investor. And if you don't want to do it yourself, I'll do it for you." That's where the "Four No-Load Buy-and-Hold Portfolios" come in, each using Merriman's suggested ten-fund strategy.

TEST-RIDE THE EXPLODE FUNDS
They "Blow Up" the 100 Largest Load Funds!

Are load funds really a waste of money? Are commissions just payola to a salesman for selling you something you really don't need—because there's a better no-load out there? The answer is yes, they're out there. But how can you find the right no-load that'll beat the load fund alternative your broker's trying to sell you? Where are they?

Many experts tell us there are hundreds of no-loads outperforming the load funds. It's no contest, says Sheldon Jacobs, editor of *The No-Load Fund Investor* and America's number one advocate of no-loads: "Load funds, by whatever name, are more costly, and thus inferior to no-loads." Moreover, *Forbes, Fortune,* and other business magazines agree.

We know that the math works against the investor. Brokers make a sale and take their commission, usually up front and right off the top. So you invest $100, but you actually have only $95 invested. Add in higher operating costs and taxes, and you're in a handicapped race right from the starting gate. The truth is, commissions are a great deal—*for the broker!*

IS THERE ALWAYS A BETTER NO-LOAD? YES, WE TESTED THE SYSTEM

But are no-loads really superior? Better yet—can you find a better-performing no-load fund *every time?* I wasn't certain. So I first tested this theory back in 1999 using the Explode Funds list on Paul Merriman's FundAdvice Web site.

Explode Funds are no-load alternatives to the one hundred largest *load* funds. No statistics were provided, so I did my own research on the numbers. I tested the data on four of the recommended no-load funds that appeared most frequently on FundAdvice.com. The four funds were Vanguard Primecap and Vanguard 500 Index, along with American Century Ultra and American Century Equity Growth. These four were recommended as better alternatives to twenty-seven of the hundred largest load funds. Bottom line: On a three- and a five-year basis, all four no-loads beat all twenty-seven load funds they were matched against. The system works.

Today there are on-line screening tools available to help investors compare funds and search for better alternatives. But that early research convinced me that *for every load fund there is always a better no-load*. Here's another way to prove it yourself—the next time your broker tries to sell you a load fund, ask for a no-load alternative! The phone will go dead.

WHICH IS BEST—VANGUARD, BARCLAYS, OR DFA? IT DEPENDS!

You can pick and stick with just one fund family and work with its funds. Merriman favors Dimensional Fund Advisors (DFA), which you can invest in only through an adviser for a fee. And according to an analysis by *BusinessWeek* columnist Robert Barker, the annual cost of managing a $1 million portfolio looks like this:

Annual Cost of a Million-Dollar Portfolio

FUND FAMILY	COST
Barclays iShares ETFs	$2,219
Vanguard no-load indexes	$2,916
DFA Funds	$9,958

The two big differences are, of course, the $6,000 added advisory fee for the DFA portfolio, and the fact that this analysis assumes that an iShares investor is a buy'n'hold investor without incurring the extra costs of active trading, added taxes, and transaction fees.

DO IT YOURSELF . . . VERSUS HIRING AN ADVISER

So why pay the extra money? That's easy: If you're really lazy, and you don't have enough confidence in one of the simple lazy portfolios that *these same advisers are offering you for free(!),* or you simply do not want to manage or even look at your portfolio, then you should entrust your money to an adviser, who may or may not use DFA funds.

But "for those with less than $50,000," says Merriman, "and *for those who simply don't want to hire investment advisers,* there are three suggested do-it-yourself portfolios available at Fidelity, Schwab and Vanguard," which include a mix of indexed and actively managed funds.

By the way, if you want some more neat on-line information on index funds, no-loads, and advisers, check out IndexFunds.com and IFA.com when you're out there looking at FundAdvice.com.

100 NO-LOADS THAT BEAT AMERICA'S 100 LARGEST LOAD FUNDS

And finally, for renegade investors who absolutely insist on picking actively managed funds on their own, before you actually buy, check out FundAdvice's Explode Funds, a tool that compares each of the top hundred load funds with a comparable no-load (saving you big commissions!).

Remember, for every load fund, there is always an equal or better no-load fund—always, whether you're looking for an index fund or even for an actively managed fund. You should never have to buy a load fund again in your life. Never. Period.

FOUR NO-LOAD BUY'N'HOLD PORTFOLIOS

source: Merriman Capital Management

DFA No-Load Portfolio

EQUITY %

12.5	U.S. Large Company
12.5	U.S. Large Company Value
12.5	U.S Micro-Cap
12.5	U.S. Small-Cap Value
10.0	Large-Cap International
10.0	International Value
10.0	International Small Company
10.0	International Small-Cap Value
10.0	Emerging Markets

FIXED INCOME %

50.0	Global Fixed Income
50.0	2-year Global Fixed Income

Fidelity No-Load Portfolio

EQUITY %

12.5	Spartan 500 Index
12.5	Equity-Income
12.5	Small-Cap Stock
12.5	Low-Priced Stock
40.0	Spartan International Index
10.0	Emerging Markets

FIXED INCOME %

50.0	Short-Term Bond
50.0	Intermediate Bond

Schwab No-Load Portfolio

EQUITY %

12.5	Schwab 1000
12.5	PIMCO Value D
12.5	Schwab Small-Cap Index
12.5	Babson Shadow Stock
10.0	Schwab International Index
10.0	Dreyfus International Value
10.0	Amer. Century Intl. Opp.
10.0	Tocqueville International Value
10.0	Dreyfus Emerging Markets

FIXED INCOME %

50.0	PIMCO Short-Term D
25.0	Schwab Short-Term Bond Mkt.
25.0	PIMCO Foreign Bond D

Vanguard No-Load Portfolio

EQUITY %

12.5	500 Index
12.5	Value Index
12.5	Small-Cap Index
12.5	Small-Cap Value Index
13.3	Developed Markets Index
13.3	International Explorer Index
13.4	International Value
10.0	Emerging Mkt. Stock Index

FIXED INCOME %

100.0	Short-Term Corp.

These four portfolios were originally developed by Merriman as buy'n'hold portfolios. As it turns out, most are also no-loads. Vanguard is all no-load. Dreyfus loads are waived at Schwab. Fidelity's two load funds work as no-loads in a 401(k). DFA funds can be purchased and managed for you only by a financial adviser for an advisory fee.

PART TWO

RECESS FUN: TESTING THE SIX LAZIEST STRATEGIES

Here's How You'll Find
More Time for the
Important Things in Life

If there's 10,000 people looking at the stocks

and trying to pick winners, one in 10,000

is going to score, by chance alone, a great coup,

and that's all that's going on.

It's a game, it's a chance operation, and people

think they are doing something purposeful . . .

but they're really not.

—Merton Miller, Nobel economist

Anybody who tells you that he understands

the American economy ought to be

sent to teach modern dance.

—Peter Drucker

Remember those boring days in school as a kid, stuck all day with all those serious teachers, shlogging through boring subjects, and doing endless boring class assignments . . . just waiting for recess, so you could go out and play? So you can go out and do what's really, really important and meaningful in life, like have fun. Remember the good ol' days!

Well, it turns out that the biggest and best benefit from putting your money in one of the laziest portfolios today is pretty much the same as going out to recess when you were a kid.

Seriously, there are so many more important things in life than personal finance and investing . . . a whole lot more. Most of you want more time with your loved ones, family, spouse, children, Mom and Dad, best friends and buddies . . . relaxing, eating out, sports, theater, church, dancing, gardening, vacations . . . without having to spend time worrying about your portfolio.

You want a portfolio that's dull and boring and works without you having to sit through any schooling about what to buy, when to sell, how to mix and allocate, what to pay, and where the heck the market and the economy are going.

PREVIEW OF COMING ATTRACTIONS— THE WORLD'S SIX LAZIEST STRATEGIES

So just to show you why and how the laziest portfolios work to give you all the freedom you need to focus on the more important things in life, here's a little preview test of the six laziest strategies before you head off to recess . . . once you understand them, you can go about your life in peace and ignore all the gobbledygook you hear from Wall Street, the mutual fund companies, and those chatterbox cable news channels like CNBC, CNN, and Fox.

And just so you don't have to worry much about this little test, here's a brief summary of the six concepts:

1. **Market timing is for chumps and chimps.** No kidding, folks, a chimpanzee throwing darts was able to create a portfolio that beat the nineties bull market for a few years. The market is totally random, irrational, and unpredictable. And it loves humbling the mighty. Try to beat it and you'll lose money. That's why market timing is a fool's game, and why trading makes no sense for America's laziest investors. Imagine, a chimp making a monkey out of Wall Street! So can you.

2. **Be frugal, save, and avoid financial obesity.** Tools like starting early, autopilot saving plans, dollar-cost averaging, frugal living, and a bunch of others are all familiar to long-term buy'n'hold investors. And underneath every single one of them is the idea of frugality—living

below your means—which we're told is a common habit of every millionaire next door.

3. **The power of compounding is explosive.** Albert Einstein, the jolly genius and Man of the Century, says that compounding is the world's most powerful force. Regular savings, expanding explosively, interest building on top of itself is money power. Another professor called it the "eighth wonder of the world." As you'll see, that's how a twenty-year-old can become a multimillionaire on $100 a month.

4. **Diversification is the lost art of being average.** Don't be greedy, be average. It doesn't take a genius to figure out that if you put all your eggs in one basket, like Enron or some silly dot.bomb—*and it goes belly-up*—you'll end up with an uncooked omelet. Remember DRIP guru Chuck Carlson's clever way of saying it: "Swing for singles." Just being average wins.

5. **Buy (quality) and hold—and you'll never sell.** Good ol' Warren Buffett says his favorite holding period is "forever"! He says the best time to sell is "never"! Okay, so there are a few minor exceptions, but if you buy quality, you'll never want to sell. Besides, as Professor Odean's research proves, "the more you trade the less you earn." So buy with the idea that you will never sell.

6. **Tortoises consistently beat hares.** Think long term: And remember Ric Edelman's amazing revelation that millionaires spend less than three hours a month on personal finance. So when you're ready, step up to the starting line and race like a tortoise. Discover how America's slowest, laziest portfolios get you on the road to retirement as a truly enlightened millionaire.

And that's our little crib sheet on the six laziest strategies designed for a lazy investor in building a lazy portfolio. Even a sixth-grader can grasp this stuff. Have fun, and please don't spend too much time on this stuff. . . . Remember, there really are more important things in life: loved ones, family, Mom and Dad, friends, your best buddy, and living life to the max.

*A blindfolded monkey throwing darts at a newspaper's
financial pages could select a portfolio that would
do just as well as one carefully selected by the experts.*

—Burton Malkiel, A Random Walk Down Wall Street

FIVE

Strategy One: Zero Timing Wins
Dart-Throwing Chimp Makes Monkey of Wall Street

DID YOU EVER HEAR THE ONE ABOUT THE CHIMPANZEE WHO MADE
a monkey out of Wall Street's top stock pickers? Maybe it was
a gorilla, or an orangutan. Anyway, it was one of the world's
primates. And by God, this primate was beating Wall Street's
best money managers!

The idea apparently originated from some remarks made
in Burton Malkiel's classic, *A Random Walk Down Wall Street.*
Malkiel is a Princeton economist who at one time served as a
member of the Council of Economic Advisers and a governor
of Amex.

Malkiel popularized the idea that a monkey could beat Wall
Street's gurus, an idea that was successfully tested by no less
than the *Wall Street Journal,* and also Raven, a chimpanzee who
was a Hollywood star. Here's how Malkiel put it in his book:

A random walk is one in which future steps or directions cannot be predicted on the basis of past actions. When the term is applied to the stock market, it means that short-run changes in stock prices cannot be predicted. Investment advisory services, earnings predictions, and complicated chart patterns are useless. On Wall Street the term "random walk" is an obscenity. It is an epithet coined by the academic world and hurled insultingly at the professional soothsayers. Taken to its logical extreme, it means that a blindfolded monkey throwing darts at a newspaper's financial pages could select a portfolio that would do just as well as one carefully selected by the experts.

Well, that was about fifteen years ago, and all kidding aside, a chimpanzee did in fact make a monkey out of Wall Street, by beating its top money managers for years after.

That's right, I'm talking about the great years of the 1990s go-go bull market, when Internet funds and tech stocks with triple-digit returns were the daily buzz around the company watercooler and at the neighborhood's weekend barbecue—*a chimp was doing even better.* In fact, any chump could throw darts against a board back then and make money.

EVERYBODY'S A FINANCIAL GENIUS IN A BULL MARKET!

I was at CBS MarketWatch.com when it went public in January 1999, in the heat of the dot.com mania. I was an editor and also wrote a daily column. In fact, that month I actually wrote a dozen columns critical of the dot.com insanity, especially when Morningstar, Lipper, and the other fund trackers announced early in January that The Internet Fund was the top performer of *all* funds in America in 1998, with an extraordinary 258 percent return.

You no doubt remember, the market was a thrill a minute,

loaded with adrenaline, and dangerously explosive. In one of my columns I called funds investing in Internet dot.coms "oxymorons." In another I compared the trend to tulipmania and other historical stock market bubbles reviewed by Professor Malkiel. They were short-term, high-risk bets that had no place in a long-term investor's portfolio. But nobody listened.

HELP—WE NEED A TWELVE-STEP PROGRAM FOR MARKET ADDICTS

In another I proposed creating an "Internet Stock Addicts Anonymous." The crash was still a year away, but the insanity was obvious, and investors were acting like drunken monkeys on a roll. The market partied on amid chanting, "This time it's different."

That month readers sent e-mails calling me an out-of-touch idiot and an old-economy fool. Nobody cared. CBS MarketWatch went public at $17 on January 14, and went ballistic. The stock closed at $91 that day, and the company was worth more than a billion. Bull markets make everyone financial geniuses, and that weekend everyone had something to brag about at the neighborhood barbecue.

And despite my challenging the absurdity of the go-go stock market, dot.coms, technology, and Internet funds, about half a million investors read my columns that month, an all-time high.

The market was really nothing more than a wild bunch of primates all throwing darts at boards called Nasdaq, NYSE, Amex, and so on.

RANDOM STRATEGIES WORK IN THE WALL STREET JUNGLE

One of my columns focused on "Monkeydex," Wall Street's first index of publicly traded Internet and new-economy stocks. All the stocks on the index were *selected by a dart-throwing chimpanzee!* Seriously, a chimp throwing darts. Malkiel's dream come true. It had just been announced in an on-line publication called the *Internet Stock Review.*

The ten stocks in the Monkeydex were "selected" by Raven, a dart-throwing five-year-old chimpanzee. Already a well-known star of film and television, Raven had decided to make a career move and was competing head-on with America's five-star fund managers for the honors as best Internet stock picker of 1999.

Tongue in cheek, I even suggested that with the strong interest in Internet technologies and the new economy, one of the exchanges would probably pick up this new index for short-term option traders. Or alternatively, investors disappointed with their Wall Street broker's advice might encourage Raven to start his own mutual fund with the latest of his ten hot tech stocks.

CHIMP'S SECRET DART-THROWING TECHNIQUE REVEALED

The mathematically inclined among you are no doubt itching to know the chimp's secret methodology. How Raven did it, of course, is a very valuable lesson for all investors in America. Some say it's all in the wrist.

Actually his technique was a sophisticated form of technical analysis. This highly gifted chimp hit ten winners on a dartboard of 133 preselected Internet stocks. Of course, any investor in the world could probably produce similar results by first pasting the eleven known Internet indexes on a garage wall and throwing darts at them.

NO EXPERIENCE, NO HANDICAP, AND NO BRAINS NECESSARY

We were told that Raven's numerous misses were understandably excluded from the portfolio. Such an exclusion decision, of course, is consistent with other, more advanced methods of stock picking because, as we all know, portfolio managers rarely discuss their losers.

Both Roland Perry, editor of the *Internet Stock Review*, and David Allsberry, animal trainer with Boone's Animals for Hollywood, assisted in Raven's dart-throwing technique.

Perry noted that "Raven had no prior knowledge of how any particular Internet related companies have been performing." Nor did the chimp handicap the Wall Street experts. Instead, he competed with them on a level playing field, *and he still beat the pants off them!*

Perry also complimented his star stock picker, noting that Raven "has talents far beyond what we ever dreamed possible and we feel certain that his picks will surprise many on Wall Street. Only time will tell how his picks pan out, but this much we can say—he is storming right out of the gate with picks like CMGI, which shot way up $95 the first six trading days."

YES, THE CHIMP MADE A MONKEY OUT OF WALL STREET!

I decided to do an independent review of the performance of Raven's portfolio. And yes, he really did make a monkey out of the best Internet fund managers.

In fact, a couple of days before the end of 1999, I reported on CBS MarketWatch that the Monkeydex beat all the major high-tech/new-economy funds with a 365 percent return. There were nineteen funds with returns of between 179 and 323 percent, including then famous leaders like Monument Internet Fund, Amerindo Technology, Firsthand Technology

Innovators, Janus Global Technology, and Munder NetNet— *and the Monkeydex random dart-throwing index beat them all.*

Sadly, Raven was working for peanuts—sorry, I mean bananas. This highly skilled chimpanzee was grossly underpaid compared to the fund industry's leading money managers and Wall Street's high-priced gurus. Raven deserved a bonus from someone!

To our knowledge, no Wall Street investment banks or Silicon Valley venture capitalists ever floated a Monkeydex IPO. Nor did the Monkeydex become an index for options traders.

BACK ON THE BANANA BOAT TO HOLLYWOOD STARDOM

Monkeydex has since morphed into another inconspicuous on-line portal. Raven is nowhere in sight. CMGI is a penny stock after peaking around $165 in early 2000. CMGI's founder is no longer a billionaire. All told, two of the Monkeydex ten totally vanished, three trade for less than a buck, and one was trading in the $3 range as of late 2002.

To his everlasting credit, however, Raven's genius lives on! Amid the wreckage of the hundreds of other dot.com bankruptcies, seven of his stock picks are still alive and well. In fact, four were trading at between $17 and $41 when I last checked in late 2002, thirty months after the Nasdaq reached its peak and crashed.

Let's hope he's back enjoying a fruitful career in Hollywood or the jungles of Borneo rather than Wall Street. Apparently he embarrassed Wall Street so badly they quietly got rid of him.

FORGET ABOUT TIMING THE STOCK MARKET—
AUTOPILOT INVESTING IS A WINNING STRATEGY

What if you're a totally inept market timer and always put your money in at the worst time? Are you throwing away your money? What if you just put your money in every month, come hell or high water? Who wins most?

The Schwab Center for Investment Research did a neat little study examining four hypothetical investors, each with a totally different investment strategy. Four buy'n'hold investors each got $2,000 annually for twenty years, a cumulative total of $40,000. Here's how their strategies worked out and how much their portfolios were worth after two decades:

- **THE PERFECT TIMER—$387,120.**
  This guy puts his money in the market at the monthly low point every year, perfectly timing the market for twenty years.
- **THE BAD TIMER—$321,569.**
  Just the opposite of the perfect timer, this poor soul buys at the worst time—the peak of the market—every year for all twenty.
- **NEVER-BUYS-STOCKS—$76,558.**
  Fear of the stock market controls. All of this investor's money goes in ultrasafe T-bills, year after year, out of fear that the market will lower.
- **AUTOPILOT INVESTING—$362,185.**
  This guy automatically invests money on the day received. This is a no-brainer for the investor, with no timing, just the good old "dollar-cost averaging," investing like clockwork according to an automatic saving schedule, like a payroll or bank account deduction plan.

The conclusion is very simple. Use the autopilot strategy, investing your money immediately and automatically *regardless of market conditions, and without "thinking" about it.*

Of course, the guy using this autopilot strategy really isn't a market timer, he's just another good ol' boy who knows instinctively that it's a huge waste of time trying to be a "perfect timer," because that *is* the dumbest thing you can do—'cause it's impossible! So save and invest on autopilot. And guess what? You'll beat the bad timer, and come close to beating the perfect timer. And remember, even a bad timer will beat a no timer who just sits on the sidelines in fear and never gets into the stock market. The no timer will lose almost a quarter million dollars.

NO, STOCK PICKING CAN'T BEAT A RANDOM MARKET

So what did we learn from the Monkeydex adventure competing in the Wall Street jungle? That Professors Malkiel, Siegel, and others are right: The stock market is totally random. Nobody has an edge, certainly not the stock pickers.

Why? Because *you can't predict anything in the financial markets!* More specifically, there were a few good lessons out of this adventure in the jungle with Raven, the now famous dart-throwing chimp who made a monkey out of Wall Street:

Random rule #1. It's the target, stupid, not the picker. Remember that wonderful old saying "In a bull market, everyone is a financial genius"? Well, the randomness of picking stocks with a dart provides an interesting corollary—and note that it is irrelevant here whether the dart thrower is *a monkey . . . or a six-year-old child . . . or a Wall Street securities analyst . . . or you!* Any one of the "family" can pick a winning portfolio if they're throwing darts at a target already loaded with winners.

Random rule #2. Actually, random pickin' ain't always random. Random stock picking is a valid selection process. And of course, the probabilities of creating a winning portfolio are increased if your "random" selections are confined to a narrow group of securities that are already high performers, rather than the entire universe of funds in the Wilshire 5000. For example, Raven's dartboard was narrowed to 133 preselected stocks in a raging bull market.

Random rule #3. Asset allocation beats stock picking nine to one. Monkeydex confirms Ibbotson Associates' 1990 study proving that more than 90 percent of a portfolio's returns are a function of your asset allocations. And less than 10 percent depend on the stocks you pick. Consequently, as Raven proved, random stock picking works just fine.

Random rule #4. Indexing beats stock picking. Independent research studies indicate that actively managed portfolios fail to outperform passive computerized index portfolios. Put more bluntly, active stock picking adds virtually nothing to your portfolio's value, which explains why better than 80 percent of all funds fail to beat their indexes in any one year, and none does it over the long term.

ASK YOUR BROKER: "CAN YOU THROW DARTS LIKE A CHIMPANZEE?"

The next time a Wall Street broker, fund manager, or financial adviser tells you he knows more about the markets and stock picking than you do, do yourself a big favor—remember Raven!

You heard me: Conjure up an image of that chimpanzee—then overlay that mental picture of a monkey's face on the expert's face, and chuckle to yourself. Remember, that so-called expert who's pitching the hype probably can't outwit a monkey, chimpanzee, orangutan, or gorilla in an IQ test, let alone the stock market! Then reflect on Professor Malkiel's sage advice in *A Random Walk:*

> Many people say that the individual investor has scarcely a chance today against Wall Street's pros . . . that there is no

longer any room for the individual investor in today's institutionalized markets. Nothing could be further from the truth. You can do it as well as the experts—perhaps even better.

I am *not* saying that technical strategies never make money. They very often do make profits. The point is rather that a simple "buy-and-hold" strategy (that is, buying a stock or group of stocks and holding on to them for a long period of time) typically makes as much or more money.

And that, folks, is language simple enough for every dart-throwing chimpanzee on Wall Street to comprehend.

The typical millionaire is, in three words: A cheap date!
—Thomas Stanley, The Millionaire Mind

SIX

Strategy Two: Frugal Saving Wins
Financial Obesity and Supersized $250,000 Pizzas

PERHAPS THE SINGLE MOST IMPORTANT LESSON YOU'LL NEED ON the road to becoming a millionaire is frugality. What? I know, *frugal* is an old-fashioned-sounding word, probably because being frugal really *is* an old-fashioned idea in contemporary America's culture of excess. Ben Franklin popularized it.

America's veered off track since Ben Franklin published his *Poor Richard's Almanack,* loaded with such words of wisdom as "a penny saved is a penny earned." Today it seems that being frugal is uncool—so it looks like being uncool is essential if you want to build a successful portfolio.

AMERICA'S BIG FAT, INSATIABLE EGO

America has a problem—a big fat demanding, insatiable ego, and that translates into financial obesity! All too many Americans are driven to excess by an insatiable need for instant satisfaction. And on top of that, our entire commercial advertising world is designed to feed this addiction to ever-greater levels of consumption.

Unfortunately, the result is that we are creating a national mind-set obsessed about current consumption rather than long-term wealth building. Here's how Thomas Stanley and William Danko put it in *The Millionaire Next Door:*

> Frugal Frugal Frugal. They Live Well Below Their Means . . . *Webster's* defines *frugal* as "behavior characterized by or reflecting economy in the use of resources." The opposite of frugal is wasteful. We define wasteful as a lifestyle marked by lavish spending and hyper-consumption. Being frugal is the cornerstone of wealth-building.

But, they add, there's a fundamental distinction between "making good money" each year and wealth building—a distinction that all too many fail to grasp:

> Most people have it all wrong about wealth in America. Wealth is not the same as income. If you make a good income each year and spend it all, you are not getting wealthier. You are living high. Wealth is what you accumulate, not what you spend. . . . Wealth is more often the result of a lifestyle of hard work, perseverance, planning, and most of all, self-discipline.

Hard work? Perseverance? Planning? Self-discipline? Well, nobody said it was going to be easy. But, folks, you either bite the bullet now or you may not have enough to chew on later in retirement when your appetite's outrun your resources—it's that darn simple.

GETTING RICH IN AMERICA—WHILE ENJOYING LIFE MORE!

One of the best examples I ever saw of the power of frugal living is in Dwight Lee's and Richard McKenzie's book *Getting Rich in America*. They give us a whole bunch of tips about how any Main Street investor can make a mental shift from current consumption to wealth building.

Their message is crystal clear. Check out the list; you can easily see a lot of frugal tips about changes you can make in the course of a day, and over the years, to help you build wealth so you can retire comfortably as a millionaire:

Building Wealth the Easy Way

MILLIONAIRE'S FRUGAL TIPS	SAVINGS
Buy used Camry vs. new one every 2 years (ages 23–67)	$869,638
Not buying a second car (30–67)	$440,632
Save $1.50/day on junk food, smokes, alcohol (18–67)	$290,363
Regular coffee & brown-bagging vs. latte (25–67)	$282,700
Not buying lottery tickets for $200/year	$106,068
Redeeming coupons, savings of $5/week (25–67)	$85,682
Engagement ring for $2,500 vs. $5,000 (at 22)	$79,801
Rolex watch, not spending $4,000 (at 30)	$68,983

Lee's and McKenzie's list is a great starting point. It covers so many of the key areas of excess in America—automobiles, lunches, snacks, smokes, drinks, luxuries—stuff anyone can cut back on if they're serious about building long-term wealth.

Yes, I know, it'll take you to a whole new level of self-discipline in order to cut back on everything at once. But hey, at least this'll get you to start thinking about where you're unnecessarily wasting money, so you can start planning ahead for a comfortable retirement.

And remember, folks, you can always start small—no extra doughnut.

TIP SHEETS ON HOW TO BE A FRUGAL KINDA GUY

There are a whole bunch of books like Allyson Lewis's *The Million Dollar Car and $250,000 Pizza* that'll give you hints on ways to cut back. There are also some great newsletters—like the *Tightwad Gazette* and the *Cheapskate Monthly*—loaded with tips and reminders.

I also wrote a few columns on CBS MarketWatch about a "Frugal Millionaire's Cookbook," a "GenXer's Hot New 'Taco Bell' Retirement Strategy," and one on why "Zen Millionaires Don't Drive New BMWs."

Another fun column is "Millionaires Just 'Ordinary Folk' at Buffett's Omaha Barbecue." One of the multimillionaires at this shindig made some interesting remarks about his fellow investors in billionaire Warren Buffett's Berkshire Hathaway fund. He estimated that the people at the barbecue were worth a total of a trillion bucks, yet they were low-key frugal folks:

> Many of these people attend Warren's party as a form of entertainment, like going to a family reunion. For example, my family first bought five shares of Berkshire Hathaway in 1968 at $22 a share, as a joke.
>
> Most people with money ain't talking. They don't drive flashy cars or live in big houses, but they're very comfortable. And they don't need a six-figure income to survive. They live very comfortably on $15,000 to $30,000 a year and still save lots of money.

A lot of this wealth doesn't show up in surveys. Undeveloped land, child's life insurance policies, all kinds of collectibles, foreign bank accounts, et cetera. For example, some family friends of Buffett, the Othmers, never showed up in the Forbes 400 but their estate ended up giving away $800 million in Berkshire Hathaway stock. The biggest problem of this comfortable 20–25 percent of the population is—how to give away their wealth.

Still, the consensus is that you don't get rich, *then* get frugal. *You are frugal, and then you get rich.*

In *The Millionaire Next Door* Stanley and Danko outline the seven "common denominators" that all millionaires have in common. And the first is: Millionaires are "frugal, they live below their means," regardless of how much they're making. They understand the wisdom behind wise ol' Ben Franklin's adage "A penny saved is a penny earned"—and they live by the modern version, a penny saved is a dollar earned, thanks to compounding.

LIVING BELOW YOUR MEANS AROUND WALL STREET

Unfortunately, the only way that Wall Street and the fund industry's active managers survive—*the only way*—is by making the investing public believe that Wall Streeters have superior stock-picking abilities and, therefore, can beat the averages . . . that they can beat the indexes . . . that Wall Street and the active fund managers can even beat the index funds.

And their Hype Machine costs them billions each year selling that message, trying to convince you that they can deliver on these promises of being "above average."

Blatantly false advertising. In fact, they fail miserably.

And they know it's false advertising. They rarely beat their indexes in the short run, and on an after-tax basis they never do in the long run. Even at the height of the 1990s bull market, with all those insane triple-digit stocks and funds, Vanguard founder John C. Bogle was able to say: "No actively managed fund has outpaced an index fund over the past fifteen years. Period."

And yet Wall Street and the fund industry are forever trying to convince American investors that they can beat the averages . . . that they can beat the indexes . . . that they can beat index funds . . . but they can't.

THE BEST WAY TO SAVE PENNIES—BUY LOW-COST INDEX FUNDS

We already know millionaires are frugal. That's what we hear about Buffett's multimillionaires. And it's a common denominator for ordinary American millionaires next door. *They all live below their means.*

We also know that a lot of conscientious young American millionaires-in-training are traveling the frugal route—doing little things like eating at Taco Bell, brown-bagging, skipping the new BMW, no credit cards, regular monthly savings, and other proven ways to live frugally and save for a bright future.

So how can you be a "frugal person" when it comes to investing?

Very simple: Buy low-cost index funds.

Low-cost index funds . . . the ultimate in cool . . . the ultimate in frugal.

EXPENSE RATIO IS THE *ONLY* RELIABLE PREDICTOR . . . PERIOD!

How do we know? The Financial Research Corporation prepared a high-priced study exclusively for fund industry insiders. The guy in charge of the study, Gavin Quill, senior

PLAY ALL FOUR QUARTERS OF THE GAME
(AND YOU WILL WIN!)

Wall Street says you need more than a $1 million nest egg and $100,000 income a year to retire comfortably. Of course they'll say that—they get paid a fee based on assets under management. They're wrong. Studies show most retire on $22,000 a year. Multimillionaires tell me they do it on $30,000.

But let's assume you want more than twice that—$4,800 a month, or almost $60,000 a year. That's about what you'd get *if* you had $1 million invested at 6 percent. Now try this: I want you to *forget about assets* and focus only on the *cash flow* you need. Remember, you don't need a million bucks sitting in a bank. What you *need* is $4,800 cash flow every month, and here's how to get it.

Think of this process as a football game, playing all four quarters over your lifetime (actually, playing all four at the same time). Sit back and I'll show you an example of how you get your $4,800 cash flow in *four* $1,200 chunks each month.

1ST QUARTER. SOCIAL SECURITY—$1,200/MONTH. Let's say you retire and get at least $1,200 a month from Social Security. You have no "hard" assets at Social Security, but that $1,200 each and every month is no different from having $250,000 invested at 6 percent.

2ND QUARTER. PERSONAL SAVINGS—$1,200/MONTH. Over the years you keep putting aside money every month in your 401(k), IRA, and pension plan. Remember: A thirty-year-old needs to put only about $150 a month into an annual IRA! Compounding does the rest. That little bit grows to more than $500,000 in thirty years, assuming a historic average 10 percent return. Even if you fall way short, you'll have enough to generate the second $1,200 on the way to a $4,800-a-month retirement cash flow.

3RD QUARTER. HOME EQUITY—$1,200/MONTH. You own your home. It keeps growing in value. *Kiplinger's* says, "Your home can be a major source of income in retirement. If you sell it and buy or rent something less expensive, the leftover amount becomes part of your nest egg." Or maybe you pay off your mortgage and own your home free and clear. Either way, your housing costs go down $1,200 a month or more. **4TH QUARTER. PART-TIME WORK—$1,200/MONTH.** Nobody retires. In fact, 80 to 90 percent of so-called retirees keep working because doing nothing is boring. No grand visions of being a successful artist. Or big-shot entrepreneur. Work a few days a week and make another $1,200 a month. And that's the equivalent of another quarter million in assets!

BOTTOM-LINE TOTAL—4 QUARTERS—$4,800/MONTH

Shift your focus: *You do not need a million bucks in assets—you need $4,800 a month cash.* Don't play the Wall Street asset-based game. You can win the game playing your way: Four quarters of $1,200 = $4,800/month!

vice president and research director of FRC, came up with two main conclusions:

1. **The best portfolio strategy is asset allocation.** "There's no silver bullet in predicting the future performance of a mutual fund. This study tells investors what *doesn't* work in predicting the future. In the final analysis, your best strategy is still to focus on portfolio asset allocation, diversification and risk assessment, *not specific funds,* it's that basic."

2. **Expense ratio is the only reliable predictor of fund performance.** Of all the predictors they researched, the FRC says that the expense ratio is the *only really reliable one in predicting future performance,* because *low-cost funds* "deliver above-average future performance across nearly all time periods."

Do you get it? Let me repeat this last point for emphasis: The only, only, *only* reliable indicator of future performance is the expense ratio. Low expense ratios indicate high performance.

And vice versa: High expense ratios indicate low performance.

So remember, a low expense ratio is the only reliable indicator of future performance. Junk like star ratings, past performance, manager tenure . . . none of the other measurements is a reliable indicator. None. Only the expense ratio.

THE FRUGAL FUND MANAGER BROWN-BAGS PEANUT BUTTER SANDWICHES

No wonder Wall Street and America's actively managed funds have hated having John Bogle around for the past several decades—he's exposing their costly game. He founded Vanguard in the 1970s on this principle: *"The manager that takes the least delivers the most."*

So you really don't need that Financial Research Corporation study to prove it—just look at the superior performance of low-cost index funds. Vanguard's been setting the pace for several decades.

And besides, the guy who started this whole indexing thing, Jack Bogle, was such a frugal cheapskate that when he was head of Vanguard, he used to brown-bag a peanut butter sandwich and apple to his corporate office because he said the prices in his own company's cafeteria were too high.

That may be going overboard on the cheapskate scale, but it's also an attitude reflected in the company's entire investment strategy—Vanguard is the master of frugality when it comes to funds, and the poster boy for cheapskate.

Now you know how to find a "frugal fund manager" (it's in the brown bag, a peanut butter sandwich), but how can you recognize a "frugal investor"? Here's how: Look around for the cheapskate who's savvy enough to buy low-cost index funds.

Think you'll never have a million dollars?
It's easier to obtain than you might think—if you're
young and patient. Thanks to the power of compounding,
a 25-year-old needs to invest only $1,720 a year to reach
seven figures by age 65. That assumes an 11 percent
average annual return. . . . For investors who start young,
most of that $1 million is interest and reinvested dividends.
By age 65, the 25-year-old has invested only $68,800,
less than 10 percent of his ending balance.

—William O'Neil, publisher, Investors Business Daily

SEVEN

Strategy Three: Compounding Wins

Einstein's Hot New Theory . . .
The Explosive Power of Compounding!

ALBERT EINSTEIN, THE FATHER OF NUCLEAR ENERGY AND *TIME*'S Man of the Century, once said, "There is no greater power known to man than compounding interest." Get it? Compounding money is more powerful than a nuclear bomb. And a guy like Einstein should know.

And yet, surprisingly, so many people seem to have a hard time grasping the power of compounding. Like it's some incomprehensible $E=mc^2$ formula.

For so many others, compounding just looks too good to be true when you see the growth. Hard to believe. So others think there's just gotta be some kind of hocus-pocus trick going on.

COMPOUNDING—IT'S BUFFETT'S LITTLE MIRACLE, TOO

Well, there are no gimmicks, compounding's a real miracle, and guys like Warren Buffett know it, too. As Simon Reynolds puts it in *Thoughts of Chairman Buffett:*

> One of the keys to Buffett's success, often ignored by his appraisers, is compounding. Berkshire Hathaway has given only one dividend; it was twenty-nine years ago and, by Buffett's own admission, is unlikely to happen again. He'd rather reinvest the money and use the miracle of compounding to his advantage.
>
> Just how powerful is compounding interest? I'll put it this way: If you put $2,000 a year into an IRA for just eight years, until you are twenty-seven, when you retire at age sixty-five the $16,000 will have ballooned to over a million dollars. You do not need unusually high returns to make good money with compound interest, but you do need to be consistent.

Please, please hear what these people have to say about the miraculous explosive power of compounding—a mere $16,000 invested for just eight years in your twenties will grow to $1,000,000 by the time you're retiring. Get it?

THE GOOD, THE BAD, AND THE UGLY TRUTH

Unfortunately, the harsh truth is that all too many people are just looking for some excuse to justify why they don't have any kind of savings and investment plan preparing them for retirement.

I'm sure you've heard a lot of different excuses—like this one: "Sorry, but I just don't have anything left over after paying all my monthly bills."

In fact, Americans sure do come up with all kinds of cockamamie excuses. For example, a few years ago a study by the Employee Benefit Research Institute and the American Savings Council grouped investors into five different personality types. It turns out that only 35 percent were seriously planning for retirement. The other 65 percent were in trouble. Listen to their excuses:

1. **(13%) Deniers.** "Save for retirement? Nope, it's a waste of time."
2. **(15%) Impulsives.** "Gotta buy that new toy! I'll save next month."
3. **(20%) Strugglers.** "I save a little, but market downturns scare me."
4. **(18%) Cautious.** "I'm confused, hate to lose, overcautious."
5. **(35%) Planners.** "I'm a regular saver and I'll retire comfortably."

Obviously, folks, your chances of retiring comfortably are going to increase dramatically if you're one of 35 percent in the "planner" category, the disciplined investors working on a million-dollar nest egg. Who are these planners? How do they think? What motivates them?

THE EIGHTH WONDER OF THE WORLD

The readers out there on Main Street America are forever teaching me a thing or two. Yes, what giants like Einstein and Buffett say is important. But what people often remember most are a couple of very special descriptions from the "man on the street," some average American who really does understand the power of compounding, *at a gut level.*

One reader sent me a long e-mail about "The 8th Wonder of the World," a parable that he'd picked up in a course at Taylor University. The other sent me a chart showing how his money will compound and grow year by year as he planned to "get rich slowwwwly" until retirement thirty-three years from now.

It's readers like these who not only teach me how simple the real world is, but also convince me that the future of America is in great hands. So if you want a simple explanation of the power of compounding—listen to the stories of these two young men.

START WITH ONE PENNY—RETIRE A MULTIMILLIONAIRE!

At Taylor University, finance professor Rick Seaman "taught the '8th Wonder of the World'—*compound interest*—using a parable that I will never forget," says Tony, one of Seaman's former students.

> **Start with just a penny.** "Seaman started the parable by asking a question. Would you rather be paid $10,000 a day to dig a ditch every day for a month? Or would you rather start with a penny and have your pay doubled each day for the same month?"
>
> **High-paid ditchdigger.** "If you chose the $10,000 and started on January 1 you would have $310,000 by January 31. Sounds great, right? It would take the average person ten years to earn that much."
>
> **Magic of compounding.** "If you took that $0.01 and doubled it each day, it was still not looking so good after the tenth day, only $5.12. Only $163.84 by the fifteenth. By the twentieth day things are looking up: You would have $5,242.88."
>
> **Long-term buy'n'hold.** "Stick it out now and reap the rewards of compound interest. On January 31 the total payout for starting with one cent and doubling it each day would be $10,737,417.60. Talk about the power of compound interest!"

Never forget the eighth wonder. "Seaman has touched many lives in the years he taught at Taylor, including mine and my wife's. His knowledge of finance and life will also be passed down to my children and hopefully their children and beyond. I think of him often and will never forget this '8th Wonder of the World' because of him. My thanks to Rick!"

COMPOUNDING HELPS YOU GET RICH SLOWWWLY

Next, Steve showed me with a simple table exactly how he was going to become a 401(k) millionaire. Keep in mind that most Web-based financial calculators don't show you the year-to-year progress, just the end result after you spend a lifetime slogging it out, one day at a time.

Seaman's parable impresses me with its simple comments about progress along the way—in particular, the seemingly teeny-tiny value buildup in the early years—and now Steve's table brings the point home rather dramatically. I like it because I'm very visual and grasp information best from graphics and illustrations, as many people do.

COMPOUNDING YOUR 401(K) INTO MILLIONS

Now listen to Steve: "Here's how my 401(k) should grow, assuming I increase my contribution by 2 percent of my salary each year until I max out. I started at 6 percent to get my full 3 percent employer match.

"Here's a few more of my assumptions: A 4 percent annual raise, and a 10 percent return on my investment. This chart takes me to fifty-nine and a half years of age, when I can actually touch the money and retire.

"I am already through year two, and I have $12,500 in my

Retirement:
The Magic and Power of Compounding
Assumptions: a 4% annual raise, employer matching, 10% growth.

AGE	401(K)
27	$4,554
28	10,274
29	17,771
30	27,311
31	39,192
32	53,747
33	71,347
34	92,408
35	117,390
36	145,501
37	177,077
38	212,492
39	252,157
40	296,525
41	346,096
42	401,421
43	463,107
44	531,823
45	608,307
46	693,371
47	787,912
48	892,915
49	1,009,466
50	1,138,763
51	1,282,123
52	1,440,999
53	1,616,989
54	1,811,853
55	2,027,531
56	2,266,156
57	2,530,079
58	2,821,886
59	3,144,425
then . . .	retirement

401(k) already. So I'm a little ahead of the game for now, but I'm willing to bet that by age sixty I'll be close to the magical $3.1 million nest egg at an average 10 percent return for the thirty-three years. Wow! I'll be happy if I can retire with that much. And this doesn't even include my wife's 403(b) or her pension! 'Getting rich slowwwwwly' works for me."

NO SAVINGS, NO NEST EGG, NO RETIREMENT . . . SO START EARLY!

The power of compounding is so simple, yet most people don't grasp it until it's too late, if ever. It works best when you start early—atomic energy on a slow fuse.

How can you harness this awesome power? Follow this one very simple rule—*start saving today, early in life, preferably in your twenties.*

Charles Schwab says that for every five years you wait to start saving for retirement, you'll have to double your annual savings. Here's how the formula works in action, in a table so simple that anybody should be able to understand the power of compounding at 10 percent annually:

When Should You Start Saving?	
AGE YOU START	ANNUAL INVESTMENT TO RETIRE A MILLIONAIRE AT 65
20	$ 1,025
25	$ 1,720—less than your annual IRA
30	$ 2,920—just $250/month, your IRA
35	$ 5,000
40	$ 8,770
45	$ 15,600—still only $1,200/month, your 401(k)
50	$ 29,000
55	$ 60,000—now up to $5,000/month!
60	$ 161,000—forget it, get a part-time job

In the first place, it should be obvious that Rule One of savings is: *Start early, and let compounding do its magic.* Anyone can do it, and it's no excuse to say you don't have a company retirement plan, because if you start early, your IRA will be enough, as you can see here.

START EARLY AND TRUST THE MAGIC OF COMPOUNDING

Professor Seaman "changed my life," says Tony, and many others would agree. And "though he's gone, his teaching on finance and life will live on through the students who were lucky enough to have him as a professor." Don't you forget his message, either.

Young Americans do understand how to harness the power of compounding. So here's a tip: Remember Seaman's parable of the eighth wonder of the world—compounding. And start with just one cent, if that's all you've got. Whatever you do, just do it, start, start saving today.

One more time: Start really early and you'll end up a winner!

You don't have to hit a home run in order to get to seven figures. Singles will do just fine.

—Charles Carlson, Eight $teps to $even Figures

You're not in a horse race. . . . If successful investors know they can't pick the right horse, what do they do? Simple: They pick every horse. For this truly is how wealth is created, and it is what diversification is all about.

—Ric Edelman, Ordinary People, Extraordinary Wealth

EIGHT

Strategy Four: Asset Allocation Wins

Diversify—the Lost Art of Being Average

REALLY, IT'S AN EGO THING—IT SEEMS LIKE MOST AMERICAN investors just can't stand "being average." We have a hero complex, a need to win, and the bigger, the better. Nobody wants to be like the rest of the crowd, just *average*.

We worship heroes, grew up with Superman and Spider-Man, Delta Force and Rambo, Wonder Woman and Charlie's Angels; we need to be numero uno, macho, a winner, a hero! We want to "be like Mike," Michael Jordan. Barry Bonds. Tiger Woods.

Settle for average? Among heroes? Are you kidding? No way!

We gotta show attitude, cockiness, power, flair, and superiority. And we gotta flaunt it.

Unfortunately, while all that braggadocio works in sports and on the big screen, trying to be a hero doesn't work in investing. Being average does.

ATTITUDE, OPTIMISM, AND CONFIDENCE—THE SABOTEUR!

Some behavioral finance professors now have research showing how this "attitude" stuff has worked its way into the investor psyche—investors now have what's called "optimism bias," also known as "overconfidence." We think we know more than we know, are convinced we've got a sure winner, even in bear markets; we bet big and set ourselves up to lose. Happens all the time, say the behavioral finance experts.

So watch out! Investors are a macho bunch. They tell us how they're beating the market (and they even *believe* they're beating it), when research studies show they are actually *5 to 15 percent* under the market. Hey guys, wake up! It's okay to bluff in poker, but in investing, the "casino" always wins.

But any way you look at it—as attitude, machismo, hero complex, or overconfidence—the fact is, the investor's own brain is a saboteur.

THE ONE KEY TO SUCCESS IN INVESTING—DISCIPLINE

Here's what it takes to beat the market. Let's look into the mind of successful traders, those who spend all day every day buying and selling, pitting themselves against the best of the best in the stock market jungle.

The elite few who are the home-run hitters are like Special Forces commandos operating behind enemy lines, because that's what the stock market is for day traders—the enemy that's working full time to beat you.

By far the best two books in this field are Jack Schwager's

Market Wizards: Interviews with Top Traders and its sequel, *The New Market Wizards: Conversations with America's Top Traders.*

DISCIPLINE AND THE NEW MARKET WIZARD

Wizards? No, we're not talking about fictional wizards like Harry Potter and the Hogwarts School of Wizardry stuff. At the time Schwager was a key officer with Prudential-Bache Securities. His books dig deep into the minds of thirty-five of America's most successful real-life stock market "wizards" to find out what makes them tick. One passage in *New Market Wizards* pinpoints the wizard's secret weapon—discipline:

> Discipline was probably the most frequent word used by the exceptional traders that I interviewed. Often, it was mentioned in an almost apologetic tone: "I know you've heard this a million times before, but believe me, it's really important."
>
> There are two basic reasons why discipline is critical. First, it is a prerequisite for maintaining effective risk control. Second, you need discipline to apply your method without second-guessing when choosing which trades to take. I guarantee you will almost always pick the wrong ones. Why? Because you will pick the comfortable ones, and . . . "What feels good is often the wrong thing to do."
>
> As a final word on the subject, remember that you are never immune to bad trading habits—the best you can do is to keep them latent. As soon as you get lazy or sloppy, they will return.

Eternal vigilance. Constant training. Top shape. Relax, get lazy or sloppy . . . and you'll lose. If you're an athlete, you'll lose your edge. If you're playing the market, you'll lose money.

DISCIPLINE VERSUS EMOTIONS IN THE DAY-TRADING GAME

Discipline—that's what it takes to create a market wizard out of an ordinary stock market trader. And you can't let your guard down for a minute, or you'll lose your edge.

It's a full-time job for the winners, and so few people have it. Out of ninety-four million investors in America, probably less than 1 percent have what it takes to become a top market wizard, a home-run hitter, an all-star. The rest of us don't have the time, or the skills, or the interest, or the self-discipline it takes to succeed as a trader.

What Schwager discovered with traders is magnified many times over with individual investors who have regular jobs forty hours a week—*so we let our emotions do the picking*. Bad idea! As Schwager points out, "What feels good is often the wrong thing to do." And even the pros can fall into that trap.

NOT ONLY SELF-DISCIPLINE, BUT ALSO PASSION, A SENSE OF MISSION

The second most important secret ingredient Schwager saw among the market wizards was a sense of mission and passion for what they do: "In talking to the traders interviewed in this book, I had the definite sense that many of them felt that trading was what they were meant to do—in essence, their mission in life."

If your "mission in life" is something *other than* a burning passion to trade stocks every day and an obsession with beating the market, then please don't think about trading part time—successful traders don't know anything else, and they play the game full time.

Even if you aren't sure whether you should give up your day job, remember the wise words of Adam Smith in *The*

Money Game: "If you don't know who you are, the stock market is an expensive place to find out." A very expensive place.

IS BECOMING A MARKET WIZARD REALLY YOUR LIFE'S MISSION?

The truth is, you're probably one of the other ninety-three out of ninety-four million investors in America who have a full-time job teaching school, working in an office or on a farm, carrying mail, working in a restaurant or retail sales, repairing cars, building homes, or doing something else productive—*something other than focusing on the stock market.*

You get all you know about investing from a quick read of the finance pages in the morning papers, maybe the *Wall Street Journal,* a flip through *Kiplinger's* and *Money* magazine once a month, maybe watching Lou Dobbs, Louis Rukeyser, Bill Griffeth, or Maria Bartiromo on cable news now and then (preferably as entertainment)—but the information you get is nothing compared to the high-priced data resources, software tools, and research and analysis efforts by Schwager's market wizards.

The fact is, most American investors lack the time, skills, and discipline to truly succeed as traders. Most of all, *they lack the interest in doing it full time—trading and investing is just not their mission in life.*

Most of us have no passion for the game of trading. We'd rather play baseball, shoot hoops, or just watch a pro game on television . . . anything other than become consumed by everything it takes to beat the market trading on a daily basis.

Face it, we just want to win enough to retire comfortably sometime in the future, with minimum effort. Not make a career of it.

FORGET ABOUT HITTING HOME RUNS—SWING FOR SINGLES

One of the best books on investing for the passive non-trader is Charles Carlson's *Eight $teps to $even Figures*. Carlson first earned his reputation as the king of DRIPs, dividend reinvestment programs, in *No-Load Stocks*—no-load because you can buy the stocks directly from a publicly held company without paying a broker's commission.

The fourth step in Carlson's *Eight $teps to $even Figures* is simple to grasp for the average passive investor who'd rather be out on the golf links, shooting hoops with the kids, or just watching a Dodgers or Lakers game:

> Swing for singles: You'll strike out fewer times and hit some home runs in the process. Selecting stocks is scary stuff. There are about 10,000 publicly held stocks and thousands of mutual funds. A lot of junk is out there waiting to snatch your hard-earned dollars. . . .
>
> You become a seven-figure investor not because of the stocks you choose, but because you invest in stocks. Approaching stock picking with this concept in mind frames the stock selection process in a less intimidating way. You don't have to hit a home run in order to get to seven-figures. Singles will do just fine.

Get it? It's all very simple, if you don't let your ego get in the way. The simple truth is, you don't have to be a stock market wizard to build a successful seven-figure million-dollar portfolio . . . you can do it with singles. It's very, very simple. You buy quality funds and stocks. You diversify. And you let them grow—*sloowly*.

PITCHING HORSESHOES IS ALL ABOUT DIVERSIFICATION

Another great professional financial adviser is Ric Edelman, author of several books that ought to be in every Main Street investor's library, in particular *Ordinary People, Extraordinary Wealth: The 8 Secrets of How 5,000 Ordinary Americans Became Successful Investors—and How You Can Too.*

Edelman also uses a simple sports analogy to get across the idea that not only can you become a millionaire by "being average," but if you do try to beat the averages and be a hero, you'll most likely sabotage yourself and lose the game. Listen:

> Investment selection has less to do with achieving wealth than you think. You see, if you really were in a horse race, the horse indeed would have a huge effect on your results.
>
> But you're not in a horse race. Instead, you're playing horseshoes. Therefore, *you don't need to pick the winner,* and it's not a winner-take-all situation. Rather, in a game of horseshoes, as I explained in *The New Rules of Money,* merely being close is good enough to win.

Edelman goes on to explain the three reasons why picking the "right" funds or the "right" stocks just "doesn't matter." First, the odds are against picking the right one of ten thousand possibilities. You have a better chance of picking the winning lottery numbers than picking the right fund.

Second, it's even harder to "pick the 'right' fund *at precisely the 'right' time.*" And finally, even if you are lucky enough to find the proverbial needle in the haystack, you'd have to gamble everything on that one fund or stock to get the big payoff—and who's stupid enough to put all their money on one fund or stock?

THE ONLY RATIONAL SOLUTION LEFT— BET ON EVERY HORSE IN THE RACE!

So what's the solution? Now Edelman goes right to the core of successful investing for the average Main Street American investor:

> If successful investors know they can't pick the right horse, what do they do? Simple: They pick *every* horse. For this truly is how wealth is created, and it is what diversification is all about.

Get it? If you want to become a millionaire investor—pick every horse in the stock market race. That's what diversification and indexing are all about.

So one more time, the message is: Create a well-diversified index portfolio that abandons the macho ego trip. You just swing for singles, get close enough, settle for being average. Because that's how ordinary people achieve extraordinary wealth using eight steps to get to seven figures and retire as millionaires.

HOW MANY FUNDS IN A DIVERSIFIED PORTFOLIO? LESS THAN TEN!

Remember what Kiplinger's annual *Mutual Fund Guide* says: If you're picking from among the best funds to start with, then all you really need for diversification is three stock funds and one bond fund—and you can forget the other 9,111 funds. Now *that's* direct and to the point. *Money* magazine asked a similar question:

> How many mutual funds should you own? According to a new study, when it comes to investing in domestic stocks, six funds are really all you need. . . . More surprising was the fact

that most of the risk reductions, about 75 percent, occurred with just four funds. After eight funds, there was very little further lessening of risk, and after fifteen funds almost none.

They also believe in choosing funds investors should target stocks of different sizes. Thus their recommended portfolio would consist of six funds: one growth fund and value funds specializing in small, medium-sized and large companies. Put the finishing touches by adding two overseas offerings—one international and one emerging markets fund.

So six is enough for the *Money* crowd. And not too long ago, the Investment Company Institute, the fund industry's trade association, reported in one of its surveys that 57 percent of all investors own three or fewer funds, 26 percent own four to six funds, and only 15 percent have seven or more. So if these investors have the "right" categories of funds in their portfolios, then American investors may have all the funds they need for a well-diversified portfolio.

And remember, folks, we already know that the Couch Potato, the Coffeehouse, and the No-Brainer Portfolios all have fewer than ten funds—*and they're all winners!*

BUY (QUALITY) AND HOLD—NEVER REBALANCE

How important is rebalancing? When should you dump a dog? Do you really need to rebalance every quarter, or even every month? *How about never?* Buffett says *never.* The three laziest portfolios agree.

If you're focused on *your portfolio and not individual funds,* if you're well diversified with index funds, if you're not stuck with a plateful of last year's "hottest funds," then you have no dogs to dump and the indexes rebalance automatically. In other words, rebalancing is a wasted effort—necessary only if you're mistakenly focused on specific funds rather than your asset allocations.

Check this Charles Schwab study. The researchers tested three rebalancing scenarios using Morningstar data. The percentages listed here are the result of annualized pretax returns from the 1990s. While they might all be lower in a bear market, the relative results would be similar:

1. **ANNUAL REBALANCING.** If you sell all funds that are in the bottom quarter of their peer group on an annual basis, you'd realize a 13.43 percent return. Alternatively, selling all funds in the bottom half resulted in a slightly lower return, at 13.27 percent. Not much difference.
2. **REBALANCING EVERY TWO YEARS.** If you wait and rebalance every two years, selling all your funds falling in the bottom quarter, the return is 12.90 percent—versus 12.86 percent in the bottom half.
3. **REBALANCING EVERY THREE YEARS.** Finally, if you wait a full three years to rebalance, your returns would be 12.53 percent if you sell all the funds in the bottom quarter, versus 12.31 percent if you sell funds in the bottom half.

Notice that rebalancing every three years versus annually drops your return only from 13.43 to 13.01 percent. So why go through the headaches of annual or, worse yet, monthly rebalancing, as many Wall Street experts advise? This research strongly suggests that you'll do just fine if you *never* rebalance. Just buy'n'hold. That is, buy *quality* and hold. Better yet, buy a well-diversified index portfolio and hold . . . and hold . . . *hold forever . . . it's sure working for the Sage of Omaha, the second richest man in the world.*

The idea is to own the stock market, own every company in America, and hold it for Warren Buffett's favorite holding period—forever. And that's the secret: Own everything, and hold it forever.

—Jack Bogle

NINE

Strategy Five: Buy'n'hold Wins

Buy Quality, Never Sell, Says Warren Buffett

WARREN BUFFETT, THE FOLKSY "SAGE OF OMAHA," WAS ONCE asked: When's the right time to sell? His answer: "Never." Never? That's right, never!

Buffett doesn't particularly take a shine to short-term stock market traders and speculators. "Do not think of yourself as merely owning a piece of paper whose price wiggles around," he said. "Visualize yourself as a part owner of a business that you expect to stay with indefinitely, much as you might if you owned a farm or an apartment house in partnership with members of your family."

That's the good old buy'n'hold investing strategy for you. You buy quality. And you hold, "indefinitely," using a well-diversified asset allocation strategy. You do not sell. Never?

Read his lips, *never.* If you buy quality, and if you're diversified—you don't have to sell.

BUY AND HOLD . . . AND HOLD . . . AND HOLD . . . FOREVER

In *Eight \$teps to \$even Figures,* Chuck Carlson adds a little more country drawl to the way he talks about this fundamental principle of investing: "Buy and hold . . . and hold . . . and hold . . . and hold . . . and hold." Heck, this one's so simple you could get in a good game of checkers while the concept sinks into your gray matter.

"Millionaire investors never sell," says Carlson. "Okay, I exaggerate. But only a little. Approximately 75% of the millionaire investors I surveyed hold stocks for more than five years. Nearly 40% of them hold stocks for ten years or more." And that's with stocks. With funds it's even easier. Buy the whole market with index funds, and never sell.

SHRINK SAYS BUY'N'HOLD PROTECTS US FROM OURSELVES

The 2002 Nobel Prize in Economic Sciences was awarded to Daniel Kahneman, a psychologist (yes, somebody other than an economist won the prize for economics). *Fortune* magazine reported that when Kahneman was "asked by a CNBC anchorman the day after his Nobel was announced what investment tips he had for viewers, he responded, 'Buy and hold.'"

Why? Because the new behavioral finance experts Kahneman speaks for tell us that we are our own worst enemy, and the best way to protect us from ourselves is to avoid playing the market altogether—"Buy and hold!"

SIX REASONS YOU CAN'T BEAT THE ODDS AT THE MARKET TIMER'S CASINO

Of course, if you really are one of those rare, elite, super-sophisticated traders, you know how to successfully make money in bear markets as well as bull, because you're 24/7 obsessed about trading derivatives, shorts, futures, options, puts, calls, and a lot of other fancy trading tools and software.

If you're one of the vast majority of investors, however—*the other ninety-three-plus million of the total ninety-four million fund investors who are basically passive investors*—the *only* real strategy for you is a buy'n'hold strategy. But just in case you ever think of jumping into trading, here are six powerful reasons why short-term trading is a very, very bad idea for the other 99-percent-plus of the investors in America, *and that includes you:*

Fact #1: The stock market is irrational and unpredictable.

Wharton School of Finance economist Jeremy Siegel, author of *Stocks for the Long Run: The Definitive Guide to Financial Market Returns and Long-Term Investment Strategies,* researched 120 of the biggest up and biggest down days in the history of the stock market. And guess what? In only thirty of these big move days did Siegel find any reason for the movement of the market.

In other words, 75 percent of the market's biggest gyrations in history were irrational! You can't second-guess them. You're trying to outguess the randomly unguessable—and that's just plain dumb!

So market wizards and amateurs like you are out there gambling in a highly unpredictable casino—the stock market—and its unpredictability makes market timing very dangerous for your financial health, as well as for the elite full-time professional traders. If you want something more predictable, become an entrepreneur: Open a scrap-metal business or a Burger King.

Fact #2: The more you trade, the less you earn.

That's right, passive investors win the race, like the slow-moving tortoise. Behavioral finance professors Terry Odean and Brad Barber of the University of California at Davis researched the portfolios of 66,400 investors at Merrill Lynch between 1991 and 1997.

The professors concluded there were two very specific factors that resulted in substantially reducing investor returns—*lousy stock-picking decisions* and *transaction costs*—and the active traders had more of both.

In fact, the most active traders averaged 258 percent portfolio turnover annually and earned 7 percent *less* annually than buy'n'hold investors, who averaged 2 percent turnover.

Stated another way, the gunslinging active traders wound up with average returns of only 11.4 percent, versus 18.5 percent average returns for the passive sideline sitters—a difference of 7.1 percent. And the main reasons for this wide difference in performance were the transaction costs created by all the extra buying and selling, plus the fact that in making a lot more trades they also increased the number of losing trades and the tax bite.

And that 7.1 percent difference makes a huge impact on your portfolio over time. Look at it this way. If you invested $10,000 at 11.4 percent, you'd have more than $85,000 in twenty years. That's okay. But if you invested the same $10,000 at an 18.5 percent rate, you'd have almost $300,000 in twenty years. Big difference, huh!

Get it? You make a heck of a lot more money "doing nothing" in a simple diversified index fund. Plus you're saving time to do other things like spend time with your family, and you're exposed to a lot less stress and anxiety. In other words, trading is a loser's game.

Fact #3: On-line trading makes it easier to lose more!

In addition, another study by professors Odean and Barber showed that investors who converted from off-line to on-line trading saw their returns drop substantially. Before going on-line they were beating the market by 2 percent. And after going on-line they fell under the market by 3 percent. So it looks as if the Internet made it easier to lose than win—a bit too easy.

Here's even better proof right from the horse's mouth, so to speak. Joe Ricketts, the founder of Ameritrade, one of the largest on-line discount brokers, told *Fortune* just before his company's IPO: "The best thing, really, for an investor to do is buy a good company and hold it. . . . Trading often and heavy is not something that makes you a lot of money. That's contrary to my own interests, but it is the truth." Apparently a lot of investors don't want to hear the truth.

Fact #4: Investors buy high, sell low—losing at top and bottom.

That's right. That is the conclusion of a Morningstar research study. Most mutual fund investors turn the investment advice of the old masters upside down—they buy high and sell low. Mutual fund investors are bad at market timing. They go *in* at the wrong time (the top) . . . and get *out* at the wrong time (the bottom).

Greed creates a buying frenzy at the top of a bull cycle. Investors jump in too late, when prices are peaking. Then they hang on as the market drops, even buying on dips, expecting short-term corrections. More drops follow as the bear chomps away at their stocks. They hold on, confused, hoping against hope. Finally panic sets in, triggering sales at the bottom.

Mutual fund investors react at the worst possible times, says Morningstar, buying at the top and selling at the bottom. Either way, they lose. The solution? Leave the market timing to the so-called experts in that game of chance. For the average investor, it's a waste of your time and money. Buy and hold . . . and hold . . . and hold . . . and hold.

Fact #5: Overly confident, we lose, deny, and fib about losses.

Not long ago a behavioral finance study reported in *Money* magazine concluded that 88 percent of investors experience a phenomenon that psychologists call optimistic bias, aka overconfidence. As a result, we often make bad investment decisions, taking on too much risk, and lose—then we hide the facts and lie to ourselves about how bad it was.

More specifically, better than half of the overly confident investors in the study who actually believed they were beating the market were trapped in a game of self-deception. It turns out they were, in fact, underperforming the market by anywhere between 5 and 15 percent below the S&P 500 . . . yet they had a mental block against seeing, facing, and admitting they'd failed.

Fact #6: Unfortunately, even winning traders don't win much.

Trading is not the get-rich-quick scheme that the hyped-up trading gurus of the world would make you believe. Yes, you can go on-line and trade for a mere seven bucks a pop. Maybe even zero brokerage fees, if your account's active enough. But as you already know, you can still make lousy picks. And you still have taxes to pay.

Trading takes full-time concentration: The successful ones live, breathe, eat trading. While the average passive long-term investor need only rebalance, buy, and sell every fifteen months or more, a short fifteen minutes will seem like an eternity for a trader. There's constant stomach-churning pressure. They eat a lot of Tums. Worse yet, trading is so intense it can easily become addictive. More than one ex-trader ends up a candidate for both Gamblers Anonymous and Debtors Anonymous.

But suppose you're one of the lucky day traders

who're making a living at the game. Be ready to give up the security of your day job, which may have medical insurance, a 401(k), a nice little vested pension plan, and other perks.

In the final analysis, successful traders who do make the commitment to get in full time rarely make more than $100,000 a year, as I recall from a study a couple of years ago. In fact, the average was less than $50,000 annually. Plus it's a solitary life. Easy to burn out. Even easier to make mistakes and lose all your winnings really fast, in one slipup or a bad streak, after building a sizable nest egg over time.

No wonder money manager David Dreman remarked in *The New Contrarian Investment Strategy*, "Market timers, if they don't die broke, rarely beat the market." If you really want an exciting life, go do something truly rewarding: Become a cop, teach inner-city kids, or join the Special Forces.

Corollary #1: Buy with the idea you can never sell . . . never!

There are a bunch of valid reasons for selling if you're already invested in stocks or actively managed funds—although neither of them is necessary for the average investor. But let's say you're already stuck in some actively managed funds. Watch out for stuff like management changes, a jump in expenses, a style shift, below-average performance for more than a year, rapid growth, and, of course, a change in your lifestyle needs.

But all that aside, if you follow one simple rule, you will *never* have to sell. The rule: *Buy quality!* As Carlson succinctly puts it:

> Millionaire investors put a positive spin on the dangers of selling. Their mind-set is the following: "If I don't sell, I'd better be right when I buy." The dangers of selling force them to make better and more thoughtful

decisions when choosing investments. This is a critical point to understand. If you could never sell an investment once you bought it, you would make better buy decisions.

SOME SIMPLE SECRETS OF BUFFETT THE BILLIONAIRE
Coke, Candy, Hamburgers, Shaving, and Tap Dancing

Buffett's billions came from a keep-it-simple philosophy: Invest in top-quality companies with products you know, and hold them forever. Buy profitable companies run by honest, competent managers who are generating lots of cash that's reinvested in the company. Listen:

Coca-Cola. "Coke is exactly the kind of company I like. I like products I can understand. I don't know what a transistor is, but I appreciate the contents of a Coke can. Berkshire Hathaway's purchase of stock in the Coca-Cola company was the ultimate case of me putting my money where my mouth was."

Hamburgers. "To refer to a personal taste of mine, I'm going to buy hamburgers for the rest of my life. When hamburgers go down in price, we sing the 'Hallelujah Chorus' in the Buffett household. When hamburgers go up, we weep."

Gillette razors. "It's pleasant to go to bed every night knowing that 2.5 billion males in the world will have to shave in the morning."

See's Candy. "When business sags we spread the rumor that our candy acts as an aphrodisiac. Very effective. The rumor, that is; not the candy."

The tap-dancing billionaire. "Money is a by-product of something I like to do very much. Every day when I get to the office, so to speak, I do a little tap dance."

Buy quality. It sure worked for Buffett. And remember, the best way of buying quality is simply by investing in a well-diversified portfolio of no-load index funds strategically allocated across the broad spectrum of the stock market.

REMEMBER, THE MORE ACTIVELY YOU TRADE, THE LESS YOU EARN

Schwager tells us that the successful market wizards are highly disciplined. Now money manager David Dreman tells us that most of us investors lack the necessary discipline to become successful active traders.

"Market timers, if they don't die broke, rarely beat the market," says Dreman. "Why don't more people beat the market? The answer is simple," he continues. "They lack discipline . . . and love to follow the crowd . . . almost always persuaded that they have seen clearly into the future. . . . Most of the time they prove wrong and it costs heavily."

So forget about short-term trading. *You will lose the game.*

There is a better solution: Buy'n'hold. Or as guys like Warren Buffett and Chuck Carlson would say . . . buy *quality* and hold . . . and hold . . . and hold . . . and hold . . . and hold . . . and hold . . . forever.

And as if to punctuate this point, while editing these paragraphs I received *The 2003 Quantitative Analysis of Investor Behavior* from the Dalbar market research firm, which has been studying investor performance for almost two decades. Their conclusion: Trading results in investors "earning equity fund returns *lower than inflation.* The average equity investor earned a paltry 2.57 percent annually, compared to inflation of 3.14 percent and the 12.22 percent the S&P 500 index earned annually for the past nineteen years." Get it? Trading means you aren't even beating inflation!

*Whether you want to believe it or not, you and you alone
have the best judgment when it comes to your money.
You must do what makes you feel safe, sound, comfortable.
You must trust yourself more than you trust others, and
that inner voice will tell you when it is time to take action.*

—Suze Orman, The 9 Steps to Financial Freedom

TEN

Strategy Six: Do-It-Yourself Wins

The Financial Nirvana Koan—
Why *Does* the Tortoise Beat the Hare?

SOME OF OUR GREATEST LESSONS ABOUT INVESTING COME FROM places you'd least expect to find them—far beyond the rigid world of Wall Street, where reality is an illusion.

In the Eastern Zen tradition, for example, the koan—an impossible riddle or paradoxical question with no real answer, other than the one you give it—is a useful tool. Zen masters use koans to jam your thinking processes, forcing you to dig deep within yourself for answers uniquely yours—to be creative, original, innovative. To be you.

The stock market is every investor's first koan. It can be stated in many ways, but this is the best adaptation of an important ancient koan for a modern investor: "If you meet the Buddha on Wall Street or CNBC, kill 'im." Tell me, what does that mean, *for you?*

This one should be easy! "The Buddha" isn't some sacred guru on cable television or a Wall Street broker cold-calling, pitching a hot stock.

SEARCHING FOR THE BUDDHA—IN ALL THE WRONG PLACES

As the ancient Zen masters will tell you, "the Buddha"— *the real Buddha*—is within you. We also know "the kingdom is within you." And you can only find it "in there." Not on cable news. Not in your broker's pitch. Not on Wall Street. It's not "out there."

How would the legendary Peter Lynch have answered such a koan? Here's a clue from his best-seller *One Up on Wall Street:*

> Rule #1 in my book, is: Stop listening to professionals. Twenty years in this business convinces me that any normal person using the customary three percent of the brain can pick stocks just as well, if not better, than the average Wall Street expert.

The Buddha is within you. When investing, trust only the still small voice—*and do it yourself.*

RABBITS, TURTLES, AND THE WISDOM OF JUST PLODDING ALONG

We find the same truths in our Western traditions. For example, Aesop's classic fable of "The Tortoise and the Hare" is a simple fairy tale offering investors great insights into the real world of investing, greater than all the fiction surrounding the surreal world of Wall Street.

For a few moments, listen closely once again to the ancient wisdom locked within this wonderful old story that has delighted children of all ages for generations. Ask yourself if you invest like the Tortoise—or the Hare. Here's a version you'll find on-line at the Ariel Funds, a fund family whose investment strategy is based on this simple wisdom, "Slow and steady wins the race." Would that more funds and more investors took this message to heart:

> One day, a fleet-footed Hare made fun of a rather plodding Tortoise. The Hare was surprised when the Tortoise laughed back. "Speedy you may be," said the Tortoise, "but I challenge you to a race and I bet I win."
>
> When the time came, both started off together. The Hare sped off from the start. In fact, he ran so quickly that he soon left the Tortoise far behind. He turned circles and flips as he raced ahead, keen and proud of his speed and nimbleness.
>
> Once the Hare reached the middle of the course, he was so far ahead, he decided to take a nap. While the Hare slept, the Tortoise plodded on and on, straight toward the finish line.
>
> Slowly, steadily, the Tortoise kept focus on his goal. When the Hare woke from his nap, he was surprised that the Tortoise was nowhere in sight. Racing to the finish line with all his proud speed, he saw that he was too late. The Tortoise was waiting there for him, a smile on his face.
>
> *Slow and steady wins the race.*

So what's the moral of this story of the arrogant rabbit and the methodical turtle? Never give up? Plodding wins? Discipline wins? So does long-term planning? Doing things your way wins? All the above!

SURFERS, TRUCK DRIVERS, DROPOUTS, ECCENTRIC RETIREES— ALL TURTLES!

Well, remember, folks, it's just a cute little fable written for kids, and just another koan—*that means the only real answer is your answer, the one you give, the answer that comes from within you.*

But one thing is for sure: Investing is definitely not as complicated as the wild, heroic racing stories told by Wall Street's rabbits. In fact, there's at least one insider who's rooting for Main Street's outsiders—Peter Lynch, a friend who once advised the turtles of the world to:

> Think like an amateur. If you invest like an institution, you're doomed to perform like one, which in most cases isn't very well. If you're a surfer, a truck driver, a high school dropout, or an eccentric retiree, then you've got an edge already.

Then, too, remember our friend Ric Edelman, who tells us that investors aren't in a horse race anyway, we're pitching horseshoes, and close enough is good enough. And not only is just being close good enough, but Edelman also explains in *Ordinary People, Extraordinary Wealth* that real millionaires don't even spend much time pitching horseshoes, either. They've got better things to do.

Real millionaires spend less than three hours a month on personal finance—that's about six minutes a day, hardly enough time for a quick glance at the business pages before turning to sports, or the arts and leisure section, or the comics.

ACCEPT THE CHALLENGE AND RUN THE RACE—RUN YOUR RACE

And at just six minutes a day, real millionaires certainly don't have enough time to read today's thick *Wall Street Journal* very closely. Or waste a lot of their precious time glued to the banal chatter coming out of CNBC, CNN, and Fox cable television all day long.

And why should they? As Charles Carlson says in *Eight $teps to $even Figures:* "Reacting to news on CNBC or any other financial media outlet is a loser's game." Probably the best expression of this theme ever was written by psychologist Wayne Dyer in *Real Magic,* one of my favorite books on this subject:

> Most of us believe that money-making is a game that is played with forces outside ourselves, forces such as the economy, the stock market, interest rates, the Fed, government policies, employment statistics and the like. But as you move along a spiritual path and begin to get a taste of the power of your invisible self, you discover that *money-making is merely a game that you play with yourself.*

Get it? Making money really is a game of solitaire. And whether you win or lose, you must accept the challenge and run the race—*your* race. Run a good race. Take total responsibility. You may as well; after all, it's *your money, your retirement, and your life* we're talking about here!

HERE'S HOW A REAL BUDDHA WINS—YOU DO IT YOURSELF!

And please remember, this is also a koan, an impossible riddle, a paradoxical question with no real answer.

As the ancient Buddha said long ago: "Believe nothing, no matter where you read it or who has said it, not even if I have said it, unless it agrees with your own reason and your own common sense."

So there is no real answer—*other than the one you give to it, on a daily basis.* And when that happens, the real Buddha—*you!*—wins, every time.

PART THREE

SIX MORE BORING, LAZY PORTFOLIOS FOR AMERICA

Say, Did You Hear the One About the New Preacher?

Independence: You need to do your own thinking.

Don't get caught up in mass hysteria.

By the time a story is making the cover

of the national periodicals, the trend is probably

near the end. . . . Never listen to the

opinions of others.

—*Jack Schwager,* The New Market Wizards

More of these index portfolios, boring variations on the same ol' theme? Yep. I'm not kidding, lots more. And for one darn-tooting good reason. We need all this, because it's so easy to forget.

My reason for reemphasizing and hammering home again and again all these dull, boring fundamentals is best told in a wonderful old story from Napoleon Hill's classic *Think & Grow Rich*.

As I recall it, the members of the parish were delighted that they had a new preacher. But after a few weeks, they were getting worried. The reverend had delivered the exact same sermon his first three Sundays at the pulpit. And after the third time, nervous eyes darted back and forth across the aisles as parishioners wondered if they'd made a mistake. Telephones were ringing off the hook as rumors kept flying—did we hire someone with some kind of memory problem?

Finally one of the deacons got tapped for the uncomfortable task of confronting the new minister. He arranged a private meeting in the parish rectory. He was mighty anxious: "Reverend, I . . . that is, we . . . well, sir, you see . . . the deacons were wondering if you were aware that you've been repeating the same sermon the last three Sundays?"

"Yes, I am," the new minister replied through piercing eyes, "and I'll keep doing it until they get the message."

SIMPLE TRUTHS TAKE LONGER TO SINK IN . . . WE NEED CONSTANT REMINDING

Investors often tell me they've been reading my columns for several years—and the reason why, they say, is because like the new minister, I repeat the same themes over and over— you have to keep repeating the basics in any field. Although I try to hook my columns into some hot news story, I invariably put what I'm working on in the broader context of long-term principles and fundamentals.

For example: I believe that what John Bogle, Warren Buffett, and Charles Schwab have to say about indexing, buy'n'hold, and value investing is vastly more important than anything any trigger-happy market timer or day trader will ever say in his lifetime. Moreover, I am convinced that at least ninety-three million of America's ninety-four million mutual fund investors would agree.

In addition, experience has taught me that the relentless noise from breaking news sources, like CNN and CNBC, easily distracts most investors from what really works in the long run. That the patient application of enduring principles ultimately works better than knee-jerk reactions to today's hot breaking news. And that principles work in both bull and bear markets, in rallies and dips, in prosperity and recession.

So why repeat? Very simple. Repetition is the best teacher

there is, next to experience. Simple truths take longer to sink in. And they seem to fade into the background so easily amid the noise of everyday life, especially if you're watching cable news. So we need constant reminders.

EXPOSED—SIX MORE REALLY SIMPLE, BORING, LAZY PORTFOLIOS!

That said, let's look at six more examples of some of the best of the boringest, dullest, laziest portfolios I can think of, hopefully told in a not-so-boring style. Hemingway I'm not, but I do feel a sense of excitement for all these critters. And I'll mix in some lighthearted entertainment while repeating and emphasizing over and over again the fundamentals that make a basic lazy portfolio "tick" in the first place:

1. **Dummies.** They also have the ultimate keep-it-simple portfolio.
2. **Dilbert's Anti-Weasel Defense Portfolio.** Plus the world's best one-page book.
3. **Motley Fools.** On-line hotshots morph into index portfolio champions.
4. **Idiot-Proof Portfolio.** For America's financially challenged winners.
5. **Trader's Index Portfolio.** He actively manages $7 billion, yet indexes his own money.
6. **Nobel Laureate Portfolio.** Duels between rocket scientists and lazy barbers.

The fact is, there are many similar lazy person's portfolios in more complicated technical and professional books.

But what impressed me most over the years is that I began seeing the simple stuff echoed in a simple way from simple sources I respected who not only weren't hiding their simplicity, but also wore it as a badge of honor—by putting on big "name tags" identifying themselves as FOOLS, IDIOTS, and DUMMIES, for example.

So here are some more variations on the core theme, some facts and figures and some entertainment from some of the financial world's best fools, idiots, and dummies, along with some parallel information on related resources, Dilbert's Weasel, and some dueling Nobel laureates.

THREE REASONS VANGUARD IS SUCH A BIG SECRET

You are going to see many more lazy portfolios with Vanguard funds. I really didn't plan it that way, and no, I'm neither on their payroll nor getting a kickback. Vanguard just emerged as some kind of secret weapon quietly used by savvy investors.

Once I got rolling with this research on lazy portfolios, I kept running across a lot of separate and independent sources that had developed their own lazy portfolios, *invariably with index funds and primarily with Vanguard funds because of the low costs.*

That's exactly what happened. So I hardly need to apologize for presenting the facts. Quite the contrary: It would be wrong to hide such important information from investors. But why was this information so secret? There are three reasons:

1. **Boring.** Index funds are really boring, so the media rarely focuses on them.
2. **No-loads.** Since most index funds are no-loads, commissioned brokers can't make a buck on them. So they will *always* push load funds, and they will *never* tell you about no-load index fund alternatives.
3. **Low expenses.** Vanguard has the lowest expense ratios, and industry research proves that low expense ratios are the *only* reliable predictor of future performance.

This message echoed loud and clear in an independent study mentioned earlier by the prestigious Financial Research Corporation (FRC) for industry insiders: *Predicting Mutual Fund Performance II: After the Bear.* The FRC studied five broad fund categories: domestic equities, international-global, corporate bonds, government bonds, and tax-free securities.

LOW EXPENSES—THE *ONLY* RELIABLE PREDICTOR OF PERFORMANCE

The eleven predictors tested by the FRC included: past performance, Morningstar ratings, expenses, turnover, manager tenure, net sales, asset size, and four risk/volatility measures—alpha, beta, standard deviation, and the Sharpe Ratio. The FRC's conclusions were quite significant—only one of the eleven predictors was of any help in predicting future performance.

That's right, of all the predictors, the FRC concluded that *the expense ratio is the only really reliable one in predicting future performance,* because funds with low operating costs "deliver above-average future performance across nearly all time periods."

Conversely, *all other predictors turned out to be unreliable—* including Morningstar's famed star ratings and the highly regarded Sharpe Ratio developed by a Nobel laureate in economics.

THE BIG SECRET—BUY CHEAP FUNDS AND YOU'LL WIN!

Bottom line: If you want predictable performance, pick cheap funds. That means no-load index funds. And since Vanguard has the lowest expenses, it should come as no surprise that its funds appear over and over in the lazy portfolios developed by so many independent sources.

And yet it does come as a surprise—in fact, a really big

secret since only 5 percent of all funds are indexed. So my hope is to expose this secret to a wider audience, because I'm convinced that this information will make Americans better investors—*and if I have to repeat this message over and over, then I will. . . .*

Say, did you hear the one about the new preacher?

So much attention is paid to which funds are at the head of the pack today that most people lose sight of the fact that, over longer time periods, index funds beat the vast majority of their actively managed peers.

—Eric Tyson, Mutual Funds for Dummies

ELEVEN

The Dummies Ultimate Keep-It-Simple Portfolio

Discover America's #1 Choice for 14 Million Dummies

UNTIL RECENTLY, AVERAGE MAIN STREET INVESTORS WERE VIEWED as financially illiterate by the experts—dummies who couldn't possibly comprehend the ultrasophisticated workings of the financial markets controlled by Wall Street.

Then suddenly the tables turned and being a dummy became a badge of honor for a new breed of do-it-yourself American! And nowhere was this revolution more evident than in the financial world, and especially in Eric Tyson's books for dummies.

Tyson's books are in a class by themselves. In fact, you can't wander into the personal finance, investing, or business section of any bookstore in America without seeing several books authored or coauthored by Tyson. I guess you'd call Tyson the financial world's number one dummy:

- *Personal Finance for Dummies.*
- *Investing for Dummies.*
- *Financial Planning for Dummies.*
- *Mutual Funds for Dummies.*
- *Taxes for Dummies.*
- *Home Buying for Dummies.*
- *House Selling for Dummies.*
- *Mortgages for Dummies.*

One of the things that I personally identified with immediately in Tyson's book on mutual funds was that he admits he "received some letters criticizing the first edition of this book for recommending too many Vanguard funds. One reader asked if I was on the Vanguard payroll," he says.

Wow, do I understand that one! The same criticisms were leveled at me on a regular basis as a columnist for CBS MarketWatch. But readers are entitled to their free-speech rights. So you just get used to it after a while.

AMERICA'S #1 CHOICE FOR 14 MILLION FUND INVESTORS

The fact is, there are only fourteen million Vanguard investors. That means there are eighty million other investors who are *not* Vanguard investors—and those eighty million are either the naive victims of the Wall Street Hype Machine, or they're Wall Street brokers who make a living off commissions—and those guys hate everything Vanguard stands for. The former rarely speak up, and the latter are vocal, defensive, and often very rude. In the 2001 edition, however, Tyson emphatically states:

I wish that more fund companies put the interests of their shareholders first, but the fact is, Vanguard is the best in this dimension. Thanks to Vanguard's unique corporate structure, it's the *only* fund company that is owned by its shareholders. Profits are returned to shareholders in the form of the lowest operating expenses in the business. For mutual funds whose performance depends heavily on the expense ratio—that is, money markets and bond funds—Vanguard is the number one choice.

So today I can say quite emphatically that Vanguard is the number one choice when it comes to any and all index mutual funds, including stock funds, as well as bond funds and money market funds.

In other words, neither Tyson, nor I, nor anyone ever need apologize for "recommending too many Vanguard funds." Heck, all you gotta do is go ask Vanguard's fourteen million investors. They'll tell you there's no such thing as too much of a good thing.

Remember, if you're a Vanguard investor, you're not on the payroll, you have an even better position—*you actually have ownership in the company!* And there isn't another dang fund investor in America who can make that same claim, other than another Vanguard investor.

WALL STREET GURUS WANT YOU TO *STAY OUT* OF INDEX FUNDS

The main reason that only about 5 percent of total investment is in index funds is simply because Wall Street can't make money on no-load low-cost index funds. It's that simple.

The Wall Street Hype Machine spends $15 billion annually to convince you that they can do the impossible—*beat the averages, that is, beat the indexes.* They not only can't beat them, but they consistently underperform by sizable margins. Tyson emphasizes another of the key reasons for this fact:

Although growing in popularity, index funds, which track the performance of the markets, still account for a small portion of total mutual fund assets. The main reason so little money is invested in index funds is because of all the ratings and ranking of funds. So much attention is paid to which funds are at the head of the pack today that most people lose sight of the fact that, over longer time periods, index funds beat the vast majority of their actively managed peers.

Index funds also seem sort of boring and ego-deflating because you're admitting that you can't beat the market, so you're resigning yourself to the market rate of return. Swallow your ego and discover the benefits of using these superb funds.

Unfortunately the Wall Street Hype Machine and the fund industry's conspiracy of actively managed funds are a great combination that fights hard to prevent full disclosure of the truth about the secrets they are hiding from the American investing public. As a result, they can continue to hoodwink naive investors and subtly cheat them out of their money by pushing substandard performers.

IF YOU BUY A NONINDEX FUND—YOU'RE THROWING AWAY 12%!

Whether Wall Street and the fund industry like it or not, as time goes on, investors are getting smarter as individuals and stronger as a group, and however the "revolution of the dummies" takes shape, it is coming, as more and more dummies, idiots, and fools are going to listen more to guys like Tyson when he says:

Index funds are perhaps the most underrated stock funds in existence. . . . The average U.S. stock fund has an operating expense ratio of 1.4 percent per year. (Some funds charge expenses as high as 2 percent or more per year.) That being the case, a U.S. stock index fund with an expense ratio of 0.2 percent per year has an average advantage of 1.2 percent per year. A 1.2 percent difference may not seem like much, but in fact, it is a significant difference. Because stocks tend to return about 10 percent per year, you're throwing away about 12 percent of your expected stock returns when you buy a non-index fund.

WALL STREET WANTS "REAL DUMMIES" AS INVESTORS . . . THEY'RE EASIER TO MANIPULATE!

When Arthur Levitt was chairman of the Securities and Exchange Commission back in the late 1990s, he spoke at an annual convention of the American Association of Retired Persons. Levitt made special note of an AARP survey of investors fifty and over. The results clearly show why brokers do not want a savvy public—because it's easier to take advantage of naive investors.

As you review these findings, imagine older relatives or friends who aren't very savvy about investing. Picture them dealing with a slick, high-pressure Wall Street shark whose main goal is to close the sale and pocket the commission:

- Eighty-eight percent of the people never asked their brokers whether they received higher commissions from one product than another.
- Sixty-four percent did not understand that higher-risk investments frequently carry higher commissions.
- Forty-eight percent did not know they could negotiate their commissions.
- Thirty-nine percent didn't even know that the broker's commission reduces their initial investment (for example, if you pay a 5 percent front-end load and invest $100, you lose $5 before you start, and have only $95 invested).
- Thirty-eight percent never asked how much the transaction actually cost.
- Thirty-seven percent didn't know that a load is a sales commission. And among women it was worse: 47 percent didn't know.

- Thirty-three percent didn't know that some firms use contests, in addition to the commissions they pay, as extra incentives to brokers.

Once investors get more information, the picture changes. For example, when asked about the conflicts of interest arising from specific questionable practices by brokers, 89 percent said they do believe it's wrong for brokers to get higher commissions for selling riskier investments.

In addition, 76 percent said they disapproved of the practice of giving brokers added incentives to sell their firm's own products. In short, once a broker is forced into full disclosure, and once the investor gets the right information, the problems inherent in these conflicts of interest become much more obvious to even a naive investor.

Get it? If you are naive enough to invest in an actively managed stock fund, you are investing in a handicapped horse that rarely beats an index fund in the short run, and in the long run will never beat it—*in short, you really are throwing away at least 12 percent of your return.*

In fact, you are throwing away at least twice that when you factor in the increased trading costs of a trigger-happy active manager in a high-turnover fund. And "if you factor in the taxes that you have to pay on your fund profits, these higher expenses gobble up perhaps a quarter of your after-tax profits." In short, you are actually throwing away about 25 percent of your profits if you invest in anything other than an index fund—something Jack Bogle and his friends have been saying for decades.

THE ULTIMATE KEEP-IT-SIMPLE PORTFOLIO FOR DUMMIES!

Tyson's respect for Vanguard index funds is most obvious in his chapter on portfolio building. He recommends several sample portfolios tailored to fit individual circumstances: retirement, inheritances, rollovers, divorces, recent graduation, a new family, and so on. And he does mention several of the best funds that do compete favorably with certain of the Vanguard funds, from fund families such as American Century, Dodge & Cox, T. Rowe Price, TIAA-CREF, and a few other solid no-loads. All good stuff.

But when the chips are down, you "want to keep things simple (without sacrificing quality)," Tyson says. How? The laziest of the lazy investors can still "establish and maintain a simple, yet solid, mutual fund portfolio by using funds of funds"—specifically the Vanguard LifeStrategy funds that are tailored to your age.

Alternatively, for retirement investments he also recommends a portfolio allocation of tax-friendly Vanguard funds in different mixes depending on your age. And three funds make up what Tyson calls "Eric's Keep-It-Simple Portfolio":

- Vanguard Total Stock Market Index Fund.
- Vanguard Total International Stock Index Fund.
- Vanguard Intermediate-Term Tax Exempt Fund.

And depending on your age, Tyson graduates the percentage of assets in bonds: from 20 percent for someone less than thirty-five years old, up to 80 percent for someone eighty-five or older. The balance of the portfolio is split two-thirds in the domestic stock index fund and one-third in international. Very simple, very basic, and clearly one solid way to adjust your portfolio depending on your age—a strategy the winning lazy portfolios believe may be unnecessary.

With guys like Tyson leading, the Revolution of the Dummies is guaranteed to beat the pants off Wall Street and the fund industry.

TWELVE

Dilbert's Anti-Weasel Defense Portfolio

Plus the Ultimate One-Page Book on Personal Finance

READY TO KISS OFF WALL STREET AND ALL THE OTHER SO-CALLED experts you're paying too much for advice that's actually lowering your returns? Ready to go it on your own? As a do-it-yourself investor?

Well, we found the perfect book for a one-book library on personal finance and investing—actually, it's a *one-page book,* if you can believe that's possible! It's also the perfect book to send to the so-called experts when you want to kiss 'em off and say bye-bye!

In fact, buy a dozen copies. It is by far better than any book ever written by or about Warren Buffett, Benjamin Graham, Peter Lynch, Burton Malkiel, Charles Schwab, or Jack Bogle.

Yes, it's that great. I'm talking about Scott Adams's *Dilbert and the Way of the Weasel.*

FIRST OFF, A DEFINITION—WHO THE HECK'S A WEASEL?

Weasels are those slippery people who live in "the Weasel Zone, the giant gray area between good moral behavior and outright criminality." Adams's book is loaded with brilliant and humorous comments about the financial weasels.

Why? Because of all the Weasel Zones, the financial world is by far the biggest—a veritable no-man's-land of weasel behavior, all day, every day. That's why the Dilbert Anti-Weasel Portfolio that I saw buried in Adams's book is so important to modern warfare on Wall Street.

So forget all you know; this book is destined to become the new American Bible of Personal Finance and Investing. Yes, that is a big claim. But trust me, I will back it up.

How? Well, at one point Adams takes off his funny hat and gets real serious. For the very first time in public, he reveals not only his secret desire to write a book on personal finance but also how—*until his great book on weasels*—humankind has been deprived of his financial genius. Why? Because his publishers came up with the strange idea that nobody would buy a one-page book.

Imagine that silliness. A one-page book: *Everything You Need to Know About Personal Investing!* But more on that later . . .

THE PERFECT WAY TO COMBAT WEASELS—PAST AND FUTURE

There are two primary ways you can use the Dilbert book to ward off weasels.

First, as a good-bye present. You'll have the great pleasure of sending copies to all those wonderful brokers and financial advisers, portfolio managers and fund gurus, analysts and television anchors who misled you and the rest of America's investing public to the tune of $8 trillion during the bubble/burst/bear cycle of the past decade . . . this is the perfect way to let them know how bad their advice was.

And second (listen closely, this is much more important), keep a copy of the weasel book near you at all times—next to your phone and your computer, in your briefcase, attached to your appointment book.

Keep it handy as a reminder. And in the future, when you have to make any decisions about money, investing, and personal finance, open it and reread it for five minutes, thinking through the pain of past advice. If you're in a big hurry, just hold the book in your hand, contemplating the weasels on the cover. The urge to seek advice from a financial weasel will soon pass!

BULL MARKETS—BREEDING GROUNDS FOR WEASELS

Yes, you really do need to keep a reminder handy. Weasels have a way of hypnotizing investors into forgetting past failures and the overwhelming damage they created in your portfolio—they hypnotize investors with even bigger promises of future miracles with your portfolio.

So you need all the anti-weasel devices possible to protect you from their hypnotic messages, handy reminders to guide your investing in the future.

Why? Because weasels multiply and breed fast in bull markets. They even tap into the little weasel in all of us. Which makes economic recoveries and bull markets dangerous to your financial health.

DILBERT'S AMAZING NEW WEASEL EQUATION

"Wherever there is money, there are weasels, usually in direct proportion," says Adams. "Someday an economist will win the Nobel Prize for discovering the exact dollar-to-weasel equation that explains our world. It will look something like this: 1 Weasel = $10. In other words, wherever there is anything of value worth $10, a weasel will appear as if by magic."

Oh my God, that means a relatively small $10,000 portfolio would attract one thousand Wall Street weasels! Imagine them attacking you, nibbling at a dollar here, a point there, a higher expense ratio, secretly increased trading costs—their little tricks go on endlessly. (Help! They're already doing it— today!)

SCOTT ADAMS DESERVES A NOBEL PRIZE IN ECONOMICS

Adams is a wise and astute observer indeed. In fact, he should be up for the Nobel Prize in Economics. Certainly the Nobel Committee has established precedent for going outside the field of economics to make an award, which makes you kinda wonder if maybe they know something we don't—that there are also too many weasels among economists today.

For example, the 2002 Nobel Prize in Economics actually went to a psychologist. So it's highly probable that any scientific connection between weasels and money will likely be made by a biologist or perhaps an anthropologist.

So why not Scott Adams the cartoonist—for being the first to observe this incredible Darwinian connection between money and weasel breeding? If the psychologist Kahneman can win the prize for "irrational investing," Adams's keen observations also deserve the prize more than most economists!

ONE WAY TO ERADICATE 4,000,000,000 WEASELS

The connection is so powerful that Adams made a most interesting observation about all the money traded on the New York Stock Exchange every day: "Weasels follow the money. If you took the same amount of money and sealed it in drums and dropped it in the ocean, 4 billion weasels would drown just trying to be near it."

That, of course, may be too drastic a solution to eradicating the Wall Street weasel problem at the stock exchange. It would be much easier and less costly to send them digital copies of Adams's weasel book.

PROMINENTLY DISPLAY *DILBERT AND THE WAY OF THE WEASEL*

The weasel book should be prominently displayed on your coffee table. Open it to his famous one-page book-within-a-book, because the wisdom in that one page matches the best of everything ever said by Buffett, Graham, Lynch, Malkiel, Schwab, and Bogle combined.

In addition, have this one-page investing "book" blown up and put in an elegant frame. It's possible it may have been written tongue in cheek—and some may tend to dismiss it because Adams slipped it into a book of humor. So I'm here to authenticate it, to tell you this one-pager is no joke—it really is one of the best books on personal finance and investing you will ever read.

Actually, it's less than one page, only 129 words, nine simple points. Rarely has any financial writer ever been so darn succinct. But unfortunately, as Adams warns, no one would buy a one-page book, not even a well-written one-page book that deserves honest professional exposure.

Adams punctuates his point with this powerful analogy: "If

God materialized on earth and wrote the secret of the universe on one page, he wouldn't be able to find a publisher."

DILBERT'S FAB-U-LOUS ONE-PAGE PERSONAL FINANCE BOOK

The idea of giving the weasel book as a gift actually came from Adams himself. So strike up the band—ruffles and flourishes, pa-leeze! Here's Scott Adams's one-page book, complete with everything you'll ever need on personal finance and investing:

1. **Make a will.**
2. **Pay off your credit cards.**
3. **Get term life insurance if you have a family to support.**
4. **Fund your 401(k) to the maximum.**
5. **Fund your IRA to the maximum.**
6. **Buy a house if you want to live in a house and can afford it.**
7. **Put six months' expenses in a money market account.**
8. **Take whatever money is left over and invest 70 percent in a stock index fund and 30 percent in a bond fund. Buy them directly from the fund company and never touch them until retirement.**
9. **If any of this confuses you, or you have something special going on (retirement, college planning, tax issue), hire a fee-based financial planner, not one who charges a percentage fee based on your portfolio's size.**

Incredibly simple: One page. Nine points. One hundred twenty-nine words. That's it. And when he says this is "Everything You Need to Know About Personal Investing," he's not kidding; it *is* all you need to know. And you sure don't need the help of Wall Street's weasels.

DILBERT'S ANTI-WEASEL DEFENSE PORTFOLIO

1. (70%) Vanguard Total Stock Market Index Fund.
2. (30%) Vanguard Total Bond Market Index Fund.

Give yourself a pat on the back—by now you've probably noticed that Dilbert's Anti-Weasel Defense Portfolio is suspiciously similar to the Couch Potato Portfolio. Well, at least the Sophisticated Couch Potato with 75 percent in a no-load stock index fund and 25 percent in a bond fund. Congratulations: You really are getting to understand the fundamentals of true lazy investing with Dilbert's remarkable new Anti-Weasel Portfolio!

IS IT REALLY THAT SIMPLE? YES, YES, *YES!*

But I can hear some of you saying: *C'mon Paul, his one-page personal finance "book" is entirely too simple. All those wonderful brokers and financial advisers, money managers and fund gurus, analysts and television anchors* must *be doing something for all that money we're paying them.*

Sorry to disappoint you, but they aren't. All those so-called experts are doing is jacking up your costs and reducing your returns. Save yourself some money—become a do-it-yourself investor and win.

EVERYTHING ELSE IS A BAD IDEA—A VERY BAD IDEA

Adams certainly has some strong convictions about this approach, warning investors, "Everything else you may want to do with your money is a bad idea compared to what's on my one-page summary.

"You want an annuity? It's worse," he says. "You want a whole life insurance policy? It's worse. You want to invest in individual stocks? It's worse. You want a managed mutual fund instead of an index fund? It's worse. I could go on, but you get the point."

So please, investors everywhere—get the point! And get a copy of *Dilbert and the Way of the Weasel*. It really is the one book all investors in America should carry with them and read before ever surrendering to a so-called investment expert. And it's also the perfect gift for all the financial weasels in your life—when you kiss them good-bye. Well, maybe not all of them; there are likely too many. Focus on the top ten weasels.

Your dream is real and available in a variety of index funds.
The biggest and best known is Vanguard's 500 Index fund. . . .
In an index fund you find 11 percent growth back-tested seventy-five
years, zero research commitment, a full knowledge of what
investments the fund is making . . . and—not to be
underrated—time to spend on other things.

—Tom and David Gardner, The Motley Fool Investment Guide

THIRTEEN

Motley Fools Morph into Index Champions

Music, Please! As Our Beloved
Fools Fall in Love with Indexing

A MOTLEY FOOL *INDEX* PORTFOLIO? YOU'RE KIDDING, RIGHT? OF course, you may reasonably ask about this incredible notion—*a fool's index portfolio*—from the kings of the fab-u-lous go-go 1990s, from America's hottest brand name in on-line investing, from the dynamic duo who popularized momentum trading on AOL as the common person's path to fame and fortune during the recent age of irrational exuberance and dot.com mania.

Yes, there is finally a pure Motley Fool Index Portfolio for America's laziest investors, and I will show you why and how it evolved. Because lessons gleaned from the evolution of this index portfolio are far more important than the portfolio itself.

This is an important story for America's remaining indexing skeptics, who are legion. For as they evolved from the dawn of the on-line revolution in the mid-1990s through the dark days of the bear market of the new millennium, until today, the Motley Fools have transformed from deferential tolerance of index funds into hard-core disciples of Jack Bogle and Vanguard, from high-flying momentum traders at all costs into respectful, conservative, disciplined, well-diversified, long-term investors. And that, folks, is a tale worth telling again and again.

MOTLEY FOOLS CAPTURED SPIRIT OF NEW INTERNET REVOLUTION

I first discovered the Motley Fools during the grand gold rush days of 1994 when on-line services were in their infancy, when high school dropouts, geeks, and nerdy entrepreneurs were having tons of fun roaming the new world of cyberspace and later making millions overnight—before Wall Street and Corporate America got their paws on that exciting new frontier.

Remember, back then CompuServe and Prodigy were bigger on-line services than Steve Case's quirky upstart, America Online. It was a fun time, perfect for a couple of lighthearted aggressive guys called the Motley Fools.

The Motley Fools really caught my eye because they captured the adventurous spirit driving the Internet. Like the rest of the on-line community, you kinda easily fall in love with the Fool Philosophy. In my first book, *The Investor's Guide to the Net: Making Money Online*, here's how excited I was when I first saw them on the America Online site back around 1994:

> **The Motley Fool:** A very popular section. Users love its witty approach. A cross between a Dan Dorfman segment, Louis Rukeyser's talk show, and a Tony Robbins infomercial. Or an Irish pub. There's a real online portfolio with trades

announced the prior day, stock tips, helpful investors forums, beginners courses, a no-nonsense library, and more.

Ah, those were the good ol' days, from 1995 until the new millennium. Oh how those wonderful Fools loved do-it-yourself stock trading! And like the rest of America, they were convinced it would never end as they rode the momentum of the ever-higher stock multiples to new levels of foolishness.

And yes, it all worked just fine in a raging bull market of the 1990s. The Motley Fools hitched a ride on America Online's star, and they both rocketed to success and glory.

MOTLEY FOOLS' NEW BEAR MARKET INDEXED PORTFOLIO

The Motley Fool Investment Guide: How the Fool Beats Wall Street's Wise Men and How You Can Too was first published in 1996 and became a *New York Times* best-seller. The founding Fools, brothers David and Tom Gardner, updated the book in 2001. Here's their delightfully naive original version of an indexed portfolio:

> The S&P 500 Index Portfolio . . . Imagine a single mutual fund whose eminently trackable performance matches market-average growth year after year, whose holdings are clearly outlined for you in advance, and that demands virtually no research. Imagine no more. Your dream is real and available in a variety of index funds. The biggest and best known is Vanguard's 500 Index Fund. . . .
>
> In an index fund you find 11 percent growth back-tested seventy-five years, zero research commitment, a full knowledge of what investments the fund is making . . . and—not to be underrated—time to spend on other things.

But alas and forsooth, America's best-known Fools then added, back in the go-go glory days of the 1990s, that thou shouldst not be satisfied with mere 11 percent rewards:

> Now let's push the ante up once more by thanking-but-no-thanking Mr. Bogle (Vanguard's redoubtable founder) and suggesting that *you look beyond his index funds*. While no one ought to accept anything less than average returns, if you're able and willing to take the risk beyond the index fund, there's a wide, wide world out there. . . .

Unquestionably the Fools showed deferential respect for Bogle and Vanguard, even though at one point they did refer to the Vanguard's basic index strategy as "Vanguard Hype." And so Fools rushed in where angels feared to tread, boldly encouraged to take on risks much higher than the boring 11 percent index fund returns acceptable to mere mortals.

FORGET THE "VANGUARD HYPE"—ANY FOOL CAN BEAT THE AVERAGES

Simultaneously, they had that cocky contrarian's edge, so prevalent during the go-go bull market, that "this time it's different," that yes, indexing was appropriate for older, more conservative Americans, but this new generation was not only different, but also way above average and would prove it:

> There's an extraordinarily important and rudimentary lesson that the majority of private investors have yet to learn: If you can't beat 'em, join 'em. If you've had trouble historically with your investments, Vanguard is there for you in a way no other fund company is. For this reason, we consider Jack Bogle a genuine modern-day hero of the individual investor despite our disagreement over the interpretation of the Efficient Markets Theory.

131

> These things said, if you *can* beat 'em, Fool, go ahead and beat 'em! *The book would end here if we thought we couldn't direct you to better than average returns.*

So when the Nasdaq was at stratospheric levels headed for 5,000 and any darn fool could make a fortune on-line—*just by following the triple-digit picks of a dart-throwing chimpanzee*—the Fools' Guide was confidently assuring Fools everywhere that while being average may be acceptable to the average Fool, the world now had a new breed of Super-Fools destined to beat the averages.

This overconfident mood propelled the Fools well into 2001, when the latest edition of the *Motley Fool Investment Guide* came out.

THE SPIRITUAL TRANSFORMATION OF THE MOTLEY FOOLS

Yes, spiritual. And definitely transformational! Flash forward a little more than a year—to mid-2002—after the bear mauled and clawed and chewed up almost $8 trillion in stock market value. Finally, the Fools capitulated. Which was not only good news, but also a signal that maybe the bottom had been reached and it was time to buy.

Capitulation? Transformation? Yes, you could see it in the Motley Fools' new book: *What to Do with Your Money Now: Ten Steps to Staying Up in a Down Market.* After many years of riding the exploding momentum of the dot.com market, the Fools were being resurrected and reincarnated as much humbler wizards—*in fact, diehard disciples of St. Jack Bogle*—offering newer, more conservative advice to a new generation of investors.

Their new book was loaded with obvious signs of capitulation, concession, confession, contrition, and surrender. But you gotta hand it to these guys for baring their souls with such a public mea culpa. They are a couple of first-class Fools who won my heart in 1994 and earned my respect in 2002. Here's why.

BEAR IS NO LAUGHING MATTER—FOOLS LEFT HOLDING THE BAG

The first noticeable sign of their capitulation and transformation was the cover photo of the authors, the Gardner brothers. It was almost the same shot as the one on the earlier *Motley Fool Investment Guide.*

But just almost. They definitely aren't smiling as much. Not as much teeth showing as in the earlier photo. A telltale sign of the bearish times. In fact, their grins look forced, and they're wearing black suits, looking more like undertakers at a dot.com wake than the successful Wall Street gurus dressing up the earlier book jacket.

Second, on the cover of the 2001 book is a chart showing the market headed up, up, and away! But on the later 2002 cover, they're "left holding the bag," literally—the cover shot shows the two brothers holding what looks like a money bag, but instead of dollar signs and bank ID numbers, there's a huge question mark on the bag—a sign of the hard times they've been through.

RETREATING VETERANS OF A BRUTAL WAR MAULED BY ANGRY BEARS

The third sign of the Fools' transformation was right up front in the dedication: "This book honors the contributions of those many people we laid off from our business in the year 2001, among them beloved friends and family members, a human congeries of passion and talent."

You gotta respect their hard-hitting realism and honesty: "those many people we laid off." You couldn't help but feel genuine sadness and reverence, as if this were an inscription in granite on a war memorial, because during the long bear market, it did feel as if we'd been at war.

In the 1990s investors marched off to battle, bands and generals leading us aggressively onward, singing loudly in praise of momentum, IPOs, tech, dot.coms, and the new Information Revolution, repeating the refrain over and over: "Yes, this time it is different!"

Then the bear and the long retreat and we became disillusioned about the meaning of this "war," with all too many opportunities to honor those who made the supreme sacrifice on the stock market's battlefields. And for that I salute the Motley Fools. Indeed, we must all honor them in stone so that future generations will never forget how brave, and foolish, we all were.

IN THE FUTURE—PENNY-PINCHING FROM *POOR RICHARD'S ALMANACK!*

What did our gallant heroes, the Motley Fools, learn? Great lessons. This war was a brutal teacher, when you assess the total damages of $8 trillion from March 2000 to the bottom. In fact, this is why their retreat is so significant, as is their transformation from total momentum traders to rather calm disciples of Jack Bogle and even Ben Franklin.

First, the Fools offer some good old-fashioned advice that sounds much like what Dominguez and Robin wrote in their ultrafrugal penny-pinchers' bible, *Your Money or Your Life*. Or better yet, ancient advice that could have come directly out of Ben Franklin's eighteenth-century *Poor Richard's Almanack*. Here is the Fools' five-point version:

1. **Reprioritize your budget.** In the 1990s nobody watched expenses.

2. **Refinance everything.** Thanks, Ben, a penny saved *is* a penny earned.
3. **Take losses and reduce capital gains.** Losses, what are they?
4. **Live below your means.** In a bear market, is there a real alternative?
5. **Get out of credit card debt.** High fees, penalties, et cetera, are killers.

The Fools would never have written such ol' fogy stuff a couple of years earlier. They'd have been laughed out of the AOL chat rooms as a couple of weenies for abandoning the aggressive take-no-prisoners momentum crowd.

THE FINALE—SIX "NEW" INVESTMENTS EVEN BOGLE COULD LOVE

But the best part of the Fools' book is their "six investments for the future," which they discovered a year or so into the bear market, and are actually old tried-and-true conservative alternatives from days gone by.

Seriously, as you read their six new recommendations, keep in mind that the Fools earlier dismissed index funds, convinced they could help Main Street investors get better-than-average returns. Alas, no more.

Evidence? Look at the six investments for the future in their wonderful new book, *What to Do with Your Money Now,* and note especially the incredible, astute addition of a bond index fund:

1. **Certificates of deposits.** After all, they're now beating the Nasdaq by a wide margin.
2. **Cheap broad market funds.** Emphasis on *cheap,* with the Fools now calling the Vanguard 500 Index and Vanguard Total Stock Market Index "investments of

the future." Get it? Indexing is the way to go in the future. Another apology to Jack Bogle.

3. **Bond index funds.** Yes, yes, bond funds! Obviously to offset a stocks-only portfolio, and an obvious acceptance of the "Vanguard Hype." They specifically mention Vanguard Total Bond Market Index. Mea culpa, mea maxima culpa!

4. **Companies paying solid dividends.** Another reversal from the Fools' momentum trading strategies in the late 1990s.

5. **Starbucks and established brands.** And they recommend other solid companies with strong brands, must-have products, sales growth, no debt, and so on. Yes, real basic companies with solid, long-term track records.

6. **Manage your portfolio for life.** Translation: No short-term trading like the good ol' days.

Bottom line: The Fools have not just capitulated, they've transformed into full-blown disciples of Jack Bogle. Today they are not simply giving lip service to index funds on their Web site and in their books—*they are one of us!*

In fact, if you look closely, it looks much like they finally wrote a book on index investing without admitting this subtle but powerful transformation. I, however, believe they deserve a big round of applause! Why? Because earlier in the go-go 1990s they referred to the Vanguard 500 Index Fund as a "portfolio"—but no bond index funds were mentioned. Now the new book not only includes but actually *spotlights* a conservative bond fund, the Vanguard Total Bond Market Index Fund. And that, folks, is a transformation of cosmic proportions that deserves recognition.

NOW THE FOOLS HAVE ONE OF AMERICA'S GREATEST LAZY PORTFOLIOS!

So now the Motley Fools actually have a real live two-fund lazy index portfolio. And it looks remarkably like—*yes, you guessed it*—the Couch Potato Portfolio. Seriously, go take a very close look: *There's the Vanguard S&P 500 Index Fund and the Vanguard Total Bond Market Index Fund!*

So congratulations, you wonderful lovable Fools, you have truly morphed into 100 percent diehard, fully indexed portfolio geniuses that Jack Bogle himself would be proud of. We applaud you!

And therefore, forthwith and henceforth, thee are now not only Master Indexing Fools, we hereby dub thee official possessors of one of America's laziest portfolios! Which is indeed a rather miraculous transformation for America's greatest momentum wizards.

Diversification means that if you divide your investments the right way, gains in one type of mutual fund can offset losses in other types of funds. One kind of fund may zig when the other zags.

—Alan Lavine and Gail Liberman,
The Complete Idiot's Guide to Making Money with Mutual Funds

FOURTEEN

Idiot-Proof Portfolios for the Financially Challenged

Slice the Pie so Your Funds Do the Ol' Zigzag Dance

WHEN IT COMES TO INVESTING, SAY A PRAYER. WE MUST INDEED thank God for taking care of all of us fools, dummies . . . and idiots in America. And thank God for Alan Lavine and Gail Liberman's *The Complete Idiot's Guide to Making Money with Mutual Funds,* which was a calm, settling voice during the insanity of the nineties Information Revolution.

And boy oh boy, do we ever need all the protection we can get. Most of us investors enter the fray about as enthusiastic (and also as naive) about personal finance and mutual funds and portfolio building as good ol' Charlie Brown is about becoming an entrepreneur and going into the snow-shoveling business in the great *Peanuts* comics. I remember this one quite well.

CHARLIE BROWN, ENTERPRISING ENTREPRENEUR IN ACTION!

The opening shot: Snowflakes are falling. Charlie Brown is out there with his shovel, ready for business (like an investor smelling a rally).

Brimming with enthusiasm, he tells Lucy: "It's starting to snow, and I'm ready. I'm going to be the first kid in the neighborhood to shovel walks. I'm going from house to house, and I'm going to shovel every sidewalk and driveway that I can find." (Rallies get the adrenaline flowing.)

"Will you make a lot of money?" Lucy asks.

"You bet I'll make a lot of money. And you think I'll spend it right away, don't you? Well, I won't," he tells her. As he continues, the snowfall begins to fade (like a rally losing steam).

YES, CHARLIE BROWN, NOW YOU CAN SAVE AND INVEST

"I'll probably put it in a savings account and just live off the interest," says a confident Charlie Brown. "Or maybe I'll buy an annuity payable at age twelve, or maybe I'll invest in some mutual funds, or even buy some stock in one of our local companies that seems to be getting bigger, or . . ."

The snow stops altogether: "Or maybe I'll . . . I'll . . ."

They look up into a clear sky, staring silently. After a bit they turn and head home, Charlie with his shovel over his shoulder.

Lucy doesn't help his ego much: "I remember reading about Abraham Lincoln, and how he used to do his homework with a piece of coal on the back of a shovel. . . ."

PEANUTS HELPS US LAUGH AT OUR WHIMSICAL FANTASIES

He cuts her off: "Forget it!" The rally must be over. The mood changes. Realism replaces optimism. Or is it pessimism? Certainly a gloomy mood.

Ah, the changing moods. What a reminder of real life. How often—*in such a brief space of time*—the world around us can so easily, so quickly, so dramatically alter our entire philosophy of life, our entire business and investment strategies, our feelings of enthusiasm, happiness, and self-worth, and can change us from master of our fate and captain of our destiny—to a victim of the whimsical and unpredictable muses roaming Wall Street.

DECISIONS AGAIN—ARE YOU A HYPERGAMBLER OR A LAZY INDEXER?

Well, folks, that's exactly why mutual funds make so much sense. You are either going to get in there and become a market timing day trader and make a full-time job out of tracking the daily, hourly, and minute-by-minute twists'n'turns of the Dow, the S&P 500, the Nasdaq, and a portfolio of maybe twenty-five to fifty stocks . . .

Or you're going to opt out of the high-risk timing-trading game and just passively invest in index funds, trusting that being average and matching the market indexes with a well-diversified portfolio are going to get you where you're going financially while you tend to the more important things in life, like work and family.

PICKIN' FUNDS ON PAST PERFORMANCE IS DANGEROUS

The Complete Idiot's Guide to Making Money with Mutual Funds is primarily a guide for savers focused on fund-picking strategies. Certain of the data and strategic ideas are a great historical reminder of the wisdom in the old caveat "Past performance is no guarantee of future results."

For example, *The Complete Idiot's Guide* has an appendix that features "The Ten Most Popular Funds," with this opening remark: "You can see why people like these funds. In recent years, they've all had double-digit returns. In addition, they all have performed well historically."

Then using Lipper data from July 2000, *The Idiot's Guide* offers readers some really exciting info about America's "ten most popular funds." These ten belong to just five fund families: Fidelity (three), American Funds (three), Janus (two), American Century (one), and Vanguard (one).

The dramatic change in their returns as we downshifted from the 1990s bull market to the depths of the bear market illustrates the extreme dangers of market timing, and offers another three cheers for passive index investing that simply tracks the market indexes along the unpredictable roller-coaster rides through bulls and bears.

TODAY'S TEN MOST POPULAR ARE RARELY TOMORROW'S

So let's take a close look at how they performed back then, just a few months after the start of the bear market . . . and how they were doing a little over two years later, deep into the bear market as the ten-year average of the S&P 500 fell from 16.0 down to 9.7 percent annually:

1. **Fidelity Magellan.** At the end of July 2000 Magellan had $105 billion in assets and was sporting a three-year average return of positive 18 percent annually. Twenty-eight months later—around Thanksgiving, in late November 2002—Magellan's assets had shrunk to $58 billion and its three-year average had dropped to a

negative 12 percent. Its ten-year average, however, was holding at 10.1 percent annually.

2. **Vanguard 500 Index.** The leading fund tracking Standard & Poor's 500 largest large-cap stocks experienced a drop similar to Magellan. At the beginning of this period, in July 2000, assets were $106 billion and returns were 16 percent. And twenty-eight months later assets had dropped to $56 billion, while the fund's three-year average returns were a negative 12 percent. The fund's ten-year average annual returns matched Magellan's at 10.1 percent.

3. **American Century Ultra Fund.** Another well-known and popular member of the top ten largest funds watched its assets drop from $41 to $18 billion while its three-year average returns sank from a positive 20 percent to a negative 10 percent through the twenty-eight-month period.

4. **American Funds.** American Funds is the third largest fund family, behind Vanguard and Fidelity, and not to be confused with the American Century family of funds. As a whole, the three American Funds among the top ten—the Investment Company of America, Washington Mutual Investors, and EuroPacific Growth Fund—fared slightly better than the other seven. Their total assets dropped from about $138 billion to $108 billion and their average returns dropped from the 12 percent range to a minus 6 percent, with their ten-year average returns still about 10.7 percent.

5. **Janus Fund and Janus Worldwide.** The Janus family of funds was one of the top performers during the late nineties *and* the hardest hit by the bear market. These two funds were among the ten largest in early 2000, with assets of $47 and $42 billion. Each lost about two-thirds of its value, dropping to $16 and $13 billion.

Their returns dropped dramatically: Janus was blazing along at 27 percent on a three-year basis in early 2000 and dropped to minus 20 percent in 2002. Worldwide dropped from a plus 25 percent to a minus 17 percent three-year annual average. Ten-year averages were 8 and 10 percent, respectively, at the end of the twenty-eight months.

There is a great lesson here! Now you can see why the so-called rule against predictability—*"Past performance does not guarantee future results"*—makes so much sense. And also why it makes sense for investors to spread their risks by indexing.

SHORT-TERM PERFORMANCE DATA IS VERY MISLEADING

Back in mid-2000, any attempt to predict the future performance of any one of America's ten most popular funds using data from the prior three-year averages was foolish and risky, bordering on lethal—obvious in hindsight, since the market as a whole lost $8 trillion through the bear market. And yet, back then, probably 99 percent of the investing public was ignoring that venerable ol' rule and assuming that past performance would indeed predict future results.

Big mistake! This doesn't mean you're an "idiot" just because you invested in any one of these funds, because most of their declines matched the declines of their peer groups. But once again, it sure does prove that market timing and economic predictions are a waste of time—and a waste of your money.

FOCUS ON LONG-TERM DATA AND DIVERSIFICATION

Perhaps a more accurate warning would be: *"Short-term* past performance is not a guarantee of future results in the *short term."*

Why? Because over time, the peaks and valleys of the *long-term* winners are what tell the real story. For example, notice that despite the dramatic shifts from three-year averages in the positive 15 to 20 percent range to a negative 10 to 15 percent range between the peak of the bull to the bottom of the bear, the ten-year average returns were still in the 10 percent range.

So what's the main lesson? Very simple: Never try to time the market; it's too much of a gamble. Create a well-diversified index portfolio that balances out the peaks and valleys over time. Period.

IDIOTS AGREE, DIVERSIFICATION IS KEY, BALANCING THE ZIGS AND ZAGS

According to *The Idiot's Guide,* "Diversification means that if you divide your investments the right way, gains in one type of mutual fund can offset losses in other types of funds. One kind of fund may zig when the other zags." And while there are sophisticated technical explanations, that's just about all you need to know about this simple idea.

Why? Well, next time you're in a Barnes & Noble or Borders bookstore check out *The Idiot's Guide* and look closely at their four basic ways to slice your portfolio pie:

1. **Aggressive investors.** You're twenty to forty-nine years old with a long horizon, so 80 percent in stocks and 20 percent in bonds.
2. **Moderate investors.** You're fifty to fifty-nine years old,

closer to retirement, so 60 percent in stocks and 40 percent in bonds.

3. **Conservative investors.** If you're sixty to seventy-four years old, you need income and some capital protection, so 40 percent in stocks, 40 percent in bonds, and 20 percent in money markets.

4. **Senior citizens.** At age seventy-five and older you should have just 20 percent in stocks, 60 percent in bonds, and 20 percent in money markets.

Simple stuff, right? Well it should be simple. Once more, let me repeat, investing is simple stuff; any idiot really can do it following the kind of simple basic advice in *The Idiot's Guide*. Remember Peter Lynch's encouraging remark: "Any normal person using the customary three percent of the brain can pick stocks just as well, if not better, than the average Wall Street expert." And that goes for you—because if any idiot can do it, so can you!

Funds charge annual expenses of 1 percent or more. Then it costs another 1.5 percent to 2 percent to buy and sell their stocks each year. It's hard to imagine them doing anything but just following the crowd, because if they don't mimic the index, they'll get beaten by it.

—Ted Aronson, institutional fund manager

FIFTEEN

Where Do Active Money Managers Put Their Own Money? In Safer Passive Index Funds!

One Honest Manager Breaks the Code of Silence

WHAT IF YOU DISCOVERED THAT YOUR FUND MANAGER (AN AGGRESsive stock trader with a high turnover ratio) not only had very little of his own money invested in his own fund (the one paying him the huge sum of $436,500 or more a year), but that he had all his own money invested in other, rather conservative funds?

That is, these guys are supposed to be investing "outside the (index) box," but they may—with their own money—be secretly sneaking back into the box, without disclosing this fact to you and the rest of their investors.

CAN YOU REALLY TRUST YOUR FUND MANAGER?

We already know that active fund managers do *not* have to disclose where they invest their own money. This is just one of many dirty little secrets that's part of the fund industry's massive conspiracy of silence. There are two compelling reasons why managers may not want to disclose this information:

1. **Lack of confidence in their own aggressive management strategy.** First, if they have too little in their own fund, it would expose their lack of confidence in their own management abilities.
2. **What if managers' own money is in conservative funds?** And second, if they had to disclose where their own money's invested *outside* their own fund, you'd probably be shocked to discover that they're aggressive with your money but a helluva lot more conservative with their own, and probably heavily indexed and in a higher percentage of fixed-income securities.

So you can imagine my excitement when I found one among the forty-three thousand money managers in America who not only talks freely about where he parks his own money, but even says he's "proud" of it. This rare find is Ted Aronson of Aronson + Johnson + Ortiz. Their team actively manages $7 billion for about fifty clients—institutional money, retirement portfolios, endowments, and corporate pension fund accounts—and they're among the best money managers in the business.

HE'S OWNED AMERICA'S FIRST INDEX FUND SINCE 1976

Imagine, actually meeting someone who bought Jack Bogle's Vanguard 500 Index Fund way back in 1976. In the beginning. Not only that, but *he still owns this dull, boring, passive fund that does nothing but sit quietly in his portfolio and track the S&P 500 index* . . . chalking up an astounding cumulative 2,000 percent since inception. No rebalancing, no trading, no monitoring . . . the ultimate laziest investor's fund.

Even more incredible: This guy, who has been investing his own money in the S&P 500 index fund "forever," is an *active* money manager, and a "quant" to boot (one of those high-tech managers who rely heavily on quantitative analysis and "rocket science").

And get this: Not only has Aronson been in Vanguard 500 Index since day one, but he *also* has all of his personal taxable accounts in ten other Vanguard index funds! And he told me, "I'm proud to say we've owned many of them for as long as they've been in existence." Now, that sure sounds like a true-blue buy'n'hold investor.

WHAT? ACTIVE MANAGER INVESTING IN PASSIVE INDEX FUNDS?

But wait a minute: Isn't all this a bit contradictory? Isn't it a bit strange that a successful, actively trading institutional money manager is putting his own personal money in dull, boring, passive index funds?

Couldn't he do better investing his money in the accounts he actively manages, where he'd presumably make more money? At least to show his clients he's confident of his ability to beat the market?

Yes, indeed, all verrry good questions! So stick with me and you'll see the very simple reasons why Aronson puts the bulk of his own family's money into eleven no-load Vanguard index funds. Listen closely, because there is a powerful lesson here for all investors in America.

$10,000 IN THE FIRST S&P 500 FUND IS WORTH $200,000 TODAY

To begin with: That darn S&P 500 index fund has served him very well. It has averaged about 12 percent annually since Jack Bogle introduced the fund in 1976, as the "First Index Investment Trust."

That means, if you've been in the fund since 1976, you've made a cumulative return of roughly 2,000 percent. Look at it this way: If you gave Bogle $10,000 in 1976, your investment would now be worth $200,000, including the original money. Twenty times as much as you put in. Now folks, that's exciting news!

And it's even more exciting to know you would have made that kind of money if you had stopped reading the newspapers, avoided on-line trading, never watched CNBC . . . and simply stuffed your shareholder documents from Bogle's totally boring, dull, passive index fund in a shoe box in your attic and never looked at them the past twenty-six years.

VANGUARD IS STILL THE DEVIL SITTING ON HIS SHOULDER

But still, that begs the real issues here: Why would Aronson—a savvy guy actively managing $7 billion for other people, clearly with the intent of maximizing returns above average—*put all his own money in a dull, boring, passive index fund?*

Why? Well, the fact is the money he manages for institutional clients is nontaxable money. And "all of my family's *retirement* money is in our funds," says Aronson, thanks to the tax benefits of retirement plans. "But because the funds trade a lot, it's *not* suitable for *taxable* investments. So all our taxable money is in Vanguard's no-load index funds."

Vanguard sets the performance standard: "My partner Kevin Johnson used to run the entire indexing show at Vanguard, where minimizing costs is crucial. By contrast, we're active managers with annual turnover of 100 percent. I never forget that devil sitting on my shoulder, meaning the low-cost passive funds. They are stiff competition. Vanguard has it nailed. *They win because they lose less. Their costs are lower. Quarter after quarter, year after year.*"

TOP ACTIVE MANAGER PICKS PASSIVE ALL-VANGUARD PORTFOLIO

So please take a very close look at the eleven no-load Vanguard index funds in the Aronson family's well-diversified portfolio. The percentages are the approximate asset allocations in his portfolio—and rather bullish, with 70 percent in stocks at a time in late 2002 when the bear was growling loudly.

(40%) DOMESTIC STOCK FUNDS
1. (5%) Wilshire 5000 (VTSMX).
2. (15%) S&P 500 Index (VFINX).
3. (10%) Wilshire 4500 Mid-/Small-Cap (VEXMX).
4. (5%) S&P Small-Cap 600/BARRA Growth (VISGX).
5. (5%) S&P Small-Cap 600/BARRA Value (VISVX).

(30%) FOREIGN STOCK FUNDS
6. (15%) Emerging Markets MSCI-EMGFree (VEIEX).
7. (10%) Pacific Stock Index MSCI-PAC (VPACX).
8. (5%) European Stock Index MSCI-EUR (VEURX).

(30%) FIXED-INCOME FUNDS
9. (10%) TIPS: Inflation-Protected Securities (VIPSX).

10. (10%) High-Yield Corporate (VWFHX).

11. (10%) Long-Term Treasury (VUSTX).

Then Aronson added, somewhat tongue in cheek, about his style of money management in the portfolio he manages: "I obviously follow a highly complex, sophisticated strategy . . . diversify . . . keep costs down . . . buy what's wounded . . . sell what's done well!"

Bottom line: When it comes to his own taxable money, however, Aronson is a real keep-it-simple, passive, boring, buy'n'hold money manager—not the same as an active trader with tax-free money.

FUND MANAGERS' DIRTY LITTLE SECRET—THEY CAN'T BEAT INDEXES

Ted Aronson is incredibly blunt when it comes to the business of active fund management where taxable money is involved. When asked why most managers can't beat the indexes, this was his reply:

> They can't. Costs. Funds charge annual expenses of 1 percent or more. Then it costs another 1.5 percent to 2 percent to buy and sell their stocks each year. It's hard to imagine them doing anything but just following the crowd, because *if they don't mimic the index, they'll get beaten by it.*

And keep in mind that unlike Aronson (he only manages institutional pension funds), the bulk of the mutual fund managers he's talking about today are investing your money in taxable accounts. And unfortunately, for them to be successful, "Turnover has to come down to superlow, like 15 to 20 percent, or taxes will kill you. *That's the dirty little secret in our business.* Because mutual funds are bought and sold *with virtually no attention attached to tax efficiency."*

As a result, actively managed mutual funds are *guaranteed to underperform the indexes* due to unnecessary loads, excessively high expenses, trading costs, and extra taxes.

The fact is, investor returns are *not* your fund managers' main concern. Managers are motivated by self-interest. They are "paid based on assets under management, not the quality of that management," says Aronson.

As a result, more assets mean that "even if some idiot hasn't matched his benchmark, his fees have doubled." So today's hungry fund managers focus primarily on increasing assets rather than investor return—after all, that's what increases their take-home pay!

ANOTHER BIG SECRET—ALL FUND MANAGERS ARE CLOSET INDEXERS

That's Aronson's conclusion about today's fund managers. They are so afraid of losing that they are "just following the crowd" to avoid getting beaten. In short, they have quietly surrendered to indexing: If you can't beat 'em, join 'em.

And Aronson is quite blunt about this: America's actively managed funds are now *"closet indexers."* And unfortunately, in the process of playing this deceptive game with our money, they're developing split personalities and getting "stupider." Why? Because they are all becoming index funds in disguise!

This costly game makes it virtually impossible for the taxable funds to beat their benchmark indexes. In fact, we *know* they can't do it, because 85 percent already fail to beat their own indexes each year, and only *one* manager has been able to beat the S&P 500 consistently every year for more than ten years.

FUNDS LIVE IN TWO SEPARATE WORLDS—*AND YOU PAY THE BILL*

It was actually quite exciting to meet one of the best active money managers in the business and discover that he's also a true-blue buy'n'hold indexer, and proud of it. And not only the proud owner of the first index fund since inception, and others from their launch date, but also proud of having his own money in an all-index portfolio.

Remember, however, that folks such as Aronson are extremely rare birds among the forty-three thousand money managers in America. Unlike Aronson, most will fight like caged animals to prevent you from finding out where they invest their own money, both how much they have in the funds they manage, and also how much they've invested in other assets. And you can easily see why: For one thing, many don't have enough confidence in their skills as managers to put too much of their own money at risk in their own fund.

And for another—they'd be pretty darn embarrassed to have you find out that they are *conservative with their own money, while aggressive with yours—the money you've invested in their fund!* Indeed, they should be ashamed for not disclosing their split-personality strategies.

I should have computed co-variances of the asset classes and drawn an efficient frontier; instead, I split my contributions 50/50 between bonds and equities [to] minimize my future regret.
—Harry Markowitz, Nobel economist

Why pay people to gamble with your money?
—William Sharpe, Nobel economist

SIXTEEN

Even Nobel Economists Prefer Lazy Theories

While High-Risk Alternatives Almost Ignite a Global Meltdown

PROFESSORS HARRY MARKOWITZ, WILLIAM SHARPE, AND MERTON Miller won the 1990 Nobel Prize in Economics for their work in developing Modern Portfolio Theory (MPT), which is the theoretical basis for the work of virtually every single money manager in America today—*including lazy investing.*

Simply put, Modern Portfolio Theory focuses money managers *on the portfolio as a whole, not the individual securities,* using diversification and asset allocation to maximize your investment returns while minimizing your risks. These economists proved that what really counts is the mix of stocks, bonds, and funds in your portfolio, not your talent for picking the best individual stocks, bonds, and funds.

Let's emphasize this again, because MPT is also the basis of lazy investing: What the MPT guys discovered is that the classes of assets and the way you slice the pie are more important in the long run than your stock-picking genius. *In fact, diversification is about ten times more important than the specific stocks or funds you pick.*

SECOND TEAM OF NOBEL ECONOMISTS USING HIGH-RISK THEORIES

In 1997 two other American economists won the Nobel economics prize for work that was at the exact opposite end of the theoretical spectrum. While the MPT trio won for a very conservative approach, Myron Scholes and Robert Merton, professors at Stanford and Harvard, respectively, won for their daring, radical, highly sophisticated, high-risk, highly leveraged hedging strategies using derivatives and various trading technologies whimsically referred to as "rocket science."

Scholes's and Merton's timing was perfect: The Internet Revolution had just moved into high gear as Netscape—the first big Internet IPO—made the first instant dot.com billionaires. Wall Street fell immediately in love with them, backing them with substantial private capital from the major Wall Street firms and their executives, as they created a rather secretive hedge fund called Long-Term Capital Management (LTCM).

NEW WALL STREET WIZARDS FOR THE DOT.COM REVOLUTION

LTCM looked like a sure bet to win—*and win big.* Wall Street's elite were so certain, they literally threw money at their hedge fund. There was no shortage of investors with the $10 million minimum required; even the chairs of Merrill Lynch and Paine Webber invested their own money.

Total capital from all sources was $4.8 billion, which LTCM leveraged to the max, ultimately controlling a portfolio of $200 billion! Unfortunately, LTCM collapsed of its own weight. As *BusinessWeek* put it, the "Long-Term Capital rocket science exploded on the launchpad" when its overleveraged portfolio backfired in fall 1998 as global markets collapsed.

MELTDOWN OF A HIGHLY LEVERAGED TEAM OF NOBEL LAUREATES

In a rapid series of humiliating meetings in August and September 1998, the head of the New York Federal Reserve Bank, Bill McDonough, stepped in to avert a global market panic. It had become obvious that LTCM, the brainchild of the two Nobel laureates, was bleeding to death.

In the end McDonough negotiated a Fed-sponsored $3.5 billion bailout of LTCM involving fifteen international banks, a buyout that essentially wiped out all investors' equity capital—as well as the reputation of these distinguished Nobel laureates.

So much for Nobel Prize winners who invent ultrasophisticated formulas and gamble with other people's money using derivatives and high-leveraged tools that result in even higher risks. In the end the Long-Term Capital Management fund proved to be neither "Long-Term" nor good at "Capital Management"!

ADVENTURES AT THE OUTER EXTREMES OF INVESTMENT RISK

So let's compare the high-flying LTCM team to the lazy MPT team, each clearly at opposite ends of the risk spectrum. To begin with, Modern Portfolio Theory is actually simpler than a deli sandwich to understand.

MPT simply tells investors they can *minimize risk exposure* through asset allocation, by spreading risks across several assets (like the winning laziest portfolios). In contrast, Scholes and Merton did the exact opposite—*they increased risk exposure* by using highly leveraged derivatives.

So when a guy like Markowitz and his buddies speak, investors should listen closely. As sophisticated as MPT may appear in theory, the application of it turns out to be remarkably simple. And I found out just how simple from my favorite *Dallas Morning News* columnist, Scott Burns.

MARKOWITZ—A KEEP-IT-SIMPLE POTATO HEAD ALL ALONG

You remember Burns, creator of the Couch Potato Portfolio—that simple two-fund index portfolio that returned an annual average of 10-percent-plus for more than a decade.

Burns was attending a conference at the University of Chicago a few years ago when Professor Richard Thaler, one of America's leading behavioral economists, asked Markowitz *how he invested his own personal retirement funds.* Markowitz's answer absolutely delighted Burns!

Here's Markowitz's rather understated response: "I should have computed co-variances of the asset classes and drawn an efficient frontier; instead, I split my contributions 50/50 between bonds and equities [to] minimize my future regret."

INVESTING HAD BETTER BE AS DULL AS WATCHING PAINT DRY!

Get it? In practice, MPT is very simple. No complicated co-variances. No fancy derivatives. No costly financial planners. Just basic do-it-yourself investing. Actually, not even that, because guys like Burns are so index-oriented they think rebalancing once a year may be overdoing it, and apparently Markowitz, the brilliant Nobel laureate, is not much different.

THE NOBEL PRIZE WINNERS' "BEAUTIFUL MIND" PORTFOLIO

By now you've probably noticed that the winning portfolio in this little comparison between Nobel economists is amazingly similar to the Couch Potato Portfolio, with 50 percent in equities and 50 percent in bonds, looking something like this:

1. (50%) Equities. Vanguard Total Stock Market Index Fund.
2. (50%) Bonds. Vanguard Total Bond Market Index Fund.

Why yes, you say, *it does look oddly familiar!* But for the time being, let's just quietly call this one the Nobel Prize Winners' Beautiful Mind Portfolio, so as not to confuse it with Scott Burns's Couch Potato Portfolio. Okay? After all, we don't want to suggest that all the brilliant mathematical formulas of these geniuses are really unnecessary when it comes to the real world. So . . . let's keep it simple, investors, real simple!

So you gotta love these Nobel laureates—they're real folks, like the rest of us. Take Paul Samuelson, for example, who won the Nobel economics prize way back in 1950. His college textbook has been a standard ever since. And he's been one of America's strongest advocates of a buy'n'hold strategy. You may remember his classic remark:

Investing should be dull. It shouldn't be exciting. Investing should be more like watching paint dry or watching grass grow. If you want excitement, take $800 and go to Las Vegas [although] it is not easy to get rich in Las Vegas, at Churchill Downs, or at the local Merrill Lynch office.

Then there's Bill Sharpe, the co-developer of Modern Portfolio Theory who received the Nobel Prize in 1990 along with Markowitz. A couple of years ago, when an interviewer asked Sharpe if he invested in broadly diversified stock index funds, Sharpe replied: "I certainly do." Then he was asked if he tried to pick individual stocks or time the market. "No," he said, "I invest in various funds, large stocks, small stocks, and international stocks."

ASTROLOGERS BEAT STOCK PICKERS AND MARKET TIMERS

Another University of Chicago economist, Eugene Fama—who may be in line for the Nobel Prize for his work developing the "Efficient Market Theory"—once expressed his disdain for active money management and market timing when interviewed in *Fortune* magazine: "I'd compare stock pickers to astrologers, but I don't want to bad-mouth the astrologers."

Where does Fama invest his retirement money? In index funds! Mostly the Wilshire 5000, he told *InvestmentNews,* with a little in other equity index funds, including small-cap and international index funds. And less than a third in value-oriented stock indexes and short-term bond funds.

THE SECRET LESSON OF THE NOBEL'S "BEAUTIFUL MINDS"

Perhaps the most amazing insight I got out of this review of the investment habits of Nobel laureates is the simplicity of their investing strategies. In fact, according to *InvestmentNews,* many college finance professors, as well as Nobel economists, prefer index funds.

In other words, whether future returns average only 5 percent . . . or 7.5 percent . . . or match the historical average of 11 percent . . . or even go back up to 20 percent annually—*it doesn't matter.* Whether we're in a bull or bear market—*it doesn't matter.* Whether the economy is recovering or tank-ing—*it doesn't matter.* Whether you pick *this* specific stock over *that* stock—*it doesn't matter.*

What matters? Shout it once again with gusto, folks—*it's the portfolio, stupid!* That's what really counts—*your whole portfolio and your asset allocations, not your hotshot stock-picking ability.*

And the same strategy applies whether you're in the cloistered halls of academia, at the trading desks on Wall Street, employed as a portfolio manager of a billion-dollar fund, in the executive suites of Corporate America, in a government bureaucracy, or in your den at home on Main Street America.

It's the portfolio, stupid. So keep it simple—use index funds like these keep-it-simple Nobel economists!

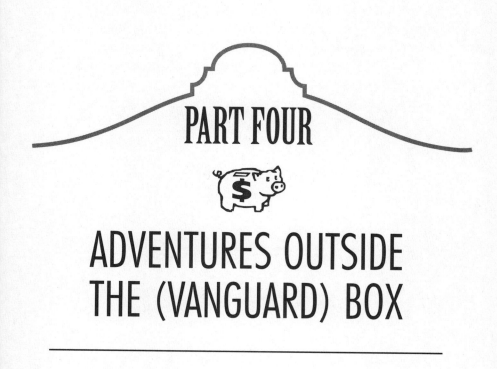

PART FOUR

ADVENTURES OUTSIDE THE (VANGUARD) BOX

When Making Money the Lazy Way Gets Too Easy for You

I wish that more fund companies put the interests of their shareholders first, but the fact is, Vanguard is the best in this dimension. Thanks to Vanguard's unique corporate structure, it's the only fund company that is owned by its shareholders. Profits are returned to shareholders in the form of the lowest operating expenses in the business.

—Eric Tyson, Mutual Funds for Dummies

By now you probably think there's a Vanguard on every corner, along with a Starbucks and McDonald's, right? And you probably believe that American investors in-the-know walk in every day to the local corner Vanguard and treat themselves to a mutual fund latte and an indexing muffin.

Wrong. Let me refresh your memory about Vanguard, the 800-pound gorilla the rest of the fund industry gives lip service to—*but secretly hates*—the scrappy underdog that Wall Street's superelite "greed-is-good" ol' boys club would love to see vanish from the face of the earth.

OUTNUMBERED, OUTSTAFFED, OUTGUNNED . . . AND STILL WINNING

Vanguard is a total anomaly in the investment world—the underdog, a renegade, a rarity, an oddball, a bizarre weirdo, a major deviation from the norm, like humans stranded on the Planet of the Apes, hobbits deep in Middle Earth, Luke Skywalker fighting the Evil Empire, George Washington's ragtag army winning the American Revolution.

Anomaly? Yes, check the numbers. Vanguard is outnumbered, outmanned, and outgunned when you look at it in the larger context of the mutual fund industry as a whole:

- **The total of all mutual fund assets is roughly $6 to $7 trillion.**
- **There is, however, only $300 billion in all index mutual funds.**
- **That means less than 5 percent of the total $6 to $7 trillion is in index funds.**
- **So index funds are no big deal in the larger scheme of things.**
- **And Vanguard manages more than $200 billion in all forty of its index funds.**
- **So Vanguard is the leader with almost 70 percent of all index funds.**
- **In addition, Vanguard's total assets are in the range of $600 billion.**
- **Which is just about 10 percent of the total money in all mutual funds.**
- **Another key fact: Only about a third of all funds are no-loads, while the remaining 65 percent of all funds are sold by commissioned brokers. Meanwhile, Wall Street acquisitions of fund companies are resulting in an increase in the number of load funds.**
- **So on the surface, indexing is not a big deal, Vanguard may not be either, and, statistically, no-loads aren't really much of a big deal today, either.**

And yet—*although numerically small*—Vanguard, indexing, and no-loads are a very, very big deal throughout Wall Street and the fund industry. Which just goes to show you that one man's vision—Bogle's vision for Vanguard—has made a huge difference.

Specifically, Vanguard's no-load index funds have become the benchmark and the standard against which every other fund, index or active, and all fund families are measured. They are the proverbial pain in the ass for the vast majority of their competition in the mutual fund industry.

EVENTUALLY *ALL* MUTUAL FUNDS GET COMPARED TO VANGUARD'S

No wonder Vanguard is the most feared and hated fund company, by Wall Street and by the major actively managed fund companies. Just look at the mutual fund statistics from any of the fund trackers.

Morningstar, Lipper, and Standard & Poor's all measure every single fund's performance against some index, and since Vanguard has a fund that tracks virtually every index, ergo, Vanguard is the benchmark for all funds.

No wonder Vanguard has fourteen million shareholders! America loves the underdog, the oddball, the renegade, the outgunned leader of the revolution! If you think about index funds, Vanguard naturally comes to mind as the obvious choice: It has the best selection of index funds.

You aren't going to find Vanguard out there on as many corner locations and as often as Starbucks and McDonald's—Vanguard is more like an elite Tiffany's or Rolls-Royce, what you could call "understated elegance."

In fact, several years ago the distinguished *Kiplinger's Personal Finance Magazine* published a feature article focused on the range of totally indexed portfolios for various ages and lifestyle needs. Vanguard index funds were the magazine's first choice across the board for every portfolio. And today Vanguard remains the first choice of fourteen million investors.

COMPETITION FROM THE ACTIVELY MANAGED FUND FAMILIES

Today Vanguard gets some competition from most of the major fund families, although none with as broad a selection to choose from in building an all-indexed portfolio. Today many of the major families have at least an S&P 500 large-cap index fund. Very few of the fund families, however, have more than an S&P 500 fund, plus perhaps a few other index funds.

Charles Schwab has nine index funds, including Schwab S&P 500; Schwab 1000, the largest one thousand companies; Schwab Small-Cap Index, the thousand second largest companies; Schwab International Index; and others.

The rest of the fund families begrudgingly give lip service to indexing with a few token index funds. Here are a few examples: Fidelity, Dreyfus, and E*Trade each have six. Scudder, American Express, and National have five. Morgan Stanley and Merrill Lynch have four. Several fund families have three. Other large no-load families, such as American Century and Janus, don't even have an S&P 500 index fund.

As you can see, most fund families simply do not offer the funds necessary to construct one of the laziest portfolios. So if you're ready to build your future around a lazy portfolio, Vanguard really is your best and only choice.

In other words, when it comes to indexing, it is virtually impossible to compete with the industry leader. The fact is, Vanguard manages 70 percent of all mutual fund assets in America, and that's that! Many other fund families offer a small selection of index funds, but none can compete with Vanguard. Vanguard's success has apparently shamed the industry into a token response.

VANGUARD'S 31 INDEX MUTUAL FUNDS

LARGE-CAP INDEX FUNDS

1. Vanguard **500 Index** (S&P 500) VFINX
2. Vanguard **Growth** Index (MSCI U.S. Prime Mkt. Gr.) VIGRX
3. Vanguard **Value** Index (MSCI U.S. Prime Mkt. Val.) VIVAX
4. Vanguard **Total Stock Market** (Wilshire 5000) VTSMX

MID-CAP AND SMALL-CAP INDEX FUNDS

5. Vanguard **Mid-Cap** Index (MSCI U.S. Mid-Cap 450) VIMSX
6. Vanguard **Small-Cap** Index (MSCI U.S. Small-Cap 1750) NAESX
7. Vanguard **Small-Cap Growth** (MSCI U.S. Small-Cap Growth) VISGX
8. Vanguard **Small-Cap Value** (MSCI U.S. Small-Cap Value) VISVX
9. Vanguard **Extended Market** (Wilshire 4500) VEXMX
10. Vanguard **REIT Index** (Morgan Stanley) VGSIX

INTERNATIONAL STOCK INDEX FUNDS

11. Vanguard **Total International Market** (MSCI-EAFE) VGTSX
12. Vanguard **European** (MSCI-EUR) VEURX
13. Vanguard **Pacific** (MSCI-PAC) VPACX
14. Vanguard **Developed Markets** (MSCI-EAFE) VDMIX
15. Vanguard **Emerging Markets** (MSCI-EMGFree) VEIEX

FIXED-INCOME BOND INDEX FUNDS

16. Vanguard **Total Bond Market** (LB Agg. Bond) VBMFX
17. Vanguard **Short-Term** (LB Short Gov./Corp.) VBISX
18. Vanguard **Intermediate-Term** (LB Inter Gov./Corp.) VBIIX
19. Vanguard **Long-Term** (LB Long Gov./Corp.) VBLTX
20. Vanguard **TIPS** Inflation-Protected Securities VIPSX

BALANCED INDEX FUND (MINI PORTFOLIO)

21. Vanguard **Balanced** (60% Wilshire 5000 + 40% LB Agg. Bond) VBINX

SOCIAL RESPONSIBILITY INDEX FUND
22. Vanguard **Calvert Social Index Fund** (Calvert Social Index) VCSIX

TAX-MANAGED INDEX FUNDS
23. Vanguard **Tax-Managed Growth & Income** (S&P 500) VTGIX
24. Vanguard **Tax-Managed Cap. Apprec.** (Russell 1000) VMCAX
25. Vanguard **Tax-Managed Small-Cap** (S&P Small-Cap 600) VTMSX
26. Vanguard **Tax-Managed International** (MSCI-EAFE) TXMGX
27. Vanguard **Tax-Mgd. Bal.** (50% R-1000 + 50% Lehman 7-Yr. Muni) VTMFX

LIFE-CYCLE FUNDS-OF-FUNDS (MINI PORTFOLIOS)
28. Vanguard **LifeStrategy Growth** (Growth Composite Index) VASGX
29. Vanguard **LifeStrategy Mod. Growth** (Mod. Growth Comp.) VSMGX
30. Vanguard **LifeStrategy Consrv. Growth** (Consrv. Growth Comp.) VSCGX
31. Vanguard **LifeStrategy Income Fund** (Income Comp. Index) VASIX

MORE ODDBALLS—ETFs, DRIPs, AND OTHER WEIRD STUFF

But, you ask, what about Barclays Global Investors' collection of index funds? We'll cover these exchange-traded index funds in Chapter 19. But you're right, the fact is, while Vanguard is America's king of indexing, Barclays has been an invisible global emperor—"The Indexing Giant Nobody Knows," said the *New York Times* in the late 1990s.

Barclays Global is a subsidiary of Barclays, the United Kingdom's number two bank, and is the world's largest manager of index funds. Yet until recently few Americans had ever heard of Barclays, because it tends to operate behind the scenes as a wholesaler of sorts, managing more than $800 billion in assets for half the world's hundred largest pension institutions.

In the past few years, however, Barclays stuck its head up

out of the trenches domestically, so to speak, and became much more visible when it began launching a series of exchange-traded funds (ETFs) called "iShares" for the individual investor on Main Street America.

Barclays now has almost eighty ETFs with about $30 billion in assets, and more planned. About thirty are international ETFs for specific regions and countries, while roughly fifty domestic ETFs cover many higher-risk sectors. So today Barclays is no longer invisible—it has become the biggest player in the ETF arena. More about ETFs in Chapter 19.

Two other fund families are heavily into indexing: Profunds and Rydex. Suffice it to say that both are tools designed primarily for sophisticated short-term traders, and make heavy use of leveraging and derivatives, including shorts, options, futures, puts, calls, and more. As a result, the average passive Main Street investor should totally ignore these fund families—*totally!*

INDEX FUNDS ARE A VERY CHEAP DATE—TOO GOOD TO BE TRUE?

Not long ago Vanguard's leading indexing guru, Gus Sauter, suggested that a high school kid could easily "manage" an S&P 500 index fund in his spare time on one of those old 286 computers operating at less than 1 percent of the speed and hard-drive capacity of today's powerful high-speed multiple-gigabyte computers. Since trading and turnover are low, you don't need that much data storage.

He was making a simple point—index funds are a "cheap date," so to speak. Which is why Vanguard can "manage" its $75 billion S&P 500 index fund as a no-load with a superlow expense ratio of 0.18.

That raises a few very serious challenges to many of the other fund families, especially the Wall Street fund families owned by publicly held corporations: Specifically, why do they have the unmitigated gall to charge so much more than Vanguard for a simple S&P 500 index fund? Are they just lacking in ethics and morals? Do they think investors are naive, gullible, and stupid? Or are they actually trying to discourage their clients from indexing?

MOST FUND FAMILIES TAKE UNFAIR ADVANTAGE OF INDEX INVESTORS

Remember, Vanguard's expense ratio is only 0.18, and it's a no-load fund. By comparison, virtually all of the other S&P 500 index funds charge expense ratios in the 0.35 to 0.70 range—two to four times Vanguard's expense ratio for the exact same fund. And many of the Wall Street fund families also tack on a front-end load.

For example, some even charge incredibly high 1.00 annual expense ratios (more than five times Vanguard's) on top of an unconscionable 4.50 percent front-end load—fees and commissions that are so outrageous and exorbitant, you can only conclude that the fund managers are in a clear breach of their fiduciary duties and are taking advantage of naive clients.

Seriously, think about it. What are these fund families doing charging so much money when they're offering absolutely no additional services? Zippo. The fact is, no *experienced* investors would be stupid enough to pay such ridiculously high fees and loads for a simple index fund if they were fully informed about the alternative.

So we can only conclude that there are a lot of Wall Street firms and big-name fund families that are deliberately—*and unconscionably*—taking advantage of inexperienced investors.

Don't let it happen to you. Here's the rule: If you are going to buy an index fund, buy the cheapest no-load. Period. If you don't buy the cheapest index funds, you are simply helping some fund managers and their hustling brokers make the payments on their sport-utility vehicles!

SOME ALTERNATIVE STRATEGIES OUTSIDE THE (INDEXING) BOX

All this said about indexing, there are many legitimate reasons why you may not be able to buy cheapo index funds. For example, your 401(k) may be managed by some fund family other than Vanguard. Or you might want to do some trading and like the flexibility of working with ETFs. Or you may still prefer investing in stocks. And so on.

With that in mind, we're going to "think outside the box"—*that is, outside the Vanguard no-load index mutual fund box*—in this part of the book, and look at some alternative lazy, cheap, and workable investment strategies that may just suit your personality a little better, and at least give you a chance to experiment:

1. **Care and feeding of 401(k)s.** Since Vanguard manages only 10 percent of America's employer-sponsored retirement plans, there's a high probability that you'll have to build a lazy portfolio with proprietary funds from some other fund company. I have a few tips on how to handle the situation.
2. **One-fund mini portfolios.** Yes, I said *one-fund*, and they do exist. They're called hybrid funds, and they work great for lazy investors. They're not index funds, but they sure are all-in-one mini portfolios with both stocks and bonds, a pseudo lazy portfolio because you do nothing. The managers do all your asset allocating and rebalancing.
3. **ETF portfolios.** Okay, if you really, really like the idea of those exchange-traded funds (ETFs) that track indexes while trading like stocks, here's one way to get

the best of both worlds: Use indexing as a passive investor *and* as an active trader, while remaining a relatively lazy person.

4. **No-load stocks.** Well, if you absolutely insist on buying stocks, then why not build your own "fund" and become your own "fund manager" using DRIPs? These are dividend reinvestment plans that, like no-load index funds, Wall Street will never tell its clients about.

5. **New "folios" strategy.** Here is yet another new way to become a "portfolio manager" of your own fund. Folios are a way of buying individual stocks in bundles, or folios, through discount brokers. This strategy may be best suited for investors interested in active trading, but take a close look if you just can't yet accept the totally lazy approach.

6. **The zero-funds portfolio.** The perfect solution for investors who don't trust stocks or bonds or funds and see bigger opportunities and fewer risks using the *Rich Dad, Poor Dad* strategies, building businesses and amassing real estate.

7. **Lazy portfolios for kids.** Okay, so this one's a bit far out, but just in case you're unselfishly thinking of your loved ones, here's a way to buy a single stock or fund and make your kids and grandkids heirs of a Rich Dad—paying for their college, *and retirement!*

So let's venture outside the box and look at some alternative ways of investing the lazy way—with load funds, exchange-traded funds, dividend reinvestment programs, hybrid funds, or zero-fund portfolios!

AND NOW—THE BIG SECRET TO GETTING OUT OF THE BOX

One last point: A savvy investor will tell you that "thinking outside the box" assumes there *is* a box, and you're in it . . . there isn't, and you're not. Believing that investing requires some kind of special or weird thinking that you don't have will blind you to your own natural instincts.

Peter Lynch had something simple and wise to say about "thinking" in *One Up on Wall Street:* "Think like an amateur. If you invest like an institution, you're doomed to perform like one, which in most cases isn't very well. If you're a surfer, a truck driver, a high school dropout, or an eccentric retiree, then you've got an edge already." You're doing just fine.

WHY FUND MANAGERS, DIRECTORS, AND OWNERS ARE YOUR ENEMIES—AND INDEXING IS THE SOLUTION

During the bear market of 2000 through 2003 investors lost almost $8 trillion, 45 percent of the market's value. But while investors were losing big-time, fund owners, managers, and directors—*the people who owe investors a fiduciary duty*—were taking huge profits out of the funds. Listen to the details:

1. **Fund investors**. While the average American fund investor lost roughly 45 percent during the three-year bear market, the fund owners, managers, and directors took in more than $200 billion annually in fees, operating expenses, transaction costs, soft money, and other hidden compensation from deals with brokers and silent third parties. Here's another gauge of the damage: While investors were losing $8 trillion between 1999 and 2003, stock funds actually *increased* their average expense ratio by a whopping 36 percent according to Morningstar data.
2. **Fund owners.** While fund shareholders lost 45 percent, the *Forbes* 400 list of America's richest people reported, for example, that the net worth

of Fidelity's two owners, Edward Johnson and Abigail Johnson, *increased from $11.1 billion to $12.3 billion between 1999 and 2002*. In a separate study of SEC prospectuses by MSN.com, we learned that the head of one fund company made $47 million in 2001, while his investors lost 43 percent between early 2000 and late 2002. Many other fund executives got big raises while the markets collapsed.

3. **Fund managers.** Overall, the salaries of fund managers *increased 35 percent between 1999 and 2001*, to an average salary of $436,500, over ten times the average American's salary. Moreover, equity fund managers with ten to twenty years' experience made $761,500 a year in the bear market of 2001. The highest-paid 10 percent expected at least $1.8 million. This data comes from a survey of about ten thousand of America's forty-three thousand managers by the Association for Investment Management & Research and the executive search firm of Russell Reynolds Associates.

4. **Fund directors.** And as if rubbing salt in the wound, we also know that fund company directors *voted themselves an average 26 percent pay raise during the bear-market years from 2000 to 2002*, according to *InvestmentNews*, increasing their average compensation to $249,500. For example, ten of Fidelity's directors were paid between $250,500 and $312,500 annually. Not bad for part-time work!

As investors, we want to believe that these people have our best interests at heart. But the truth is—they don't. Their personal interests come first, and all too often they get overly greedy at our expense. They are not living up to their fiduciary duties.

Fund owners, managers, and directors are your enemy—*you cannot trust them*. And you're kidding yourself if you let your guard down and think you can. Your best protection is an index fund, because, for one thing, indexing at least allows you to avoid actively managed funds.

There are a lot of places to put your money, but—based on our analysis of the stock market over the past two decades—none compared with an employer-matched 401(k) plan. If you had invested $100 a month for the past 20 years in your 401(k), it would have outdistanced any other investment vehicle.

—SmartMoney *magazine*

SEVENTEEN

The Care and Feeding of Your 401(k) Plan

Here's How You Can Work with Fidelity, Schwab, or Anyone Else

WHEN YOU'RE PICKING FUNDS FOR YOUR TAXABLE INVESTMENT portfolio and your IRAs, you can invest in anything you please. Not just Vanguard funds, but *any* of America's ten thousand funds and eight thousand stocks. But there's one area in which you may not find a single Vanguard fund—your employer-sponsored retirement plan, affectionately known as your 401(k), or your 403(b) if you happen to be working for a nonprofit, such as a university, school, or hospital.

Recent years have seen roughly $1.75 trillion invested in America's four hundred thousand 401(k) plans, according to the ICI, with forty-five million employees participating, about half of all who are eligible.

And about three-quarters of the money was invested in

stocks, including 51 percent in stock mutual funds, 19 percent in company stock, and 8 percent in balanced funds. Of the rest, 10 percent was in guaranteed investment contracts, 5 percent in bonds, 4 percent in money markets, and a few percent in others. From a diversification standpoint, that's probably too much in company stock and not enough in bonds.

FIDELITY IS AMERICA'S BIG 401(K) KAHUNA

The biggest of the 401(k) plan managers is Fidelity Investments. They manage about $478 billion, almost 30 percent of the market, according to an *InvestmentNews* survey. Wells Fargo Bank manages another $278 billion, and Vanguard is third with $147 billion. Together the three dominate about 50 percent of the 401(k) market.

Each of the other 401(k) managers in this business has $80 billion or less of assets under management. The bigger ones include such well-known names as Schwab, T. Rowe Price, Putnam, Invesco, American Express, State Street Global Advisors, and the American Funds (Capital Research & Management Co.). All told, the top ten companies manage more than two-thirds of America's 401(k) money.

In other words, the odds are that Vanguard funds won't come up in your 401(k) plan. Instead, you'll be picking funds from Fidelity, T. Rowe Price, Schwab, or some other fund family that's managing your company's 401(k) plan. So I'll give you some general tips on what to do in this widely varied arena.

YES, THERE ARE LOTS OF EXCUSES FOR AVOIDING YOUR 401(K)

First, before we talk about portfolios and funds, a big reminder—no savings, no compounding, no nest egg, equals no retirement. Get it? Listen closely: Unless you save some money, you've got nothing to buy and pick funds with! So if you haven't begun yet, start saving money on a regular basis. Discover why the 401(k) is one of the best investment deals available to you.

Your 401(k) plan is such a great deal—and yet, so many employees never take advantage of this great giveaway. Competing personal needs is a common excuse for not saving (food, rent, medical, vacation, new car, etc.). Many never even bother to enroll at all. And of those who do invest, when they leave, most simply cash out and spend the money, instead of rolling it over into a self-administered, tax-advantaged IRA. So they lose all the tax benefits.

Others overload on their own company stock, contrary to the advice of virtually every professional adviser. Others use the excuse that 401(k)s are down along with everything else during the bear market—forgetting they could have invested in bond funds and received all the benefits.

YOUR BIGGEST MISTAKE—NOT MAXING OUT YOUR 401(K)

Despite these pitfalls and excuses, *the biggest mistake you can make is to stop investing in your 401(k)*. Listen to Warren Buffett's amusing remarks about this strange behavior among American investors:

> When hamburgers go down in price, we sing the "Hallelujah Chorus" in the Buffett household. When hamburgers go up, we weep. For most people, it's the same way with everything in life they will be buying—*except* stocks. When stocks go

down and you can get more for your money, people don't like them anymore. That sort of behavior is especially puzzling. . . .

Remember something I said earlier: If you start at age twenty-five and invest just $1,720 a year (much less than your annual IRA!), you'll have a million bucks when you retire at sixty-five, assuming an average 10 percent return through bull and bear cycles. Even if you wait till age thirty-five to start, you can reach your million-dollar goal investing just $2,920 a year—*thanks to the magic of compounding.*

SOUNDS TOO GOOD TO BE TRUE . . . BUT IT ISN'T!

Another big reason a lot of employees don't invest in their 401(k) is that they don't see the tremendous gift being handed to them. They apparently think the deal is "too good to be true." A few years ago I read this story from Eric Schurenberg's very informative book, *401(k)—Take Charge of Your Future:*

> Suppose a stockbroker called you and pitched an invest-ment that he claimed would shave thousands off this year's tax bill, earn a guaranteed return of 25% to 100%—*instantly*—and not generate a penny of future income taxes until you decided to sell. If you were smart, you'd mutter something about the securities regulators and hang up.

Don't hang up, because this one's a legitimate deal of the best kind:

> Chances are, though, you've already been pitched this investment or something very like it—by your employer, not by your stockbroker. The investment, of course, is your 401(k) plan. Your company may call it something different: the savings plan,

capital accumulation plan, retirement program, or the like. But under any name it is one of the rarest of creatures in the financial world: an investment that sounds too good to be true—and happens to be true anyway.

Why is your 401(k) too good to be true, yet true anyway? Very simple: If you're in a 28 percent tax bracket, you're automatically saving 28 percent on your taxes right up front on every dollar you contribute—you're reducing this year's taxes! And at 28 percent, that means you're already beating the average returns from the stock market. So you're way ahead of the game even if you just put your contribution in a money market account.

BOSS'S MATCHING CONTRIBUTION IS FREE MONEY, A BONUS, A GIFT!

Not only that, but many employers also match what you contribute, somewhere between a quarter for every dollar to dollar-for-dollar matching. That's free money, a bonus, a gift, a winning lottery ticket! So you're making another 25 percent up to maybe a 100 percent return on your money, immediately.

Hey, I bet you'd grab it in a heartbeat if the boss labeled it a "bonus" or "gift" instead of a legalistic term like "matching contribution." Please don't throw it away! Grab every penny that the government and your employer want to give you. Go for the max and accept this free wonderful gift.

SIX REASONS YOUR 401(K) IS THE PERFECT INVESTMENT

The chances are very likely that you'll be able to make adjustments in your plan sometime soon. Most plans permit periodic changes. So when the opportunity comes up, please push aside all your skepticism and remember these six key advantages to 401(k) programs:

1. **Discipline with autopilot savings.** Thanks to automatic payroll deductions, you have a perfect way to help you stay disciplined. Which is great, because failing to save regularly is a huge problem for most of us, given the seemingly endless demands on our money.

2. **More take-home pay thanks to tax-deferred contributions!** Your contributions will increase your take-home pay—and at the same time you'll reduce this year's tax bill by the amount of money you put into the system, up to the legal limit. This will be $15,000 annually very soon.

3. **Employer matching is a gift,** usually ranging somewhere between 25 and 100 percent of your contributions. For example, for every dollar you put up, your nice employer could put up fifty cents. With this incentive, why would you not max out?

4. **Uncle Sam defers taxes on future earnings.** Yep, the tax on every dollar of return that you reinvest and let accumulate in the plan is deferred, so your nest egg grows faster by reducing your tax bill further.

5. **Dollar-cost averaging buys more.** This may be your single best reason to keep on investing in bull and bear markets. As Warren Buffett says, for the same amount of money you get more shares of a stock when the price is down. So in the long run, it pays off to keep investing.

6. **Transferability.** Once the boss's money is vested, the money's yours. All of it. And what if you go to a new employer? Things get even better. You simply roll over your account, either into an IRA—where you have vastly more freedom to invest in virtually anything—or into your new employer's plan. And you get to keep all your tax-deferral benefits.

These six benefits usually result in returns that will exceed anything you can do by investing the same amount of money directly in the stock market—just from the mere decision to save and invest in your 401(k). Such a deal!

YOUR 401(K) IS THE PERFECT MONEY MARKET FUND— 53% RETURNS!

So here's the one core rule you must remember above all else: *"Max out your 401(k) contributions."* This is one time Uncle Sam and your employer are playing Santa Claus. You can't possibly do better in the stock market. Even if your employer's only matching the minimum of 25 percent, if you couple this with a 28 percent tax break, that's a return of more than 53 percent. *Where else can you get a 53 percent return on your money, even if you leave it in the 401(k)'s money market fund!*

In fact, here's how *SmartMoney* magazine put it: "There are a lot of places to put your money, but—*based on our analysis of the stock market over the past two decades*—none compared with an employer-matched 401(k) plan. If you had invested $100 a month for the past 20 years in your 401(k), it would have outdistanced any other investment vehicle"—and that included IRAs, large-cap portfolios, taxable no-load funds, variable annuities, and "any other investment vehicle."

In fact, as an investment, your 401(k) plan really does sound too good to be true. Yet the truth is, your 401(k) really is the best investment around! As *SmartMoney* summarized it, "The best advice is the simplest: Max-Out. Put as much into your 401(k) plan as your employer allows you to." Just do it!

GETTING OUTSIDE THE BOX WHEN YOU'RE STUCK IN THE BOX

Not too long ago I read a *Money* magazine article on how to "Avoid the Five Big 401(k) Mistakes." The biggest mistake I recall was not paying enough attention to the asset allocations in your 401(k) portfolio. In fact, many people not only ignore asset allocations but also get flippant, picking and forgetting the hottest funds of the moment. Do your homework, and focus on the portfolio.

A few years ago one of the biggest complaints I heard from investors was that the selections were just too darn limited in their 401(k) retirement programs. In the average plan, workers got a choice of a measly ten or twelve funds—which was absurd with a total of ten thousand funds to choose from, many of which would be better choices. That's not always the case today. In fact, the problem now may be that you have too many choices. Here are the main structural alternatives:

1. **Limited selection of proprietary in-house funds.** This means you get a take-it-or-leave-it selection of eight to twelve funds from the Wells Fargo Bank, Putnam, Principal, or whoever else may be managing your 401(k) plan.

2. **Proprietary plus supermarket access to other fund families.** Here Fidelity, T. Rowe Price, Schwab, or some other manager may offer you some of their own proprietary funds, for example. In addition, they offer you access to their "supermarket," a network of funds offered from other fund families that might include, for example, Baron, Dreyfus, Janus, Legg Mason, PIMCO, and others. Schwab's no-transaction-fee supermarket is called OneSource, and Fidelity has an extensive "NTF" network.

3. **Self-directed brokerage account as add-on to basic plan.** There's one great new innovation that can be added to virtually any 401(k) plan, even an old-fashioned one

with a limited selection of ten funds, for example. I'm talking about the "self-directed brokerage account" option. This gives you a window with *unlimited* access to the entire market, allowing you to invest in any stocks, funds, and bonds—just as you would in any normal brokerage account.

Keep this option in mind if your company's stuck in an old-style plan with limited choices. Instead of forcing executives and board members to get rid of an entire plan and hire a new plan manager—which might be met with a lot of resistance—you can simply request that one new option be added to the existing plan.

WARNING: SMALL INCREASES IN 401(K) EXPENSES AND FEES CAN EAT BIG CHUNKS INTO YOUR RETIREMENT NEST EGG

Watch your 401(k) fees like a hawk. Management consultants Hewitt Associates ran the numbers for *USA Today:* A small increase may not seem like much, but down the road you'll pay dearly. Let's say you have $50,000 in your 401(k) and expect an annual return of 8 percent. Here's how small changes cut into your retirement:

		BALANCE AFTER		
Fees	5 YEARS	10 YEARS	20 YEARS	30 YEARS
0.5%	$71,781	$103,052	$212,393	$437,738
1.0%	70,128	98,358	193,484	380,613
1.5%	68,504	93,857	176,182	330,718

Notice that a jump in fees of 1 percent reduces your nest egg from $437,738 to $330,718 over thirty years—a loss of $103,920! So keep a close watch on those management fees; they'll eat up your retirement before you get there. Get in your 401(k) manager's face. They're already charging you too much.

BUILD A COUCH POTATO PORTFOLIO AT YOUR FIDELITY 401(K)

As strange as it may sound, there is also a way to build a simple two-fund Couch Potato Portfolio in a Fidelity 401(k) plan using Vanguard and other index funds, *without* adding the self-directed brokerage feature—which normally costs $30 to $100 or more. Using this new option, you can invest in Vanguard and any other funds through a Fidelity, T. Rowe Price, Schwab, or any other 401(k) plan.

Here's how it works. According to Schwab's 401(k) experts: Today, most fund providers use an "open architecture" system. This enables the manager to offer funds of other companies *without the added expense of a brokerage window*. Thus, Fidelity (for example) has the ability to "record-keep" any Vanguard or other funds.

YES, YOU CAN EVEN SNEAK VANGUARD INTO A FIDELITY 401(K)

In fact, I understand that the Vanguard 500 Index Fund has already been requested and is being offered in various Fidelity-managed 401(k) plans. Using this alternative, employees can avoid extra transaction fees, because a Vanguard fund simply becomes another option along with the Fidelity funds.

Once set up, employees will still have a limited list of proprietary funds from the plan manager (Fidelity, for example), with perhaps only two or three Vanguard funds—*but if the options selected by the company are the Vanguard Total Stock Market Index and Vanguard Total Bond Index, for example, then the employees would have access to the ultimate lazy portfolio, the two-fund Couch Potato!*

So if you want Vanguard funds in your Fidelity-, Schwab-, or T. Rowe Price–managed plan (or vice versa), just ask your benefits department's record keeper to add the two basic Vanguard funds to your plan's choices. Most 401(k) managers can record-keep Vanguard funds—or any others.

Neat trick, huh! Unfortunately, most employees *and employers* don't know about this option—for obvious reasons. After all, the fund family that has the management contract isn't going to volunteer the information. Remember, it has a monopoly, and out of self-interest you can expect them to do whatever is necessary to keep the 401(k) choices limited to their own proprietary funds. Still, a group of activist employees can change all that.

BEST BUYS FOR 401(K)S FROM THE *SMARTMONEY* SET

First, let's take a look at some of the better proprietary funds. Most of these funds appeared in a special feature on SmartMoney.com called "Best and Worst 401(k) Funds" (just remember, lists like this tend to change frequently). Still, these plan managers control perhaps two-thirds of the total 401(k) assets and are likely to work hard to maintain performance levels.

Relatively speaking, these particular funds represent some of the best in each particular plan. They may not, however, be better than similar funds in another plan managed by another fund company. Of course, the simplest way to make a decision is to pick funds that come closest in style to one of the lazy portfolios, since every 401(k) plan is different, tailored to a particular company and its employees:

1. **American Express.** AXP Bond A (INBNX); AXP Growth A (INIDX); AXP Dimensions (INNDX).
2. **American Funds.** American Balanced (ABALX); Income Fund of America (AMECX); Investment Company of America (AIVSX); Washington Mutual Investors (AWSHX).

3. **Fidelity.** Fidelity Growth & Income (FGRIX); Fidelity Fund (FFIDX); Fidelity Aggressive Growth (FDEGX); Fidelity Blue Chip Growth (FBGRX); Fidelity Contrafund (FCNTX); Fidelity Growth Company (FDGRX); Fidelity OTC (FOCPX).

4. **Invesco.** Invesco Balanced (IMABX); Invesco Blue Chip Growth (FLRFX); Invesco Dynamics (FIDYX); Invesco Select Income (FBDSX).

5. **Janus.** Janus Fund (JANSX); Janus Balanced (JABAX); Janus Growth & Income (JAGIX); Janus Worldwide (JAWWX); Janus Overseas (JAOSX); Janus Twenty (JAVLX).

6. **Merrill Lynch.** Merrill Lynch Growth Fund A (MAFGX); Merrill Lynch Global Alloc. A (MALOX); Merrill Lynch Pacific A (MAPCX); Hotchkis & Wiley Total Return (HWTRX).

7. **Putnam.** Putnam Investors A (PINVX); Putnam Opportunities Y (PNOYX); Putnam Vista A (PVISX); Putnam Voyager (PVYYX).

8. **T. Rowe Price.** T. Rowe Price Equity 500 (PREIX); T. Rowe Price Balanced (RPBAX); T. Rowe Price Equity-Income (PRFDX); T. Rowe Price Blue Chip Growth (TRBCX).

9. **Schwab.** Schwab 1000 (SNXFX); Schwab Total Bond Mkt. Index (SWLBX); Schwab MarketTrack Conservative (SWCGX).

10. **Vanguard.** Vanguard 500 Index (VFINX); Vanguard Total Bond Mkt. Index (VBMFX); Vanguard Growth & Income (VQNPX); Vanguard Primecap (VPMCX); Vanguard U.S. Growth (VWUSX); Vanguard Wellington (VWELX); Vanguard Windsor II (VWNFX).

11. **Wells Fargo.** Wells Fargo Growth Balanced I (NVGEX); Wells Fargo Equity Income I (NVIEX); Wells Fargo LifePath 2030 (STHRX).

Another word of caution: Picking the top performers is not going to protect you against a bear market. Building a lazy portfolio with a balance of bond and stock funds is a better solution to balance ups and downs. In addition, the funds offered by many fund families aren't a broad enough selection necessary to create a well-diversified lazy portfolio, such as the Coffeehouse or No-Brainer Portfolio.

If your selections are limited, a conservative investor should consider one of two strategies. First, you could simply pick the funds that best replicate the two-fund Couch Potato Portfolio: one based on a broad stock market index such as the Wilshire 5000 or the S&P 500, the other based on a total bond market or intermediate bond market index.

Alternatively, play it safe and pick a hybrid fund. Hybrids such as perennial favorite Dodge & Cox Balanced are one-fund mini portfolios with a mix of stocks and bonds to balance out the volatility of bull–bear cycles. I'll tell you more about this real neat option in the next chapter.

BEST-BUY PORTFOLIOS FROM THE DEAN OF NO-LOAD FUNDS

Another excellent resource is Sheldon Jacobs's newsletter, *No-Load Fund Investor,* which the *USA Today* newspaper called "the best single resource for the average fund investor," and justifiably so. This newsletter has one incredible monthly feature that's worth the subscription price alone.

In the back of each issue of the *No-Load Fund Investor* you'll find six model portfolios using funds from Vanguard, T. Rowe Price, Fidelity (proprietary funds only), the Fidelity NTF (includes non-Fidelity funds in Fidelity's "no-transaction fees" network), and the Schwab NTF network. The two NTF portfolios include hundreds of funds from many families. Jacobs offers his "Best Buy" fund recommendations for each of these five portfolios. He also adds a sixth, the "Master Portfolio," which includes his selections of the "best buys from *any* source."

Jacobs's selection of just four fund companies—Vanguard, T. Rowe Price, Fidelity, and Schwab—is significant. Why? Quite simple. Because Jacobs is widely regarded as the "dean of no-load funds" and a man of unquestioned skill and integrity. The fact that he narrows his model portfolios to these four families suggests to me that they are also four of the better fund families in the 401(k) management business, and as such provide funds that form a solid basis for building a top-performing portfolio.

In addition, each of the six portfolios has three sets of asset allocations—Wealth Builder, Pre-Retirement, and Retirement—which adjust for age, with the bond allocation increasing and the stocks decreasing as you approach retirement.

THE MASTER WEALTH BUILDER—WHEN YOU CAN BUY ANYTHING

Obviously, if you have a 401(k) plan with self-directed brokerage option, you should consider the Master Portfolio since you have access to all financial markets. Here's one sample Master Wealth Builder Portfolio that might be put together through your self-directed "window":

MASTER PORTFOLIO: WEALTH BUILDER
1. (10%) **Baron Small-Cap** (BSCFX).
2. (10%) **Berger Mid-Cap Value** (BEMVX).
3. (30%) **Vanguard Total Stock Market Index** (VTMSX).
4. (10%) **Artisan Mid-Cap Value** (ARTQX).
5. (10%) **Longleaf Partners International** (LLINX).
6. (5%) **Vanguard Short-Term Corp** (VFSTX).
7. (25%) **Strong Ultra Short Bond** (STADX).

Jacobs notes that a $10,000 investment in this portfolio in 1988 would have grown to $44,855 over a fifteen-year period that included three years of the recent bear market. In addition, the Pre-Retirement and Retirement versions of his Master Portfolio also grew roughly the same amount, although they had different allocations and several different funds from the Wealth Builder version. As with all portfolios, however, remember that it's not the specific funds you pick, *it's your asset allocations that create a winning portfolio.* And here, Jacobs is making that allocation for you.

MAX OUT AND BUILD YOUR OWN LAZY PORTFOLIO

Finally, it's impossible to cover all 401(k) plan offerings in a constantly changing economic and market environment. But whatever you do, don't let the large selection of funds throw you off track; *stay focused on the portfolio* and make the funds fit in your laziest asset allocations.

In other words, stick to two basic principles. First and foremost, max out your 401(k) every year, no matter what. Even if you just invest your 401(k) contributions in a money market fund, you'll still be making a darn good return thanks to the tax benefits; and it's even better if your employer adds a matching contribution.

Second, think positive, do some research, and work with what you have until you can change the plan. Build a well-diversified portfolio with the funds available in your 401(k)— funds that clone the ones in our lazy portfolios. Get aggressive and demand that your company and plan manager provide all the funds you need to clone a lazy portfolio! Better yet, pay for a self-directed brokerage window and invest in the real thing. And if you're ever in doubt, pick a hybrid fund with a solid long-term track record, such as the ones in the next chapter.

Most people have it all wrong about wealth in America.
Wealth is not the same as income. If you make a good income
each year and spend it all, you are not getting wealthier.
You are living high. Wealth is what you accumulate,
not what you spend. . . . Wealth is more often the result
of a lifestyle of hard work, perseverance, planning,
and most of all, self-discipline.

—Thomas Stanley and William Danko, The Millionaire Next Door

EIGHTEEN

Happy Hybrids: One-Fund Mini Portfolios
One-Stop Shopping for the Laziest of Lazy Investors

I KNOW WHAT YOU'RE THINKING—ISN'T THERE AN *EVEN SIMPLER solution* than the Couch Potato, Coffeehouse, No-Brainer, and all the other lazy portfolios?

After all, every darn one of the three laziest winners has *at least two* funds, and some could totally exhaust a poor soul loading up with as many as ten funds. Too many to fit in Scott Burns's microwave at one time!

The fact is, for many truly lazy investors, two funds is one too many, too complicated, and too taxing. They want to keep it simple, *real* simple, and lazy.

The one-fund portfolio is what those fund industry geniuses call the "hybrid" because it is a fund that acts like a mini portfolio—*investing in both stocks and bonds, and some cash*—just as you would do if you were doing all the work yourself picking two to ten funds for one of the other laziest portfolios, as in the Burns-Schultheis-Bernstein trio of winners.

LOVE 'EM OR LAUGH AT 'EM—HYBRIDS ARE BOOORING!

There are two kinds of investors. First are those who love hybrid funds, because they're boring. And then there are those who laugh at hybrids, and for the same reason—*because they're boooring!* Regardless of which half you're in, you know they make a great lazy investor's portfolio because the ideal hybrid fund acts like a whole portfolio, diversifying between stocks and bonds for you.

You don't hear much about hybrids because they have no pizzazz, no entertainment value for "real American" investors who need the action and love the thrill of the daily drama on CNBC. The sophisticated investor thinks hybrids are kid stuff, a little like training wheels on your first bicycle. But every time I start talking about the laziest portfolios, someone will bring up hybrids as "one-fund portfolios" that do the same job. So here they are.

LEVELING OUT THE BULL—BEAR ROLLER-COASTER RIDE

Hybrid lovers want peace of mind and will give up points for it. And they get peace, because hybrids act like tranquilizers for people who don't trust Wall Street. Hybrids fill that prescription. When they're working right, they'll put you to sleep—in bear markets *and* in bull.

Here's why. Morningstar says the roughly eight hundred domestic hybrids actually beat the S&P 500 by 11 percent in the bearish days of 2000, with a positive 2 percent return. No heart-stopping 50 to 90 percent drops as with the dot.coms, techs, and even some sad blue chips.

And yes, those same hybrids did underperform the broad market in the bull years from 1995 to 1999, but still, they were in positive territory every single one of those years, ranging from 9 to 25 percent. Moreover, the average annual return of the conservative hybrids was a solid 10 percent for the past ten years, with many beating the broad market.

Hybrids may be the perfect funds for many investors for one simple reason—you get professional managers doing three key things that most investors have found to be virtually impossible with their own portfolios lately—picking stocks and bonds, timing the market, and allocating between asset classes.

AMERICA'S TOP-FOUR ONE-FUND MINI PORTFOLIO CATEGORIES

How do they do it? Very simple—by mixing bonds in with stocks, creating a mini portfolio in a single fund—"one-fund portfolios," I call them. No, they won't do as well as an all-stock fund in a bull market. But they also won't do as poorly in a bear market.

They try to level out the peaks and valleys. And that trade-off helps you sleep better. So they're perfect for passive investors who have better things to do with their lives than watch CNBC.

Hybrids actually cut across a number of fund categories: balanced funds, asset allocation funds, life-cycle funds, and funds-of-funds. In fact, you'll even find excellent hybrids with oddball names like Oakmark Equity-Income and T. Rowe Price Capital Appreciation, as well as some growth and income funds and convertible bond funds tossed into Morningstar's hybrid category. Why? Because the term *hybrid* is loose enough to include virtually any fund that has both equities and fixed-income securities in its portfolio.

1. **Balanced funds—they level out unbalanced cycles.** Think of them as overly protective parents. They know exactly how much your portfolio needs in each category; that way you can go out and play, and let them do the

worrying about market timing and cycles. After all, they are pros, and they know how stocks and bonds move up and down in counterbalancing cycles.

Balanced funds have a *fixed* percentage or range in each category. For example, 60 percent might be in equities and 40 percent in bonds. And the managers usually have flexibility to adjust between the two types of securities—in other words, they rebalance your portfolio for you. Here are a few winners:

Dodge & Cox Balanced is one of the best, a no-load hybrid currently managing about $10 billion in assets. In fact, this was the one hybrid that readers sent in as their *unsolicited write-in vote* as an alternative to the Couch Potato, Coffeehouse, and No-Brainer lineup—so you know it's a winner.

Launched in 1931 during the depression years, Dodge & Cox Balanced keeps about 60 percent of the portfolio in value stocks and about 30 percent in investment-grade debt securities. The expense ratio is under 0.53 and turnover less than 25 percent, which minimizes capital gains for investors. The fund returned 15 percent during 2000, averaging more than 13 percent the prior decade; even in the bearish days of 2002, when the fund was slightly into negative territory, it was still beating the S&P 500 by 15 percent, as were many hybrids.

The two giants among these boring balanced funds are also solid long-term performers, with long-term average annual returns of better than 10 percent. Both are no-loads. **Vanguard Wellington,** launched in 1929, is the largest balanced fund with around $20 billion of assets. The second largest, **Fidelity Puritan,** has been around since 1947 and manages about $19 billion in assets.

Of note is the fact that the long-term returns of

both these balanced funds are within a point of their high-profile siblings, the Vanguard 500 Index and Fidelity Magellan, but with only about half the volatility.

2. **Asset allocation funds—when you can't cut the pie.** Don't be fooled by hybrid name tags. Asset allocation funds are actually quite similar to balanced funds, but with much more flexibility in reallocating among categories. Still, the average returns of these asset allocation funds are relatively close to those of their balanced siblings.

For example, **Fidelity Asset Manager** is one of the top five hybrids, a $10 billion no-load fund launched in 1988. The fund's annual averages for the past decade have been fairly close to those of its sibling Puritan. Similarly with **Vanguard Asset Allocation Fund,** another of the top five hybrids with $7 billion in assets. The fund's longer-term returns hover close to those of its sibling, Wellington. Also check out the **Schwab MarketTrack** funds and the **TIAA-CREF Managed Allocation Fund.**

3. **Life-cycle funds—pick a target date and go with the flow.** No, they're not exercise equipment, like StairMasters. They're designed to perform as portfolios for certain age groups, and they usually come in sets of three or four—for example, Fidelity's four **Freedom Funds,** designated Fidelity Freedom 2010, 2020, 2030, and 2040; and Vanguard's four **LifeStrategy Funds,** designated Growth, Moderate Growth, Conservative Growth, and Income.

The longer your time horizon to retirement, the more aggressive these funds are, with higher stock allocations. Then, as retirement approaches, their fixed-income allocations increase. So they're great for the laziest investors—you leave both the short-term and also the long-term rebalancing to fund managers.

Altogether, there are fewer than one hundred life-cycle funds. And they've attracted only about $20 billion in assets, about the size of Vanguard Wellington or Fidelity Puritan, suggesting that the public isn't overly excited about life-cycle hybrids. Maybe they're just *too* darn boring. And don't let category names confuse you—the Fidelity Freedom funds, for example, are classified as asset allocation funds and funds-of-funds as well as life cycles.

4. **Funds-of-funds—but keep it all in the family.** These hybrids diversify by investing in other funds, rather than investing directly in stocks and bonds. Also, there are two kinds of funds-of-funds. The larger fund families have funds-of-funds investing in their own funds, with only one layer of management fees.

For example, check out **Vanguard STAR,** the largest fund-of-funds with $8 billion in assets. Like most of the better hybrids, it was beating the S&P 500 by more than 10 percent during the bear market while averaging slightly under the benchmark over the long term. Other examples include **T. Rowe Price Spectrum Growth** and its siblings, as well as the Fidelity Freedom and Vanguard LifeStrategy funds.

There are also independent funds-of-funds that invest in funds outside their small fund families. As a result, they're forced to add a second layer of management fees, and as a result they tend to underperform the competition. Avoid them.

TRAINING WHEELS AND TRANQUILIZERS

Roughly $250 billion is invested in hybrid funds: a small fraction—perhaps 5 percent—of the $6 to $7 trillion in all mutual funds. Nevertheless, they serve a very important role for certain types of investors: New investors. Small portfolios. Anxious people. And investors with little or no interest in tracking the market—the laziest investors.

But for all these types, the added peace of mind is a welcome trade-off. Remember, the lower returns in bull markets are more than offset by higher-than-market returns in bear markets.

WARNING—AVOID MARKET TIMING HYBRIDS, TOO BUSY

Watch out for the market timing hybrids that become more enticing than Victoria's Secret lingerie ads when things are dropping. I don't want to mention any of them by name, but if you look at any on-line screening of hybrid funds, you'll likely see terms such as *market neutral, long/short,* and *bear* in their names.

Whatever you do, look past those sizzling market timing hotshots, regardless of how good their short-term returns look during down cycles. They won't do well in bull markets. They were created for market timers and day traders who love to gamble using shorts and derivatives, leveraging, hedging, and otherwise engaging in outguessing the economy and *betting against the market*—but unfortunately that assumes you can predict which way the market's going in the first place. For most investors, that's a guessing game for losers.

For many years fund tracker Morningstar lumped the more aggressive market timing hybrids in with the lazy conservative hybrids. Morningstar recently separated them into two categories, making it easier to pick lazy winners. Great move, because the aggressive ones come with much, much higher expenses, loads, and turnover ratios.

My advice for the average Main Street investor? Avoid these bear hybrids like the plague. Stick to their conservative cousins, the four categories above.

EXTRA WARNING—MANY HYBRIDS HAVE VERY HIGH EXPENSES

Keep in mind that most of the hybrids are *actively managed* funds. They come in a wide range, from hybrids that passively track indexes and usually have lower expense ratios (around 0.30 percent), to heavily traded hybrids with ridiculously high expenses (from 1.30 to more than 3.00 percent).

Whatever you do, check out their expense ratios and other costs, and compare them to the expenses in one of the lazy portfolio winners before buying any hybrid fund.

DODGE & COX BALANCED—ALL-AMERICAN MASHED POTATO FUND!

There's some real nice down-home country charm to some of the best of the happy hybrids, at least the conservative ones. In a way, the best ones are almost like seeing the two-fund Couch Potato Portfolio merged into one fund.

And for the fun of it, you could say this little "merger" created the "Mashed Potato" Portfolio—or maybe the "Smashed Potato" Portfolio, because the investor never has to rebalance, they do it for you (and you certainly can't get any lazier than that!).

Which of the hybrids is best? No question, Dodge & Cox Balanced stands out. It consistently beats the S&P 500's long-term average, often by a percent or two. And as I've already noted, readers made this ol' workhorse (it's been around since 1931) the number one write-in candidate in the laziest portfolio contest. So I'd have to award Dodge & Cox Balanced the distinction of being one of the top five laziest portfolios in our contest.

One final note: Remember that the conservative low-cost hybrids clearly have a very important role for many investors with special needs—such as novices. And people with short-term goals. Also, investors with ultralow risk tolerance or relatively small portfolios. And, of course, investors with little or no interest in following the market—the laziest of all investors.

NINETEEN

The ETF Zoo: Spiders, Qubes, Diamonds, Webs, Vipers

Wild Menagerie Trades Like Hot Stocks in Marvel Comics

THE ANCIENT BIBLICAL STORY OF NOAH'S ARK REMINDS ME OF today's new world of ETFs or exchange-traded funds. ETFs are breeding like animals . . . but I'm getting ahead of myself!

Remember biblical times. Warnings of a global flood. So Noah builds a huge ship big enough to hold two of every species. They're herded on board. No problems. No competition. No overload. No fighting. No eating everything down the food chain (Noah had a well-stocked galley).

Then the flood hits. Rough seas. But the ark stays afloat (Noah was a great shipbuilder). Animals behave. The storm finally subsides. Cheering. Solid landing. Happy ending. End story. Life goes on.

ETFs ARE WILD ANIMALS—FUN TO WATCH, BUT TOUGH TO TAME

Today it's a whole different story. Forget all those congenial twosomes on the ark—we've got a zoo run wild. Mayhem in the menagerie. We've got hundreds of index mutuals, plus all the ETFs with cute names like Spiders and Qubes, Webs and Vipers, Diamonds and HOLDRs. Dumb names . . . stupid pet tricks!

ETFs are wild animals crowding around the deck. Trainers and handlers cracking their bullwhips. Bumping, pushing, snarling. Man, when the perfect storm hits, there's no modern Noah who's gonna want these angry beasts on board. Too many. Too dangerous. And too tough to understand, let alone figure out *how to build an ark—I mean, portfolio—out of them.*

OVERSTOCKED! TOO MANY WILD ANIMALS CROWDING THIS ZOO!

Yes, indexing is in danger of running amok, at least with all the new exchange-traded index funds. Don't get me wrong; with about $100 billion invested in domestic ETFs—which are growing in popularity as people get to know them better—they are a great alternative to index mutuals for more sophisticated investors.

But you gotta wonder if maybe they're drowning in their own success—or rather excess. It's a distinct possibility. Why? Investors are left with too many darn confusing ETF choices today! It's overwhelming for a lazy investor.

One of the biggest problems I see is all their silly cartoon-character names—Spiders, Diamonds, Webs, Holders, Qubes, Vipers. Too cutesy. Most of these silly name tags were invented during the manic 1990s bull market, when lighthearted comic-book names fit in with the Marvel superhero mentality of that era when hot-and-fast trading was popular.

The guys inventing ETF names must have been hyperactive teenagers at heart with heroes like Spider-Man, Qube-Boy, Diamond-Lady, Varooming-Vipers—but these are definitely *not* images designed to attract passive, conservative investors.

THE SECRET TO SUCCESS—IGNORE THE NAME TAG, FOCUS ON THE INDEX

Okay, we need to get back to emphasizing the underlying value here—and, yes, there really is a lot of value for you under the comic-book name tags. So keep an open mind and let's take a close look.

The value lies primarily in the fact that an ETF is the best of both worlds: It tracks an index like a mutual fund. Plus you can trade it like a stock, at any time during the day (but you pay a brokerage commission for each trade). As I said, right now it's not easy to figure out what "animal" is under the comic-book names—however, once you get the hang of it, you've got a tiger by the tail!

An all-ETF indexed portfolio makes a lot of sense if you have a psychological itch to trade part of your portfolio now and then, but you still believe that indexing really does beat active trading. You want the best of both worlds—a solid, quiet home life, plus an occasional trip to Vegas to let your hair down and have a good time gambling. Right?

ETF PORTFOLIOS—FOR LAZY INVESTORS WHO AREN'T ALWAYS LAZY

So here's the perfect solution, a switch-hitting portfolio. You get both a boring, conservative, low-cost, long-term, buy-and-hold portfolio—*plus* the total flexibility of having fun playing in the stock market whenever you choose. How? By building an all-ETF indexed portfolio. That's right, buy nothing but exchange-traded funds, 100 percent ETFs.

So here's how this new strategy works with an all-ETF indexed portfolio: Put 90 percent in untouchable ETFs—money that you just cannot afford to lose—for retirement, college funds for the kids, emergency funds, etc.

And the remaining 10 percent you put in a separate account of mad-money ETFs that you can trade with wild abandon. Just make darn sure that it's *money you can afford to lose, because you probably will.* Think of it as a vacation trip to Vegas, where your losses are offset by the entertainment value.

FIRST STEP—YOU ALLOCATE YOUR BOND ETFs

Although ETF experts will tell you that ETFs work for both buy'n'hold investors and active traders—in bear markets as well as bulls, dips and rallies—the visible absence of bond index funds in many of these portfolios suggests that they are mainly used by active traders. So please remember, you still do need some fixed-income bond funds in order to build a successful all-ETF portfolio.

My advice: Calculate your bond ETF allocations first. Buy them first *and sit on them.* No trading. Whether you're a twenty-year-old college grad or a sixty-year-old retiree, make darn sure you focus on fixed-income funds *before* equities. Then and only then look at stock ETFs.

The bond ETFs are newer, but solid. Especially check out these four Barclays iShares, which include short-, intermediate-, and long-term Treasury bond ETFs, and one corporate bond ETF: Lehman 1–3 Year Treasury Bonds (SHY); Lehman 7–10 Year Treasury Bond Index (IEF); Lehman 20+ Year Treasury Bond Index (TLT); and the iShares GS $ InvesTop Corporate (LQD). There are also some other comparable bond ETFs to pick from. You can check some of the ETF Web sites, such as IndexFunds.com, for the latest additions, updates, and prices.

YES, YOU CAN ALSO USE REAL BONDS OR BOND MUTUAL FUNDS

Keep in mind that while I'm showing you how to construct a sample all-ETF portfolio, you obviously don't have to have a "pure" all-ETF portfolio. For example, you could invest directly in bonds or bond mutual funds, rather than these suggested bond ETFs, and just use ETFs as a substitute for your stock ETFs or stocks—you know, use your imagination and mix it up!

Moreover, when it comes to stock ETFs, obviously you can also have some stocks, some stock mutual funds, and some stock ETFs. But remember, the more you mix and match, the more complicated your portfolio will get, and *the less lazy it will be.*

But for the moment, we're focusing on exchange-traded funds—*which combine some of the best features of stocks and mutual funds*—as an alternative. And I want to show you how to build a flexible portfolio out of these fabulous ETFs.

NEXT, AFTER BOND ETFs—ADD 90% IN STOCK ETFs

Once you have set aside your fixed-income allocation, it's time to diversify the remainder of your money across the stock ETFs. For example, if you have a $100,000 portfolio and you put $40,000 in fixed-income bond ETFs first, then you'll be allocating the remaining $60,000 to stock ETFs.

That means you will have 90 percent ($54,000) in retirement stock ETFs—*which you never risk*—and the remaining 10 percent ($6,000) is your high-risk trading account to gamble with. Get it? Ten percent. Any more is too risky.

1. **(45%) Large-cap stock ETFs.** Start with your large-cap allocation. The biggest and oldest (launched in 1993) is the SPDR or Standard & Poor's Depository Receipts

(SPY), affectionately called the "Spider." The Spider tracks the S&P 500 index just like a typical S&P 500 index mutual fund. There are also Value (IVE) and Growth (IVW) versions of the S&P 500, if you want to skew your portfolio more toward value stocks versus growth stocks.

There's also a Barclays iShares S&P 500 (IVV). And if you prefer the blue-chip Dow 30 Industrials, buy the "Diamond" (DIA). Other large-cap variations include the Fortune 500 Index Tracker (FFF) and State Street's streetTRACKS U.S. Large-Cap Growth (ELG).

2. **(30%) Mid-cap and small-cap stock ETFs.** This "piece of the pie" will probably be focused on these ETFs: For mid-caps, the S&P 400 Mid-Cap Spider (MDY), and the iShares S&P Mid-Cap 400 (IHJ). For small-caps, Barclays iShares Russell 2000 (IWM), and iShares S&P Small-Cap 600 (IJR). Note that both the mid-caps and small-caps also have growth and value ETFs if you want to get fancy, something truly lazy investors hate to do.

Alternatively, you could use Vanguard Extended Market VIPER (VXF), which is the whole market less the biggest five hundred stocks. Or just keep it simple and forget about splitting allocations among large-, mid-, and small-caps by investing in Vanguard's Total Stock Market VIPER (VTI), which tracks the Wilshire 5000, the whole cotton-picking stock market.

3. **(15%) International stock ETFs.** For a large-cap international exposure, consider iShares S&P Global 100 (IOO). If you want exposure in the developed markets, try iShares S&P Europe 350 Index (IEV), iShares MSCI UK Index (EWU), or iShares MSCI Japan Index (EWJ). There are a whole bunch of smaller regional and individual-country ETFs, but

you're better off staying more broadly diversified and in the developed countries.

FINALLY, YOUR ETF TRADING ACCOUNT—USING SECTOR ETFs

Now comes the hot, racy part of your portfolio allocation, to satisfy the itch to do a little day trading now and then, or the need to buy or sell before the end of a day (remember, normal mutual funds are priced once a day, at the end of the day, and that's the price you buy or sell at, regardless of when you place the order during the day). It's important to acknowledge this and deal with it directly—and ETFs give you the flexibility.

Public interest in ETFs skyrocketed in the 1990s with the launching of the tech-heavy Nasdaq 100 index ETF, the "Qubes" (QQQ). In fact, the Qubes and the S&P 500 ETFs together accounted for more than 80 percent of *all* ETF investments at the peak of the bull market—like elephants and lions dominating this jungle.

Interest has faded somewhat, but Spiders and Qubes are still the favorite ETFs, with about 60 percent of the total. Most of the other ETFs, now more than a hundred, appeal mainly to active stock market sector traders, and about 85 percent of them have assets of less than $1 billion, and they are more volatile than index mutual funds.

FIVE MAJOR SECTOR ETFs FOR YOUR TRADING ACCOUNT

Here are some hot sector ETFs worth your consideration in building a portfolio. Just remember, you probably need to pick only a few out of the whole batch, and the pros will tell you to pick sectors you're familiar with. If you put a gun to my head and demanded a recommendation, I'd say split your 10 percent trading account into five pieces, picking one ETF in each of these five sectors. As you gain experience, adjust.

1. **Technology.** SPDR Technology (XLK), iShares Dow Jones U.S. Tech Index (IYW), and iShares Goldman Sachs Technology (IGM). Also look at the Merrill Lynch HOLDR series: Software (SWH), Wireless (WMH), Semiconductors (SMH), Telecomm (TTH), Broadband (BDH), and Internet (HHH).

2. **Health care.** iShares Dow Jones US Healthcare (IYH), iShares Nasdaq Biotech Index (IBB), Holders Pharmaceuticals (PPH), and Holders Biotech (BBH).

3. **Financial.** Financial Select Sector SPDR (XLF), iShares Dow Jones Financial Services (IYG), and iShares Dow Jones Financial Sector (IYF).

4. **Basic sectors.** Sector SPDRs: Basic Industries (XLB), Consumer Staples (XLP), Consumer Services (XLV), Financials (XLF), Cyclical/Transportation (XLY), and Utilities (XLU).

5. **Real estate.** Consider iShares Cohen & Steers Realty Majors (ICF), iShares Dow Jones Real Estate (IYR), and streetTRACKS Wilshire REIT Fund (RWR).

ETFs' low expenses, which are in the 0.10 percent range, are an invitation to frequent trading. A word of caution, then: Rebalancing and frequent additions through dollar-cost averaging can run up your costs due to brokerage commissions. Some Web sites help limit this risk through batching with other small purchasers.

But in general, an all-ETF portfolio works best with large, infrequent lump-sum additions and long holding periods. Otherwise, no-load index mutual funds will be less costly.

AN ALTERNATIVE TO SECTOR ETFs—FIDELITY'S SECTOR FUNDS

As an alternative, you might also consider putting your mad money account with Fidelity and its thirty-nine sector funds. You have more choices, and all your trading would be easily managed through one source backed by many experienced sector research analysts.

Remember, whether you go with sector ETFs or Fidelity's sector funds they are simply an alternative for investors who don't (yet) trust lazy investing and just can't give up the idea of occasional trading.

But be forewarned: According to my research on the performance of these sectors as a whole, the winners and losers balanced out over time. For example, *the combined returns of all Fidelity sector funds were roughly equal to the S&P 500.* Meanwhile, you have to spend a lot of time and incur transaction costs playing the sector trading game—*so this is definitely not a lazy portfolio!*

Moreover, you darn well better be ready to compete against the pros who track and understand which sectors are favored over the long-term economic cycles—a risky gamble.

WARNING: HIDDEN COSTS ADDED ATOP THE EXPENSE RATIO

Are the costs of an ETF really cheaper? Let's focus specifically on the Vanguard 500 Index and some of the comparable S&P 500 ETFs. Are the ETFs really a better deal than the index mutual funds simply because their published expense ratios are in the 0.10 to 0.12 percent range? *Not really, if you add in the costs of active trading.* And you need to add in *all* the other costs:

• ETF trades trigger brokers' commissions—$15 to $85 per trade.

- Investors pay the bid–ask spreads—from $0.06 to $0.50 per share.
- Brokerages charge quarterly fees on small accounts— about $15.
- Premiums and discounts can result in price-to-NAV (net asset value) spreads.

So add in all the extra transaction and ownership costs, and even the cheapest ETFs may end up costing you several times a basic S&P 500 index mutual fund, *especially if you get into active trigger-happy trading.*

In fact, the total costs of an ETF are probably more like 1.00 percent for a onetime $10,000 investment with an on-line discounter, or about 1.60 percent for a broker-assisted trade. Compare this to 0.18 percent for the Vanguard mutual fund that tracks the S&P 500 and is a no-load (no commissions).

THE ONLY WAY TO WIN WITH ETFs? BUY'N'HOLD!

A research study by economists at Stanford and MIT "found that the Vanguard 500 index fund outperformed Spiders from 1994 through 2000," according to *Forbes.* "Lesson: The only way to own ETFs that brings you ahead of index funds is to *buy* a lot of them and *hold* on to them. Trading ETFs, as many do to a fault, will hurt your returns." Trading costs are the big culprit.

Blindly switching to ETFs from index mutual funds—simply because their published expense ratios are lower—may not be such a hot idea. The expense ratios may be lower for ETFs, but total costs are higher. Still, if you're building a long-term passive portfolio with little or no trading, the lower costs may eventually pay off.

WHAT'S RIGHT FOR YOU? ETFs OR INDEX MUTUAL FUNDS?

So much for individual ETFs. Now comes the big question—is an all-ETF index *portfolio* really any better than one made up of traditional index mutual funds? William Bernstein made his own independent analysis of this question on his EfficientFrontier.com Web site.

Bernstein compared eight of Vanguard's index mutual funds with eight of Barclays' iShares ETFs, both sets tracking the same indexes. After adjusting for expenses and tracking errors, he concludes: "The result is a *dead heat*... and this is no ordinary tie score, it's the equivalent of shooting eight even rounds with Tiger Woods."

Then after reviewing some of the advantages and drawbacks, Bernstein wraps up with this observation: "I'm still wary, but cautiously optimistic. I wouldn't fill my portfolio with ETFs yet; however, the day may come when they are a solid competitor to the traditional open-ended index fund."

EITHER WAY—INDEXING IS AMERICA'S BEST-KEPT SECRET!

Meanwhile, the index mutual funds are still the preferred choice of most *passive* index investors—the last time I checked, out of $6 trillion in assets, the index mutuals were about $300 billion *or 5 percent of the total of all mutual funds.*

And 70 percent of the total index funds were Vanguard index funds. By comparison, the total invested in ETFs was about $150 billion worldwide—versus that same total of $6 trillion in funds.

In other words, indexing is the best-kept secret in the financial world—whether you're looking at a traditional index mutual fund or an exchange-traded index fund.

And even though this new ETF menagerie of wild animals is wild, unruly, and reminiscent of Noah's Ark, ETFs obviously have a powerful and growing place in the investment world—because they offer a lot of advantages. Moreover, I like them for yet another reason: Because of their dual roles, they are competition for both stocks and funds, giving savvy investors better alternatives.

INDEX MUTUALS—STILL THE PREFERRED CHOICE OF PASSIVE INVESTORS

But this zoo needs a better public relations job. ETFs may be understood by institutions and active investors. But the newness of these securities and their comic-book name tags make them a bit confusing to the average passive investor.

In the final analysis ETFs are more complicated than mutuals—frankly, I have a tough time figuring out what to do with so many options! Give me a simple two- or ten-fund portfolio of index ETFs.

For example, Barclays iShares has a broad enough selection of indexes that could help you duplicate any one of the three winning laziest portfolios from the Barclays list while you forget all about the other sector and single-country global ETFs; you just don't need to make it that complicated. Keep it very simple to win.

So for now, Bernstein's right, ETFs need to mature. Meanwhile, average passive investors will likely want to continue building their index portfolios out of mutual funds for the near future until they get more familiar with the ETFs as another alternative that may or may not work in their particular case.

WARNING: YOU MAY LOSE YOUR STATUS AS A LAZY INVESTOR!

So what do I think of the emerging world of ETFs? In simple terms, just this: Once an investor starts carving up his portfolio so he can trade 5 or 10 percent simply because he loves trading, that's kinda like an alcoholic thinking he can have just one drink. Open the door and it's tough to close. Transaction costs will increase; returns will likely drop.

Exchange-traded funds are what members of the anonymous programs call a dangerous "slippery slope." They are best suited for the more active traders. And whatever entertainment value there is in active trading, transaction costs are real economic costs that will definitely reduce your overall returns the more actively you trade. In other words, if you are trading ETFs, don't kid yourself: *You're not really a lazy investor.*

BOTTOM LINE: IT'S NOT MUTUAL FUNDS *VERSUS* ETFs, IT'S STILL THE PORTFOLIO, STUPID

But in the final analysis, please remember—*your most important decision is not whether you invest in mutual funds or pick exchange-traded funds*—the key to successful portfolio building still rests on your asset allocations.

Always keep that in mind—*it's the portfolio, diversification, and your asset allocations, not the specific funds you pick.* And that means you must know how the underlying indexes work within your overall portfolio needs and lifestyle.

*Many people say that the individual investor has scarcely
a chance today against Wall Street's pros . . . that there
is no longer any room for the individual investor in today's
institutionalized markets. Nothing could be further
from the truth. You can do it as well as the
experts—perhaps even better.*

—Burton Malkiel, A Random Walk Down Wall Street

TWENTY

DRIP-DRIP-DRIPping with No-Load Stocks
Start Your Own Fund—Be Your Own Manager

SOME SAY INDEX FUNDS ARE AMERICA'S BEST-KEPT SECRET. However, insiders will also tell you that no-load stocks are the best secret on Wall Street.

No-load stocks might be just perfect for you if your ego still believes that index funds and being average are for wimps, that funds just aren't macho enough for you, maybe even un-American—especially if you believe that *ownership* in Corporate America is the way of a "real American"!

Or maybe you just don't like the idea of paying a broker or letting any fund manager pick stocks for you when you know you're a pretty good stock picker, and know that you can do a better job and beat the pants off the pros.

NO-LOAD STOCKS ARE WALL STREET'S BEST-KEPT SECRET!

You just gotta pick the stocks, all by yourself. You feel it in your bones, like a calling from beyond; it's part of your psychological makeup. And you gotta do what you gotta do! You refuse on principle to turn the picking over to some broker making big commissions or to an overpaid fund manager.

You still want to pick the best possible stocks *for the long run,* because a little voice tells you that Buffett's got the right idea—*buy quality and never sell.* And you are certain you can do as well or better than the average pro.

So "Start Your Own Fund" using DRIPs (Dividend reinvestment programs), says Vita Nelson, editor of *Moneypaper,* a newsletter specifically about the wonderful world of DRIPs—which she says are the "best-kept secret" on Wall Street.

Why are DRIPs Wall Street's best-kept secret? Very simple: Because Wall Street won't tell you about them. And why not? Because Wall Street can't charge you any commissions on these "no-load stocks," as Charles Carlson calls them in his book by the same name.

The subtitle of Carlson's book *No-Load Stocks* makes it clear why they're called no-load stocks, because with DRIPs you'll find out "how to buy your first share and every other share directly from the company—with no broker's fee." *Get it—no-load stocks.* Good advice from the "King of DRIPs," the editor-publisher of the *DRIP Investor* newsletter and author of several great books on investing, including *Eight $teps to $even Figures.*

PERFECT INVESTMENT FOR LONG-TERM STOCK PICKERS

To begin with, mutual funds are generally recognized as the "perfect investment," says my ol' buddy Bill Griffeth, CNBC anchorman and author of *10 Steps to Financial Prosper-*

ity. And if you combine that idea with DRIPs, then guess what, you get to be the manager of your own fund!

No brokers, no fund managers, no fund-rating services, no exchanges, no commissions, and no hassle. So using DRIPs to create your very own "mutual fund" lets the big secret out of the bag and becomes another possible way to structure a lazy portfolio.

It's actually very simple. Dividend reinvestment programs—affectionately known as DRIPs—are already offered by many major U.S. corporations. Today well over a thousand major companies have DRIP programs.

And most of these DRIPs are blue-chip members of the Dow Industrials and Standard & Poor's 500—companies like Coca-Cola, Disney, ExxonMobil, Home Depot, Pfizer, and Walgreen. Plus you'll find a lot of solid foreign companies offering DRIPs, including Allianz AG, AXA, Barclays PLC, GlaxoSmithKline, Royal Bank of Scotland, and Toyota Motors, all administered through ADRs (American Depository Receipts) handled by American banks.

IMMEDIATELY INCREASE YOUR RETURNS BY 30% OR MORE

With DRIPs you can also save the fee you'd pay to a money manager at one of the Wall Street firms like Morgan Stanley or Merrill Lynch to buy ten stocks for you and just hold them indefinitely while you keep paying that ridiculous 1.5 to 3.0 percent annual asset management fee.

And there are similar savings compared to mutual funds: If you do it yourself and act as your own fund manager using DRIPs, you'll save 1.4 percent, the operating expenses the average fund manager charges. Plus you'll also save all the hidden transaction costs that active fund managers run up, especially the high-turnover, heavy-trading managers. And best of all, of course, you'll cut out your broker's commission. All of which is lost money—down the drain.

How much more in your pocket? Lots! Think of it this way: Historically (since 1926) stocks have returned an annual average over 10.0 percent. So if you save 3 to 4 percent on management and brokerage costs, the 10.0 percent goes to the bottom line—*your bottom line*—and directly into your bank account. And that means a potential increase of 30 percent or more in your portfolio's return, your pocket, your retirement nest egg!

INVESTORS END-RUNNING WALL STREET'S CODE OF SECRECY

"DRIPs have grown increasingly popular with individual investors," says Joe Tigue, editor of *S&P's Dividend Reinvestment Plans Annual Directory.* "A no-brainer [and] many more will be seen before long as companies jump on the bandwagon." Tigue reiterates that the "big attraction of DRIPs is the commission you save on brokers . . . brokers go broke." So you can be sure Wall Street will never mention them as a way to invest.

No wonder the editor of *Moneypaper* calls them Wall Street's best-kept secret. No wonder Wall Street lobbies hard to make darn sure the SEC won't let corporations advertise them—if this "secret" ever got any widespread publicity and was regularly advertised, brokers would go broke!

DRIP YOUR WAY INTO A $1,000,000 PORTFOLIO
Fortune Says, "Suddenly, It's Hip to DRIP!"

As double taxation of dividends moved into the spotlight, *Fortune* magazine ran an article, "Suddenly, It's Hip to DRIP," calling these dividend reinvestment programs a "powerful compounding tool," because dividends are automatically rolled over into more stock. DRIPs are a *fab-u-lous* deal in any event, and if dividends eventually become tax-free, DRIPs become an even better deal.

PROS SCREEN 1,000 DRIPS TO PICK THE 5 WINNERS

Fortune asked Chuck Carlson, editor of the *DRIP Investor*, to help pick America's "best DRIPs." The process Carlson used in screening the thousand-plus companies in his database is worth noting:

> Carlson searched his data base for companies with [1] above-average yield and [2] a long track record of growing dividends. To increase the chance of price appreciation, he further screened for stocks that are [3] trading below their five-year P/E ratio, are [4] expecting profit gains of 5% or more in 2002, and that [5] have fallen at least 15% since March 2000. That winnowed the list to nine names.

Fortune then went one step further and talked to several fund managers and analysts about the nine in order to narrow the list down to the five best—*for that moment, anyway.* And they were: ChevronTexaco, General Electric, Pfizer, Morgan Stanley, and Bank of New York.

And it's so easy to start with these guys: ChevronTexaco and General Electric will let you get in on their DRIPs for just $250. GE lets you stay in for as little as ten bucks a month. Of the five, Morgan Stanley is the priciest at $1,000 to start and $100 a month. But they are still a great deal, at this moment in time—*that's just about what you'd need in order to retire a millionaire, if you start in your twenties and trust compounding!*

TEST-DRIVE BEFORE YOU TAKE THE PLUNGE AND START DRIPPING

My advice is that since the *results*—but not the *methodology*—of screening and selecting the "best DRIPs" will probably change over time, you may need some help. So if the idea of DRIP investing does appeal to you as the kind of lazy investing that'll work for you, then you should read a couple of Carlson's books on DRIPs and subscribe to his *DRIP Investor* for a few months before you take the plunge and get "dripping wet"!

FIVE RESOURCES TO GET YOUR DRIPs DRIP-DRIPPING ALONG

Yep, it's so easy to get started. All you need is a single share of stock, because DRIP programs are available only to existing investors of a company.

Fortunately, there are several organizations with Web sites that'll sell you single shares, and there are ways to avoid paying commissions even on the first share. Moreover, some major companies, including Pfizer, GE, and ExxonMobil, are now letting *non*shareholders enroll in their DRIPs after a minimum $250 initial purchase, so it's easy to start from scratch.

For more information on the details, here are five sources on DRIPs, each with newsletters, books, directories, and Web sites that will help you get started:

- *DRIP Investor* newsletter.
- *Moneypaper* newsletter.
- AAII: American Association of Individual Investors.
- NAIC: National Association of Investors Corporation.
- *Standard & Poor's Directory of DRIPs.*

So far, so good. If these DRIP experts are right, building your very own diversified portfolio with DRIPs is a slam dunk, easier than rolling off a log.

There are several great references, on-line and in print,

that'll get you on a fast track to being your own "fund manager." First off, you should do Internet searches on Google and Ask.com. Better yet, for a quick jump-start, check out Charles Carlson's supersimple brochure *Dividend Reinvestment Plan Starter Guide*, and then dig into a couple of his books, *Buying Stocks Without a Broker* and his best-seller, *No-Load Stocks*.

EIGHT KEEP-IT-SIMPLE STEPS TO JUMP-START YOUR DRIP FUND!

Here's a short summary of Carlson's eight steps to get you up to speed, and if you want more information go to his *Guide* for details on these incredibly simple eight steps for "getting started in DRIPs":

1. **Select the best companies.** Solid companies with long-term prospects.
2. **Research the plan's specifics before investing.** They differ widely.
3. **Buy the first share of company stock.** And do it in your name.
4. **Wait for the stock certificate.** So you're a shareholder of record.
5. **Tell the company you want to join the DRIP plan.** Ask for enrollment forms.
6. **Receive the company's DRIP enrollment form.** Carefully fill it out and return it.
7. **Know the company rules on optional cash payments.** Read the prospectus.
8. **Keep good records.** Cost basis, annual dividend income, et cetera.

Now isn't that real darn lazy? So now you're enrolled in the company's program, and you can start sending them your monthly savings checks. You can even make it a painless automatic deduction from your back account. Yep, this is definitely a slam dunk.

ONE STOCK DOES *NOT* A PORTFOLIO MAKE—GOTTA DIVERSIFY, TOO!

Okay, you're on your way to being your own mutual fund manager—with one stock. That's just one small step on the path. Virtually every mutual fund expert will tell you that diversification is the key to successful investing—and that's true with DRIPs, too. One stock does not a portfolio make!

What *does* make a portfolio? You can do it with just ten quality stocks with solid long-term track records. Carlson recommends a number of portfolios for different investors with different lifestyle needs and levels of money to invest, with starter portfolios from a two-stock $100 portfolio to an eight-stock $2,300 portfolio. The two-stock portfolio is made up of Dollar General and Walgreen. And here's the eight-stock starter portfolio with the ten-year growth of $1,000 invested in 1992:

The No-Load Stocks "Starter Portfolio"

COMPANY NAME	10-YEAR TOTAL RETURN
Medtronics, Inc.	$8,187
Popular Inc.	6,543
Walgreen	5,739
Pfizer Inc.	5,653
Dollar General Corp.	5,470
ExxonMobil Corp.	3,200
Regions Financial Corp.	3,156
Walt Disney	1,499
	$39,447

In other words, this portfolio was generating average annual returns of 16 percent and cumulative returns of 393 percent for a ten-year period, and that includes three years of the bear market.

So you gotta admit, this is a pretty darn good performance when you stack it up against the performance of the broad market benchmark—the S&P 500—for the same period. For example, if you had invested $1,000 in an S&P 500 index mutual fund, or a comparable exchange-traded fund, the ten-year cumulative returns were less than 170 percent, with average returns of under 10 percent annually.

NO-LOAD STOCK PORTFOLIOS—LESS DIVERSIFIED THAN MUTUALS

Of course, you'll have to live with the fact that each of the eight stocks you're picking represents a relatively large 12 percent of your portfolio. That's a lot allocated to each individual stock.

Compare that to the professionally managed mutual funds, which are often diversified across fifty to a hundred or more stocks. So obviously you'd have much broader diversification in a traditional mutual fund than you would creating and managing an eight-stock "fund" by yourself.

JUST ONE MORE REASON YOU DON'T NEED WALL STREET

For many investors, however, that risk is well worth it. Carlson and the other DRIP sources provide many more model portfolios, with asset allocations to fit the needs of most investors. True, you probably will still need to add some bond funds to create a balanced portfolio that best suits your lifestyle, so you should consider sticking with an established index bond fund for that slice of your portfolio.

Remember, if you're a confident and savvy do-it-yourself investor willing to research the companies and their DRIP programs, and if you're convinced you can do at least as well as the 85 percent of fund managers who can't beat the market indexes any one year, you owe it to yourself to seriously consider this "best-kept secret."

WALL STREET'S BEST-KEPT SECRET IS NOW OUT OF THE BAG!

Bottom line: Okay, *maybe* a portfolio of eight DRIP stocks isn't a pure mutual fund. *Maybe* you aren't going to put in the same amount of time as a full-time professional fund manager. And *maybe* your new "fund" won't be diversified quite enough.

On the other hand, just *maybe* a no-load stock portfolio better suits your inner psychological need to get close to the companies and their stocks. And just *maybe* you can pick stocks for an eight-fund portfolio all by yourself—*better than the pros.* Put it all together, and just *maybe* you'll sleep better with this unique kind of lazy portfolio.

*Whether you win or lose, you are responsible for your own results.
Even if you lost on your broker's tip, an advisory service
recommendation, or a bad signal from the system you bought,
you are responsible, because you made the decision to listen and act.*
—Jack Schwager, The New Market Wizards

TWENTY-ONE

You Wanna Be the Next Super-Mario?
"Folios" Will Make You a "Fund Manager"!

I'LL BET SOMETHING LIKE THIS GOES THROUGH YOUR HEAD EVERY time you look at fund performance stats: *Those dumb fund managers don't know what the hell they're doing. I can manage a fund just as well, and cut my costs too.*

Wanna try? Here's another possibility! Plus it's easy and it's cheap. For a few hundred bucks a year you really can create *and manage* your own fund. Just log onto Foliofn.com and you're in business—America's new Mario Gabelli, our next legendary fund manager. Call it "Joe&Jane Lunchbox Early Retirement Fund," or whatever makes you feel in charge and proud.

NEW FOLIOS' LOW FIXED PRICES MAKE TRADING EASY

Foliofn.com is the brainchild of Steven Wallman, a former SEC commissioner who wants "to do to the mutual fund industry what Charles Schwab did to the old fixed commission structure—rip it up," as *Forbes* put it in calling Wallman and his Foliofn one of the top fifteen innovations of the year in 2002. Because folios have a "system for replacing the traditional fund with automated portfolios that the customer manages from their own computer." Quite a compliment, quite an innovation—for active investors.

Seriously, you'll save money, they say, because you'll break even with the fees you pay when compared to an average 1.23 percent mutual fund expense ratio on a portfolio of $30,000 or more. So obviously you'll save even more as your assets increase.

GO AHEAD, TEST-DRIVE YOUR NEW "FUND"—WITH $1,000,000!

Still skeptical? You can test-drive your new career as a fund manager for nothing down. Set up a watch folio and learn how to become a fund manager by tinkering with a portfolio of up to fifty stocks from a menu of thirty-five hundred. Buy, sell, monitor returns, rebalance. Start with a million bucks, if you want. Later you assemble the right stocks and settle down to a passive, buy'n'hold investor.

Monopoly money, of course. But hey, it's a free education. Think of it as a fast-track mini MBA home-study course to hone your innate skills as a fund manager—before you sell all your real mutual funds and get into this innovative new (port) folio management. Take a month or two testing your skills on this trial run, and you'll be ready to invest real money and become a real fund manager.

YOUR PERSONAL TRADING MENTOR—THE FOLIO WIZARD!

You can start from scratch and build your own folios. The flat fee is $14.95 a month for one folio or $149 per year (double that if you want three folios). That gives you five hundred commission-free "window trades" a month, executed twice a day. If you want timely market trades, you'll pay a low discount brokerage commission.

Better yet, start with the demo. I went through the demo, and actually found it extremely easy. And versatile, with three basic ways to create these folios. Start with their "Folio Wizard," which questions you about your lifestyle goals and risk tolerance, then offers stock suggestions.

SHARPEN YOUR SKILLS—100 READY-MADE FOLIOS TO PLAY WITH!

While you're still in the *I'm-just-thinking-about-it* stage, I strongly suggest you explore their ready-made folios. That's the fun part of this mini MBA course in "how to become a hot-shot fund manager."

To begin with, there are a hundred ready-mades in eleven major categories, including media favorites like the *Money* 30, *Forbes* Super 100, and *Fortune* 50. Plus foreign-country and regional folios. They also have ready-made folios in the major asset classes, everything from large-cap growth to small-cap value: Sectors. Dividend stocks. Dogs of the Dow. REITs. ETFs. Folios based on analysts' recommendations, such as highest buy ratings and earnings growth. And bond folios of all kinds.

THE WIZARD'S READY-MADE FOLIOS—ALMOST LIKE INDEXES

In addition, Foliofn.com even has a "back-test" tool to help you analyze each folio! Plus fab-u-lous graphing tools to compare your folios to various indexes, as well as breakouts of the folio's sector compensation and fundamentals, like price/earnings ratio, market cap, beta, volatility, and dividend yield. You'll even find what amounts to a limit-order tool, and a chart that compares the current performance of all these folios from best to worst.

You might even look at each of these folios as special "indexes" helping you create your own "index fund," while giving you the added flexibility of becoming a portfolio manager who can modify the "index"—which you can't do with a Standard & Poor's, Russell, or Wilshire index fund, for example.

CUSTOMIZE ALL YOU WANT—YOU'RE THE MANAGER!

That's right, you can customize all you want. It's like going to Sizzler's restaurant and buying a basic T-bone steak dinner. You start with the ready-made folio, then just subtract and add all the side dishes from the salad bar and dessert tray. You have total control. You customize the whole menu, mixing and matching to suit your personal tastes.

The list of the hundred ready-made folios is a mini MBA education all by itself. Even if you finally decide to stick with traditional mutual funds, you can learn a lot from exploring these ready-mades. *It's like looking inside a fund manager's brain.* So stop and look closely.

Once you have the folio set up, you can buy, modify, sell, and rebalance the entire portfolio or individual securities. And when you sell or rebalance, you can even designate one of eight tax-planning strategies that optimize your objectives, and even test your decision before taking action. And the paperwork is all in one place for the IRS.

SOCIALLY RESPONSIBLE FOLIOS FOR GOOD GUYS IN WHITE HATS

My interest in folios got started after writing a column on socially responsible funds. Foliofn.com suggested I look at their socially responsible portfolios. I looked at their "Environmentally Responsible" and "SRI [Socially Responsible Investing] Large-Cap" folios.

Even if you are hard-core in this arena, you might not like the fact that five of the stocks in the Environmentally Responsible folio have p/e ratios above 40. No problem. If that's your threshold criterion, you can easily omit them. Other specific screens can be used to omit the stocks of inappropriate companies.

The selections in these particular folios are made by the Investor Responsibility Research Center (IRRC), an independent organization that evaluates fifteen hundred companies based on their compliance with sixteen social-responsibility screens, with no revenues from tobacco, alcohol, military weapons, gambling, animal testing, and similarly controversial activities.

If you decide to go directly with a socially responsible mutual fund and let it do all the stock picking, buying, and selling, check out the Social Investment Forum, which also evaluates socially responsible mutual funds. SIF is a leading shareholder advocacy organization pushing corporations toward greater social responsibility.

TOOLS FOR BUY'N'HOLD INVESTORS? OR JUST ACTIVE TRADERS?

The American Century fund family is now an investor in Foliofn. In addition, they are breeding competition from big guns like Fidelity and E*Trade who are toying with the business. On the downside, the mutual fund industry's trade group, the Investment Company Institute, has asked the SEC to start regulating folio sites as "mutual funds."

So where's the folio phenomenon headed? Early in the bear market, *Mutual Funds* magazine warned that the folio trend could make mutual funds obsolete. Oh hmmm, we've heard the same warning in past years about DRIPs and ETFs, and yet traditional mutual funds just keep growing.

Fidelity Insight newsletter publisher Eric Kobren also thinks that folios are just another passing fancy. Yes, folios do seem to be a revival of the active trading mentality made popular by the on-line discount trading craze in the 1990s go-go years. Yes, it's a more sophisticated portfolio management tool, but the folio isn't really any big technological advance.

It's possible that within a few years every major brokerage, mutual fund family, and financial adviser—*and who knows, maybe even the 401(k) plans*—will have a variation of these folio tools, for their in-house staffs if not for their clients. Schwab, however, has already test-marketed and rejected its folio product. Actually, I don't see folios as much of a threat to mutual funds—another minor alternative, but certainly no major competitor.

MUTUAL FUNDS—STILL THE BEST CHOICE FOR TRULY LAZY INVESTORS

Fund portfolios are complicated enough, especially for the passive investor. Yes, *Forbes* and *Mutual Funds* magazines have both hinted that folios could dramatically alter the mutual fund world—but frankly, I get exhausted thinking about all the work involved to create and stay on top of a folio! They feel like just another hula-hoop fad.

Still, I admit, I'm quite fascinated by folios. They are innovative. But when the novelty wears off, you have to conclude that they're more appropriate for active investors and traders than for passive, buy'n'hold, lazy investors.

Most investors just don't have the time, interest, or expertise necessary to fool around timing the market and picking the "right" hot folio of stocks. This is definitely *not* a game for the truly lazy investor, regardless of how it sounds.

YOU'RE NOT A REAL FUND MANAGER, BUT PRETENDING IS FUN!

So let's get brutally honest: Word games aside, a "folio" of stocks is not a real "mutual fund." Close, but no cigar. Folios are not funds and you're not a manager no matter how the media spins the name tag to lure investors back into playing the market. A real actively managed fund hires full-time pros to manage the beast, not part-time amateurs.

These "folios" of stocks are just that, bunches of stocks. And the owners are just more average Main Street Americans playing the market with their bunches of stocks. Period!

Of course that's perfectly all right, if that's what you want to do—play the market—*but you're not really a mutual fund manager.*

The truly lazy investor will do far better with a well-diversified portfolio of two to ten easy-to-understand index funds that you can forget about for months at a time while you go about your life. Remember, you just want to sleep well and hopefully—if you're lucky—retire on time. Get it?

A TEST FOR WANNABE
MARKET TIMERS AND DAY TRADERS
"You Got What It Takes, Hotshot?"

There are about ninety-four million investors in America. Very few—maybe a million—have what it takes to be a successful trader. The vast majority, ninety-three million, simply do not have the time, or the skills, or the guts, or the interest necessary to be a successful market timer and trader. Still, you may be one of this rare breed.

Here's a short test to help you decide if you have what it takes, as an alternative to a buy'n'hold strategy. If you mark all of these ten statements "true," you should consider becoming a timer and active trader:

1. I HAVE LOTS OF TIME TO TRACK THE MARKETS AND TRADE. (T) (F)

Market timing and active trading are very time-consuming. In *Ordinary People, Extraordinary Wealth,* Ric Edelman says typical millionaires spend about six minutes a day on personal finance. They're busy focusing on their careers and families, not trading.

2. THE MARKET'S IRRATIONAL, BUT I CAN HANDLE UNCERTAINTY. (T) (F)

Economist Jeremy Siegel studied the 120 biggest up and biggest down days in history. In ninety of these days he found *no* logical reason for the move. Trading is psychological warfare. To win you need the discipline to stick with whichever technical timing system you select, no matter how unpredictable the outside world appears.

3. YES, IT'S OKAY IF I LOSE MONEY. (T) (F)

Most investors love winning, hate to lose. But savvy traders believe it's okay to lose money. They know the world's unpredictable, the game's risky, you win some, you lose some. But long experience and discipline give them the confidence of knowing they'll win more than they lose.

4. I'M VERY DISCIPLINED AS A MARKET TIMER. (T) (F)

"Market timing works," says money manager Paul Merriman, "and it works well for people who actually practice it as a discipline. In theory, every investor is capable of following the discipline of timing. But not everybody has the right emotional makeup to do timing right. In real life, most people who try are ultimately unsuccessful."

5. YES, I CAN HANDLE LOSING STREAKS. (T) (F)

There are all kinds of sophisticated computer timing systems. But none is perfect. They deal with probabilities. So traders are always making "mistakes," getting in or out too soon or too late. Can your ego handle the endless mistakes, even a series of big ones?

6. BREAKING NEWS DOESN'T DISTRACT ME. (T) (F)

Most people will tell you timing doesn't work—Wall Street, mass media, fund managers, and financial planners. But we know timing does work—for some people. Whether they're winning or losing, these winners ignore CNBC, CNN, and the financial press, and stick religiously to their trading system. Period.

7. I NEVER BUY HIGH AND SELL LOW. (T) (F)

Not unless you go short. Morningstar research shows mutual fund investors are bad at market timing, tending to buy at the top and sell out at the bottom. Greed triggers a buying frenzy at the top of a cycle. Fear creates a selling panic at the bottom. They lose both ways.

8. I MAKE QUICK DECISIONS, WITH NO REGRETS. (T) (F)

Successful trading demands quick decisions. Unfortunately, most people have difficulty making decisions, even when they know they have to. Mistakes add up, and the negative results will haunt you.

9. I CAN LIVE COMFORTABLY ON $50,000 A YEAR. (T) (F)

Trading is not a get-rich-quick scheme. And paradoxically, cheap on-line trades increase trading activity, risk, and losses. Even the best full-time day traders rarely make more than $100,000 a year. The average is less than $50,000. And it's a solitary game.

10. I'M NOT OVERLY CONFIDENT, NOR IN DENIAL. (T) (F)

Behavioral finance studies indicate that 88 percent of investors have an "optimism bias." Their overconfidence leads to bad investment decisions and losses. But they still tell themselves they're beating the market, even though, on an after-tax basis, they're often under the market by five to fifteen points.

STILL THINK YOU CAN BEAT THE ODDS? YOU MUST BE KIDDING!

Finance professors Odean and Barber of the University of California at Davis studied 66,400 investors between 1991 and 1997. They concluded that bad stock picking and transaction costs substantially reduced returns. The most active traders averaged 11.4 percent, versus 18.5 percent for passive investors. Worse yet, trading on-line also reduced returns. So if you think you're really different, go for it—but only if you scored ten "true" answers on the above test!

*At the current rate of wealth creation, by the year 2005, out of
100 workers at the age of 65, only one will be wealthy
($5 million net worth or more), four will be financially
independent ($1 million to $4.9 million net worth),
41 will still be working, and 54 will be dead broke.*

—Mark Alch, How to Become a Millionaire

TWENTY-TWO

The Superpowered Zero-Funds Portfolio

Rich Dad Says . . . Invest in You, Inc!

NOTICE WALL STREET'S RETIREMENT ADS LATELY? NOBODY'S
young. But they're not really "old" either. They're smiling,
gray-haired alive folks. And they're doing what'll help them
retire with a comfortable income.

How about you? Want to retire *young and rich?* Oh, you do?
Then stop doing what you're doing! Today. Seriously. You're
doing it all wrong. Working at a job? Stop! Investing in mutual
funds? Stop! All wrong. Stop all that now!

HOW TO GET RICH—*REALLY RICH?* THINK LIKE AN ENTREPRENEUR!

America has about seven million millionaires out of a pop-
ulation of roughly 283 million people. But those few million-

aires (among whom are a few hundred billionaires) own more than 90 percent of America's wealth. Many of the other 276 million will struggle in retirement.

So if you really want to retire young and rich, you gotta start thinking in a radically new way. How? *Think like an entrepreneur*—think about leveraging OPM, other people's money.

In *Retire Young, Retire Rich,* Robert Kiyosaki and his partner, Sharon Lechter, tell us, "Leverage simply means the ability to do more with less"—like borrowing a million bucks to build and own an apartment complex or local business.

STOCKS AND FUNDS TOO RISKY—EVEN IF YOU DIVERSIFY

Kiyosaki is a great promoter, encouraging everyone to take the path of the entrepreneur: "I retired at age forty-seven without a single share of stock or a mutual fund. To me, *mutual funds and stocks are too risky, even if you do diversify. There are better ways to invest for retirement.*

"The reason less than 5 percent of all Americans are rich," Kiyosaki continues, "is because only 5 percent know how to use the power of leverage." The rest are afraid of the risks of leverage. Or they abuse it.

According to Kiyosaki, the average American uses very limited leverage. Their mind-set is stuck on working forty hours a week for a modest salary. Enduring that life for forty years. Saving a modest amount. And investing in mutual funds for a modest 10 percent. If you're lucky, says Wall Street, the money just might compound to a million bucks after decades of hard labor. If you're lucky.

And if you think you're aggressive (but still working for Corporate America), your salary-oriented mind-set might even rationalize that you're "leveraging" your money in leveraged funds, such as hedged and enhanced index funds.

Or you might convince yourself that you're leveraging

your money by trading on margin, or playing with puts and calls, options, futures, and other derivatives that theoretically help you do more with less.

YOU'RE NOT GETTING RICH—YOU'RE MAKING "THEM" RICHER

Fat chance! You are kidding yourself, my friend. You're not thinking like the rich: "People who work hard have limited leverage. If you're working hard physically and not getting ahead financially, then *you're probably somebody else's leverage,*" Kiyosaki warns. You're an employee making "them" rich. Or perhaps an active day trader making your brokers rich.

And worse yet, even if your money is in long-term retirement accounts like IRAs and 401(k)s, says Kiyosaki, "then others are using your money as their leverage." They'll retire young and rich. Not you. Or they won't retire, they'll just keep having fun getting richer and richer—leveraging on your hard labor, for decades.

STOP WORKING FOR "THEM" TODAY— START WORKING FOR YOU, INC.!

Get it? The vast majority of Americans are working their butts off helping *someone else get rich.* You too. You're working your butt off, praying you can at least retire when you're old and live modestly, if you're lucky. Lucky, because only one in three Americans is saving enough to retire, ever.

What's a modest retirement today? Ask a retirement planner. It means retiring at roughly 70 percent of your highest salary, probably no more than $50,000 a year.

And while that 70 percent may seem modestly comfortable for you (because endless Wall Street ads have convinced you that's enough), it ain't rich in the same way Kiyosaki thinks of rich. So most investors aren't rich, *and most won't retire young.*

YOUR JOB IS BLOCKING YOUR PATH TO GETTING RICH

What would make you rich? It's not just the money, it's a state of mind, says Kiyosaki. It's not just being financially independent when you retire so you never have to work. First, "find the leverage that works best for you"—the kind of leverage "you can use to acquire and create assets to allow you to get ahead financially faster."

That's the secret goal of the entrepreneur—*to acquire and create assets* by leveraging other people's money.

It also means that you stop thinking about IRAs, 401(k)s, and company pension plans. You stop thinking about stocks and mutual funds. And you stop thinking about a job working for "the man"! All that guarantees only that you'll retire old and live modestly, not retire young and rich.

Whoa! Do you really have to give up your day job? Kiyosaki's Rich Dad's answer is emphatically, Yes! "The problem with having a job is that it gets in the way of getting rich."

So if you wanna get rich, your odds increase dramatically if you take that first big risk, quit that job you're clinging to for security, and work for "You, Inc."!

FIRST, YOU RETIRE EARLY . . . THEN YOU GET RICH!

Kiyosaki's entrepreneurial strategy works in two stages. First, he had enough assets so he was financially independent in his late forties. He had accumulated passive assets generating about $100,000 a year, enabling him to retire young. But he wasn't rich at this point, merely financially free.

So here's the big second stage as you rocket to Jupiter and Mars: "You retire young in order to get rich," by leveraging yourself. "*Forbes* magazine defines rich as $1 million or more a year in income," says Kiyosaki. "We were not yet rich when we retired. . . . After retiring, our plan was to spend time investing and building businesses." Today Kiyosaki and Lechter fit the *Forbes* definition.

A strategy in two stages: You retire young first. And that gives you time to get rich. This plan is obviously not for employees of Corporate America. It is not about investing in government-approved retirement plans. And not about mutual funds.

Instead, Kiyosaki's *Rich Dad, Poor Dad* books teach people how to use leverage to create assets—in particular, businesses and real estate—"that work hard so you don't have to." His ideas will be familiar to anyone who has read *The Millionaire Next Door,* in which the authors wrote that "the majority of the millionaires we interviewed said it's nice to invest in the market, but the mother lode of investing is in their own business."

MOST OF US AREN'T CUT OUT FOR THE ENTREPRENEURIAL JUNGLE

Should you follow Kiyosaki's strategies? Listen: I'm not saying you *should* quit your job, become an entrepreneur, and start building businesses, or developing real estate, or whatever you'd have to do to create "assets that work hard so you don't have to."

The fact is, most people are not psychologically cut out to be entrepreneurs. They don't have the interest, drive, and edge that it takes to make it in business for themselves. It takes a special breed to make it in the entrepreneurial jungle.

Besides, research studies tell us that most people just aren't willing to make the sacrifices it takes to become rich, let alone truly rich. They have a different life path, and they must honor it. In their minds, there are far more important things in life than getting rich. In fact, if they are browsing through a bookstore, they probably wouldn't even pick up a book with a title like *Retire Young, Retire Rich*, let alone read it!

YOU'VE GOT A TIGER IN YOUR TANK—STRUGGLING TO BREAK FREE!

But still I challenge you to at least ask yourself the bigger question: *Why am I in the job I'm in? Am I in my career by default? Or by choice?*

And if you don't know, you owe it to yourself to read at least one or two of Kiyosaki's *Rich Dad, Poor Dad* books—then choose your own career path, *consciously*. In Corporate America . . . or working for You, Inc. You owe it to yourself. Don't continue working in a career or business by default. You have but one life to live—*make it yours!*

I strongly suggest you read Kiyosaki's books with an open mind, regardless of who you are. You may find that secretly you *are* an entrepreneur—that you would be far happier and more in line with your true destiny if you quit your job with all its false sense of security, if you forgot all about building a retirement nest egg by investing in mutual funds for the next thirty years—*and took the risk of investing in your biggest and best asset, You, Inc.!*

Millionaires who have a high creative intelligence often make one very important career decision correctly: They select a vocation that provides them with enormous profits, and very often this same vocation is the one they love. Remember, if you love what you are doing, your productivity will be high and your specific form of creative genius will emerge.

—Thomas Stanley, The Millionaire Mind

TWENTY-THREE

Lazy Portfolios for Not-So-Lazy Kids
Get a Kid to College and a Million-Dollar Retirement!

PEOPLE OFTEN ASK ME WHAT FUNDS ARE SPECIFICALLY DESIGNED to pay for a kid's college. Or what are the best funds to build a million-dollar nest egg for their retirement?

Once again, the short answer is: You're putting too much focus on picking the "right" funds, and *not enough on starting early, on saving, and on the pure magic of compounding.* That's the lesson kids need to learn—*and learn fast and early, before the bad habits set in!*

Remember "Action Step #1. Start Saving Now" from Chuck Carlson's *Eight $teps to $even Figures.* Carlson says he spends "a lot of time on step one, for good reason. It's the most important of all. You can't get to the other seven steps without starting. Oftentimes it is the most difficult step. You may have to break old habits and start new ones."

In other words, start early with your kids, *before the bad habits set in.*

THE FUTURE OF AMERICA—OUR BIGGEST AND BEST INVESTMENT

Listen up, parents and grandparents: You have all kinds of options to save for your kid's college. The proliferation of tax-advantaged section 529 plans—*every state has one*—has made parents' jobs much easier if they start saving the day Mom and the new baby are coming home.

Under most conditions there are no taxes until the children pull out money for college, and then it's at *their* low tax rate. And some plans let you put in well over $100,000. The options are as varied as the states—just remember, if you start saving early and plan right, you'll have all the money you need.

And yes, it takes a lot of dough. Keep in mind that each child now costs the parents about $350,000 from infancy through high school—everything, including diapers, snacks, lessons, Nikes, wheels, school supplies, you name it. And by 2020, getting your child four years at a top university will cost you about a cool quarter million; half that at a good state college.

WOW! $5,000 AT BIRTH GROWS TO $2,451,854 AT RETIREMENT!

Here's another way to finance the kids—from cradle to grave, with a good education along the way. Financial planner Ric Edelman, author of *Ordinary People, Extraordinary Wealth,* offers a simple alternative that you should be thinking about. He calls it the RIC-E Trust, short for "Retirement InCome—for Everyone Trust."

Okay, so the name's a little flashy, but the plan makes a lot of sense. And I'm bringing it up here for a very, very important reason—because Edelman's trust is helping me hammer home the power of *starting a saving plan early* and *letting the magic of compounding* do the rest of the work. So listen closely to Edelman's simple explanation of the simple magic in this simple solution:

> When it comes to children and savings, most people only think about college costs. That's great, and worthwhile, too. And if you start early, you won't have to struggle as much to pay for college when those bills arrive. But what's the real purpose of sending a youngster to college?
>
> It's to get an education so your child can get a good job. Then, with a good job, they can earn a decent wage so they can save for their own retirement, like you, and hopefully live comfortably in their later years. Well, why not cut-to-the-chase and put some money away for their retirement when they're young, too?
>
> Think about it . . . if you set aside $5,000 for a newborn for 65 years . . . and if you didn't touch that money the entire time . . . and if that money was able to earn a 10% annual return . . . you'd have . . . more than $2.4 million!

Then Edelman goes on to describe how such a legal trust can save you taxes and take care of college—plus leave enough money for the kid to retire on very comfortably. Yeah, I know, you're saying, *Hey, this is too good to be true. Just $5,000 at birth and this wonderful child goes to college and still has enough left over to retire as a millionaire?* Trust me, it's true.

Edelman adds this note about the power of compounding. The $5,000 grows to $2.4 million at a 10 percent average rate of return. At 12 percent it would grow to $7.9 million by age sixty-five. On the other hand, at a conservative 8 percent it grows to just $743,899, and might also affect the amount available for college tuition earlier. Still, you can see the huge leveraging effect of compounding over a lifetime. Keep that in mind in the following story.

SIBLINGS GOT $1,000 AT BIRTH—NOW THEY'RE MULTIMILLIONAIRES

Here's another true-life story that will further encourage you to start saving early for your kids—*and grandkids*—while trusting the incredible magic of compounding. I got this first-hand from Sam when he turned sixty. In fact, his "secret formula" has worked so well (thanks to his grandfather's vision sixty years earlier) that he's passing it on to his grandkids, investing money for them at birth. Listen to Sam's inspiring story:

> **Grandparents gave $1,000 at birth.** "When we were born my grandparents put $1,000 in a mutual fund for my sisters and then for me. After all, back in 1938 when I was born, $1,000 was a lot of money! It represented half a year's income for most people. My grandparents were not well off. Comfortable, yes; well off, no. What they did for each of us was a definite sacrifice on their part."
>
> **Compounded for sixty years.** "Now I'm sixty years old and I haven't touched it yet, although I do have to pay the taxes, *but the taxes are paid out of the dividends.*"
>
> **His fund is now worth $1.8 million.** "How's it doing? Well, not bad. Not bad at all. Last statement showed just a bit over $1.8 million. It was invested with Fidelity for some years, and is now divided between Vanguard, American Century, and Janus."
>
> **And his sister's fund is worth about $5 million!** "My older sister's original thousand dollars was put in a different fund. And when she turned sixty-five she finally decided to tap into it. She had a touch under $5 mil-

lion. My fund is an ultraconservative one; her fund was more aggressive."

Passed it on to our children. "So I did the same for my kids, only we put in $5,000 as the starting amount. Older boy is now thirty-two and his account shows about $138,000. Give him another twenty-eight years and I suspect he'll have his million plus inflation damage."

Raising the ante for the grandchildren. "We have our first grandchild on the way and have decided to start them out with $10,000. And both my children's and grandchildren's money is going into one of the top no-load families."

YES, YOU CAN ALSO DO IT WITH NO MONEY DOWN!

You can't help but admire the insight and love Sam's grandparents had back when he and his sisters were born, during the Great Depression and the tough days just before the Second World War.

Sam's story also touched a chord in me. I was raised by grandparents through high school, in the years following the Second World War. They were retired. Money was tight. There was no $1,000 at birth. But there was a lot of love and guidance. I worked odd jobs and always seemed to have money. We lived off Grandpa's gardening and Grandma's canning and cooking. Seems every day they passed on a little wisdom and a sense of values that you just can't buy.

My case was a little different from Sam's: Between my grandparents' spiritual support, the Marine Corps, the GI Bill, scholarships, loans, and part-time work, I got ten years of invaluable higher education—and with that, I got all I'd ever need to prepare for retiring in the distant future. Which I guess is at least anecdotal proof that investing in education is probably the best investment in America's future, *and also in your kid's future retirement.*

MORE THAN MONEY—AN INSPIRED VIEW OF A BRIGHT FUTURE

Sam's grandparents and my own grandparents were two sets of great people, so I was pleased when he followed up a few days later with this postscript:

Inspiration. "Last night at a family get-together the exchange you and I had prompted quite a discussion. There were a couple of points made that I'd like to pass on. The operative word for most of the evening's discussion was *inspiration,* as you used it."

Focusing on the horizon. "If there is inspiration here, we all concluded, it was the *farsighted attitude of our grandparents.* After all, most of my cousins and one of my sisters used the money for college."

Discipline. "For the very few of us who did not (for whatever reasons) it was *discipline more than farsightedness,* and in my case a desire to honor my grandparents' wishes."

No regrets. "Today, neither my sister nor cousins who used the money long ago have any hint of envy or regret. They accept that a few of us were able to leave the money alone, and that was that."

No handouts. "But neither do they display any hint that they expect the government to solve their problems (if they have any)."

Instill responsibility. "The inspiration definitely came from our grandparents, who tried to instill in us a sense of self and of responsibility."

Original stocks sold. "No one remembered (if we ever knew) which stock we were gifted. The stock was sold when I was very young, and the money put into a fund that my father invested."

Now professionally managed. "When it was turned over to me, I invested in different stocks and funds until the early 1980s, when I realized I was not very clever at such things. It has been in funds ever since, though switched a few times, and is now with a professional."

BUILDING CHARACTER MORE IMPORTANT THAN BUILDING A PORTFOLIO

Sam went on to relate this key aspect of the discussion I had sparked with his family:

The second strongest theme of our discussion was this: Today so many people want a quick fix for all their shortsightedness and self-indulgence. They want someone to tell them or show them a fast, painless way to "get it together" in life. And I'm not saying that I haven't been guilty of this short-term thinking as well.

The $1,000 gifts at birth obviously had a huge impact on Sam and his siblings and cousins, because there apparently was an intangible, near-spiritual experience that accompanied the money, yet went far beyond the relatively minor one-thousand-dollar gift each received:

So often today, values like character, honor, and sacrifice seem to be just lip service. The *inspiration* I got was definitely from my grandparents. Those qualities were alive and well in them, may they rest in peace. But do your readers have forty, fifty, or sixty years to get it together? Do they have the patience in this intensely commercial culture? There's the rub.

Focus on the long term—and patience!

START EARLY BUILDING A LITTLE PORTFOLIO, TRUST COMPOUNDING, BUT MOST OF ALL—INSPIRE THEM, HELP THEM BUILD CHARACTER!

If it's so easy, and cheap, to plan for your children's college education, even for their retirement, why don't we? Why? Frankly, it's a big mystery. Here we see clear evidence that a mere $1,000 invested sixty years ago is worth $1.8 to $5 million today. And yet too few people get it, too few people have the foresight and wisdom of these folks—even with the advantage of today's 529 plans and trusts such as Edelman's.

More Americans need to shift from short-term consuming to long-term planning, saving, and investing. And remember—it ain't the money. Teach your kids and grandkids how to build character, do the right thing, and live with integrity while helping them plan for the future. That you cannot buy.

WHAT A FORMULA: KIDS + COMPOUNDING + CHARACTER = GREAT WEALTH!

It is one of the best investments you'll ever make, and it won't cost much if you start early enough, teach character, and trust the magic!

PART FIVE

WHEN LAZINESS FAILS YOU AND YOU'RE ITCHIN' FOR SOME ACTION!

Mad Money, PMA, and
Other Cures for Your Brainstorms

Your memory is more a recording of emotions and feelings of events than a recording of facts. . . . You want to believe that your investment decisions are good. In the face of evidence to the contrary, the brain's defense mechanisms filter out contrary information and alter the recollection of an investment's performance.

—John Nofsinger, Investment Madness

Imagine this scene: Suddenly you find yourself uneasy, your breathing quickening. A panic attack? No. Excitement! *You're itchin' for some action!* It can happen to anyone, even the more passive of investors, at some point when life gets too good, too serene, too boring, too lazy. Guaranteed. We're all susceptible to old habits, good and bad. Some more prone than others. Some even get addicted to the thrill of playing the markets.

Believe me, it is going to happen. Markets go up. Markets go down. Stock prices rise and fall. Breaking news stories scream of opportunities—and warnings. You "hear" voices demanding immediate action. You get anxious, feeling the need to do something . . . *anything!*

Actually, we're born with a feeling that we must "do something" when things are off center and need fixing, which seems to be the only constant in life. Call it the American way, the entrepreneurial spirit, the human condition. Deep in our souls each of us believes that by "doing something" we can fix the problem—even if it's the entire stock market.

KRISPY KREMES, QUICKIES, AND A RED-HOT MUSTANG

You know what I'm talking about: Something triggers "the urge," turns you on. You get excited. Suddenly being passive, doing nothing, just doesn't feel right. You have the urge to buy, sell, trade that hot stock—*you're itchin' for some action!*

It's much like that irresistible urge following the whiff of fresh Krispy Kreme doughnuts that's calling you, screaming: *Forget the diet!* Or some seductive music, the excitement of your sweetheart's scent, and a *let's-get-it-on* nod. Or any other "too-good-to-pass-up" offer to buy something you've always wanted, when a voice whispers: *Now, now! I gotta have it right now!*

That irresistible urge. And once again, your brain chemistry kicks into overdrive, overriding all that fail-safe rational long-term programming in your system, heading straight for immediate gratification, passing "go" like a rocket and into the action—for the doughnut. The quickie on the kitchen table. That superhot red Mustang.

VARROOOOOM! YOUR SUPERCHARGED BRAIN'S ROARING, RACING!

So what do you do? Logically, rationally, scientifically you know that lazy investing is the solution. For the average Joe and Jane Main Street know in their heart of hearts as well as their reasoning brains that a pure and simple diversified port-folio of passive index funds beats all that hyperactive jumping in and out of the market, and all the frantic efforts at picking the "right" stocks and sectors. Even know it's just a big waste of time and money.

But the truth is, the markets are not logical, or rational, or scientific. *And neither are our brains.* Emotions run the markets, emotions run our brains. Not logic. Not rationality. Not science.

So what do you do when you're itchin' for action? When you get a hot tip? When the market just keeps dropping? When you see yet another list of the "Ten Best Funds," and you don't have any of them . . . and you have a couple of funds that are losers . . . even though they were on somebody's "Ten Best" list last year (but you can't remember where you saw it)? What do you do?

Well, obviously the best solution is to get as lazy as possible and build one of the laziest portfolios I've already outlined. But that's not working in this scenario. *You're itching for action!*

HOT BRAINS, MAD MONEY, AND TWELVE STEPS TO FREEDOM

You need a contingency plan for when the urge hits and it's scrambling your brain. When you feel like another you is taking over and throwing caution to the wind. When you're convinced it's time to forget all this passive buy'n'hold talk, I've got a game plan for you—but it depends on whether it's a short-term urge or a chronic urge that's trying to sabotage you.

1. **Brain chemistry and brainstorms.** Find out what the new science of neuroeconomics is saying about how the stock market and the news media can control your brain chemistry and result in irrational, misleading, and costly investment decisions. Once you've learned about your brain reactions, I have some simple short-

term countermeasures that can offset the brain's going bonkers and making stupid moves.

2. **Create a mad-money portfolio using Vegas rules.** Yes, you can have your cake and eat it, too. You can create a passive buy'n'hold portfolio with index funds—and also keep a little mad-money portfolio on the side to satisfy that irresistible urge to play the market when "the urge" pops up unpredictably. But you will need some discipline, and I'll show you a simple rule to instill it and limit your bets.

So read on. I have a few ideas that'll get you thinking in advance about how to deal with your emotions when that urge to buy, sell, trade, or otherwise play the market takes over your brain.

Yes, there'll even be moments when the rational side of your brain knows the chances are pretty high that *any action* you take may make things worse because of your emotions—but you can't seem to stop yourself, it's as if you're possessed by an outside force. Trust me, you can still win, and I'll give you a few clues how.

If it's true that investing is so simple, then why do people wind up losing money on stocks, view the market as a major gamble, or feel too intimidated to invest in the first place? . . . Because every emotional drive associated with money gets played out in investing: The longing for security, the guilt engendered by greed, the quest for power and self-esteem, the fear of being abandoned, the search for love, the dream of omnipotence. And when these constellations of emotions intersect with the churning, manic depressive mood gyrations of the market itself, the result can be financially dangerous.

—John Schott, M.D., Mind Over Money

TWENTY-FOUR

Sssssizzle . . . Fizzzzzz . . . That's Your Brain Frying on a Hot Stock

WHEN YOU'RE ITCHIN' FOR ACTION, YOUR BRAIN CHEMISTRY IS KICKing into high gear, heating up, accelerating, short-circuiting, overriding all your rational, long-term planning—and going for immediate gratification. Gimme action! All you hear is: *Gotta have my Krispy Kreme . . . a quickie . . . that new hot red Mustang!*

Grandma was right: It really is "all in your head." Everything. In fact, teams of economists, psychologists, and physicians are today proving that she was right. *They're actually looking into our heads, watching our brain chemistry in action.*

They call this new science "neuroeconomics," a marriage of brain science and economics. Or more accurately, *the science of irrational investing.* There were less than fifty of these guys around for their first national conference held in 2002.

THEY'RE HOT STOCKS BECAUSE THEY'RE SIZZZLING!

Here's how *Wall Street Journal* columnist Sharon Begley described what these neuroeconomists "see" when they look in our heads. She covered their conference in a fascinating little article, "This Is Your Brain. This Is Your Brain on a Surging Stock." Listen:

> At a brain-imaging center in Massachusetts, a team of scientists that includes one of this year's Nobel laureates in economics makes functional magnetic resonance imaging scans of volunteers' brains. When people anticipate rewards, the fMRI shows, the circuits that switch on are the very ones that go wild when you anticipate a delectable chocolate truffle, sex or (in the case of addicts) cocaine.
>
> At a lab in Virginia researchers measure brain activity in subjects who cooperate to maximize gain. By comparing it with the activity in people who take the money and run—but wind up with less dough—the scientists are unearthing the neuronal basis for the fundamental trust that underlies financial transactions.

Although there are less than a hundred of these neuroeconomic scientists, the importance of their work is growing. As economist Paul Zak of Claremont Graduate School puts it: "To understand economic decisions, you need to understand the brain."

IS YOUR BRAIN WIRED FOR WEALTH? OR ARE THE WIRES CROSSED?

This new science of neuroeconomics is emerging in conjunction with behavioral finance, the psychology of financial decisions. *Money* magazine's Jason Zweig also wrote about the new science of neuroeconomics in "Are You Wired for

Wealth?" He believes brain chemistry research shows considerable promise in helping you, me, and the rest of America's investors understand:

> Why we chronically buy high and sell low, why "predictable" growth stocks sell at such high prices, why it's so hard to understand our own risk tolerance until we lose money, why we keep buying IPOs and "hot funds," despite all the evidence that we shouldn't, why stocks that miss earnings forecasts by a penny can lose billions of dollars in seconds.

The Journal elaborated on another specific example of the kind of findings emerging from this research—of what makes the brain itch for action:

> The brain seizes on even the slimmest evidence of pattern. After only a couple of repetitions of some event, the anterior cingulate begins to fire in anticipation of another: As a result, we're convinced that the stock that beat profit forecasts two quarters in a row will do it a third time.
>
> And if it doesn't? Then neurons in emotion-processing regions fire like crazy, generating a sense of anxiety and dread, researchers at Duke University report. Result: When a nice, reliable stock misses its earnings target by even a little, investors abandon ship in a fury. Often the longer a stock has held up, the worse the beating, because the longer a pattern has persisted, the more alarmed the brain gets when the pattern is broken.

Remember the 1990s? A perfect example of the pendulum swinging both ways! Hot stocks and funds with high multiples, increasing. The momentum pushing the price higher and higher into the stratosphere. Then the pattern breaks. Earnings drop. Multiples fall. Prices sink.

THE ULTIMATE DRUGSTORE PHARMACY—YES, IT'S YOUR BRAIN!

At the peak of the bull market one on-line broker's ad showed an obsessed investor so addicted to trading, so absorbed in his monitor, and so oblivious to the world around him that he wasn't even paying attention to a couple of fire-fighters handling a blaze behind him in his living room. And the brain reacts the same way to bear markets.

Norman Cousins, author of *Anatomy of an Illness,* often referred to the brain as a pharmacy, a chemist's shop, a natural manufacturer of drugs that affect our health and control our moods. Oh, how right he was.

In fact, anything can stimulate it into action—surges, dips, hot tips, economic reports, stock alerts, Fed meetings, you name it. The brain is a clever machine that often overrides common sense, good judgment, long experience, and even the facts when it's chasing a short-term thrill—like a hot stock.

YES, INDEXING WINS—BUT YOUR BRAIN LOVES THRILLS AND CHILLS!

So what should you do? My advice: Do nothing. Wait. Defer action. But not everyone can. Yes, many investors are naturally conservative. Their brains will trick them. They will stay focused on their long-range strategy, no matter what kind of exciting hot tips they hear on CNBC or from their broker.

But many other investors are naturally addicted to the thrills and excitements of the marketplace—their brain's chemistry will flood itself with the addictive neurochemical dopamine, feeding on ever-higher doses, triggering irrational behavior, and eventually sabotaging itself. Begley hints at why the name *dopamine* accurately fits the drug—because it makes people act like dopes:

We get a dopamine surge when we anticipate a nice, healthy 4% return on a money-market fund. But dopamine neurons get extra juiced when a long shot comes in—and the addictive nature of dopamine makes us willing to take financial risks for those long shots. *We whip out our checkbooks for managed mutual funds even though, historically, few beat the indexes.*

Did you hear that? Right out of *The Journal:* Our brains' natural chemistry is one of the main reasons we make the mistake of chasing actively managed mutual funds—even though all the evidence proves they rarely beat index funds!

DOPAMINE IS MAKING DOPES OUT OF EVERYBODY!

But why? Because once the dopamine takes over, surging through the system, common sense and logic go out the window and the brain starts making irrational decisions, and mistakes, often big ones.

And behavioral finance experts add that emotionally charged investors riding a high on dopamine believe action is necessary to relieve their anxieties . . . so they seize control . . . get into action . . . start "doing something" for the sake of proving they are in control . . . anything to chase the thrill. No wonder we make big mistakes.

Studies by Morningstar and others prove that market anxieties make investors buy at market peaks. They are anxious because they missed the run-up, and fear they'll miss the next big run-up. Then later, feeling stupid, they jump in at the bottom and sell when their fears turn to panic. So they lose by buying in at the top. And they lose *again* at the bottom. Bigger mistake.

YOU NEED A BIG DOSE OF POSITIVE MENTAL ATTITUDE—GET ONE!

Here's one of the best ways to keep your emotions from sabotaging your portfolio and your life. Pick up a book and meditate—*any book!* Read from a book of affirmations, or the Bible. Anything filled with a positive mental attitude and inspiration. Or just pick up a good novel and go to the back porch and read.

Yes, you do need a dose of positive thinking. I'm reminded of Chuck Salter's *Fast Company* article on survival in which a Special Forces instructor with twenty-six years' service said: "If you have a guy with all the survival training in the world who has a negative attitude and a guy who doesn't have a clue but has a positive attitude, I guarantee you that the guy with a positive attitude is coming out of the woods alive. Simple as that." The same applies here.

You can overcome the anxieties and fears in your brain. You can survive and win with PMA—a "positive mental attitude," as Napoleon Hill called it a long time ago in a financial and business context. Believe you will win and you will, even if you don't have a clue about the market, the economy, or the inside tricks of professional traders. PMA creates winners.

DRIVE YOURSELF TO DISTRACTION—AT YOUR FAVORITE BOOKSTORE

Here's another trick you can use when the itch acts up—turn off your computer, get in the car, drive to your favorite bookstore, and cool down. Go and browse. Have a latte and muffin. Distract yourself—and *avoid making decisions.* Just getting out of the house is a perfect avoidance strategy, a way to turn off your brain's chemistry set and dilute the dopamine flooding your brain.

Read a book on gardening or golf. Or leaf through *Archi-*

tectural Digest, Scientific American, or some other magazines you'd normally pass by. Or calm yourself with a book on rational investing, like Thomas Stanley's *The Millionaire Mind* or Ric Edelman's *Ordinary People, Extraordinary Wealth.* Or just grab *anything* close at hand and start reading.

Too simple? Nope. One nice thing about books is that they'll divert you from the kind of self-destructive knee-jerk reactions so many of us have when, for example, the panic sets in while we're reading some hot news in a daily newspaper or watching bad news on CNBC, Fox, CNN, or MSNBC (just turning off the tube should help).

Alternatively, if you can't stop, exercise, sweat, hike, swim, shoot hoops, wear yourself (and your brain) out physically.

WHEN ALL ELSE FAILS, SAY A LITTLE PRAYER— IT WORKS FOR THE WEALTHY

If the itchin' continues, say a prayer before you act. It worked for Andrew Carnegie, Henry Ford, Thomas Edison, and the other five hundred captains of American industry and finance that Napoleon Hill spent a lifetime studying for his books like *Think & Grow Rich, Success Through a Positive Mental Attitude,* and *The Science of Success.*

And it worked for Sir John Marks Templeton, founder of Templeton Funds and a very rich man. Maybe it'll work for you. Here's Templeton's key principle of investing: "If you begin with prayer, you will think more clearly and make fewer mistakes." And that's your goal—fewer mistakes. So try praying when nothing else works. You got nothing to lose and everything to gain.

Whatever you do, remember that when it comes to the stock market, your brain chemistry is not your friend—but you can do something about it. When it turns you on—*do something, do anything to distract yourself until the brain chemistry cools down.* Don't let your "dopey" mind take over and force you to react to external events in the market and the economy. Become a truly lazy investor.

The best thing, really, for an investor to do is buy a good company and hold it. Trading often and heavy is not something that makes you a lot of money. That's contrary to my own interests, but it is the truth.

—Joe Ricketts, chairman and founder, Ameritrade discount brokers

TWENTY-FIVE

Plan B: How Investors Learn to Live with Two Brains and a Split Personality

You Need Dual Portfolios: Untouchables Plus Mad Money

BUY'N'HOLD GOOD. MARKET TIMING BAD. FOR A LONG TIME I HELD tenaciously and dogmatically to that non-negotiable position. *Buy'n'hold good, market timing bad.* But is that right?

Well, maybe not. Maybe a bit too rigid. Why? Stick with me on this one, because I got this bright idea after exposure to the esoteric worlds of neuroeconomics and behavioral finance—and a dentist's office. Yes, a dentist.

Psychologically speaking, humans don't have "one brain," we actually have many "brains." And not just the often-mentioned left-brain/right-brain hemispheric split—*that is, left logical, right creative.* Our brains are more like computers; we all tend to compartmentalize our minds into separate brains, like multiple hard drives, partitioning off sections that rarely bother to tell each other what they are doing.

IF YOU HAVE TWO BRAINS—YOU MAY NEED TWO PORTFOLIOS!

Actually it's like having a split personality, or even multiple personalities. In a strict psychological sense, however, these terms connote pathologies, something "bad." However, I'm using the terms more in the layperson's vernacular, to describe the way almost all of us humans divide up our brains to cope with today's overload of information, along with a need to present different identities to different groups—at work and at home, for example.

The idea first came to me when *Fortune* profiled a dentist a few years ago in a story about the new on-line brokers and traders. Between patients this doctor would disappear into his "Pentagon war room," armed with three PCs, eight monitors (two locked on CNBC and MSNBC), plus tons of high-tech support equipment, where he was making two hundred trades a month! That was his "mad money" (trading accounts)—roughly $100,000, or about 10 percent of his portfolio.

Now get this: The doc was a savvy, disciplined combination investor-trader. Because he also kept 90 percent of his money earmarked "untouchable," locked up in solid stocks and funds, isolated from his high-risk trading, and under his broker's control. He stopped trading much once the bear market was in full swing, but the idea of a two-portfolio strategy got me thinking.

SCHWAB RESEARCH UNCOVERS SCIENTIFIC BASIS FOR DUAL PORTFOLIOS

This idea about how the two brains of a human adapt and work together to create two separate portfolios gained considerable scientific authenticity during an interview I did about the same time a few years ago with Schwab's chief investment strategist, Daniel Leemon. Here's what he told me:

> I remember one of the first focus groups I sat in on and listened to when I came to Schwab: They were supposed to be mutual fund investors. You know, conservative, buy'n'hold, mutual fund investors under age forty. But when the moderator started asking them about investing, after listening to the first twenty minutes of the discussion, you would have thought these were momentum, high-tech day traders!

So I asked him, "Do you mean all those buy'n'hold investors were acting just like day traders?" Leemon agreed:

> Yes, they all had 90 percent of their money in mutual funds. They put a little bit in every month. And they *never thought about that 90 percent and never looked at it.* But with the other 10 percent, they were playing high-tech stocks, and that was the stuff they talked about because that was the fun part!

Get it? "The stuff they talked about," the exciting stuff that they could gab about at the watercooler in the office. Over cocktails. At parties. With buddies at lunch: "That was the fun part," *the stuff that made them feel alive!*

True, the bear market has slowed most of them down, temporarily. But realistically, we know the itching remains in many investors, ready to spring into action given the first bullish opportunity. So the idea of dual portfolios has become a practical way to protect your retirement nest egg while having a little trading fun along the way—even if it's expensive entertainment.

INDEX FUNDS TOO DARN BORING FOR CNBC, FOX, AND CNN

Now get this—we rarely talk much about the other 90 percent of the "stuff"—that boring, plain-vanilla 90 percent. Why? Well . . . because it is boring. It just sits there year after year after year. Gathering dust (and money). Making a mere 8 percent, 10 percent, maybe even 12 percent some years. Like Vanguard's original S&P 500 index fund that's made over 2,000 percent since its launch in 1976.

But who cares? It's just not exciting. Let's face it, folks, Vanguard is downright boring, like a slide show of Uncle Joe's latest fishing trip. As Gary Gensler and Gregory Baer said in *The Great Mutual Fund Trap:*

> Asset allocation is boring. Diversification is boring. Index fund managers are the earth's most boring guests. So you don't often hear about these things in the media—it doesn't make for good reading or viewing!

Nor is there anything to brag about when you need to show off for clients and coworkers, or when you want to brag about how you're beating the market at a neighborhood barbecue. Certainly nothing exciting like the blow-by-blow contests reporting the latest hot stocks on CNBC. Boring is boring. We don't even talk about it in our sleep.

SSSSH—ACTIVE TRADERS HAVE SECRET UNTOUCHABLE PORTFOLIOS

In a *Forbes* article on trading, some of the top professional money managers were asked where they invested their own cash. All were surprisingly conservative. In fact, we saw some of the strongest endorsements of buy'n'hold strategy from these well-known leaders in the hot-and-heavy trading world:

1. **Jack Schwager,** author of *The New Market Wizards.* Here's one of America's leading money managers admitting to the world that "I tend to be sloppy with my own investment portfolio. Frankly, I think dollar cost averaging is the best way to change my ways."

2. **Dan Tully,** former Merrill Lynch CEO. "I'm not smart enough to know the top or the bottom of the market. People who have tried to pick the last year, five years, even ten years, have all missed one of the greatest markets in history. I'm conservative, rely on dollar cost averaging and use a long-term disciplined approach."

3. **Jonathan Hoening,** author of *Greed Is Good: The Capitalist Pig Guide to Investing.* Today he's a high-risk hedge fund manager. When he was working as a high-stress futures trader in the Chicago pits at the peak of the 1990s go-go bull, he told *Kiplinger's* that his "own portfolio is about 40% bonds because he figures that a 6% bond backed by the U.S. government with inflation under 3% is a pretty good return."

Six percent is a "pretty good return"? And acceptable to a "capitalist pig"? Yes! And that was at the peak days of the insane dot.com market.

That's hardly what you'd think of as a "greedy pig" investment strategy! And yet Hoening's remarks are to me proof positive that all mere mortals operate with split brains, because trading Treasury futures all day in the Chicago pits is worlds apart from holding boring Treasury bonds to maturity.

Of course, the split-brain concept also makes sense when you recall Chuck Carlson's simple strategy in *Eight $teps to $even Figures:* "You get rich in stocks, and stay rich in bonds."

TWO-PORTFOLIO STRATEGY FITS SPLIT-PERSONALITY INVESTING

Simply stated, here's how a two-portfolio strategy works for street-smart investors who just cannot yet comprehend the simple wisdom of passive index investing.

You start by simply partitioning your brain—*and your portfolio*—into two parts that don't even have to talk to each other, and let each one of them invest using two totally different sets of investment criteria. You might want to distinguish them as rational and irrational, or more kindly by their risk profiles or, as I call them, untouchable and mad money.

Brain #1 (90%) invests your untouchable portfolio.
This part of your investment portfolio is treated as if it's locked up in a bank vault, compounding for retirement or some other long-term goal. And untouchable. You can't touch it! You should even require two signatures, yours and that of a very conservative investment adviser. That way, the 90 percent is protected from aggressive risk taking and invested in relatively conservative securities (like Hoening's 6 percent bond funds!).
Brain #2 (10%) invests your mad-money portfolio.
This money is for risky, aggressive, short-term day trading, for taking chances on high fliers, investing in emerging markets and new issues. This is money you can afford to lose if your bets go sour, so it may also be tapped into for some fun weekends in Vegas or buying lottery tickets.

Another important criterion with this mad-money portfolio: Your total bets rarely exceed 10 percent of your mad-money assets at any one time. The winnings you can brag about at cocktail parties, and the losses you quietly write off on your tax returns.

TRADING WON'T MAKE YOU MONEY, BUT IT'S FUN, LIKE VEGAS

As Joe Ricketts, chairman and founder of Ameritrade, admitted to *Fortune*, "The best thing, really, for an investor to do is buy a good company and hold it. Trading often and heavy is not something that makes you a lot of money. That's contrary to my own interests, but it is the truth."

Still, Ricketts's warning sure didn't keep investors away—tens of thousands of investors still believe they can beat the market. And the fact that Ameritrade still has a market cap of more than $3 billion is even more evidence of the human need to function with two brains.

The reason I've made a big issue about this need to create two portfolios is just my commonsense observations of people. Advocating buy'n'hold to the absolute total exclusion of active trading is like insisting people can't get married unless they're virgins—too rigid. You gotta allow for the exceptions to the rule, because that's human nature.

SURRENDER TO THE TRUTH— YOU ALREADY HAVE TWO SEPARATE BRAINS

Of course I still believe that most investors just do not have the time or inclination to stay abreast of the stock market—and even if they did, transaction costs would still eat up their gains—so a buy'n'hold strategy works for them.

But on the other hand, the new field of behavioral finance clearly shows that investors actually do make investment decisions as if they have two separate brains that think totally differently and may not even communicate with each other.

We pretend we believe in Wall Street's time-honored "rational investor" theory, then go on our merry way led by our other brain, the split brain, the irrational side of our personality. The "rational investor" is a joke, a disguise, because nobody wants to admit how totally irrational investing really is.

OKAY, YOU'VE GOT TWO BRAINS—USE A TWO-PORTFOLIO STRATEGY!

So I decided that it's best to accept this reality and develop at least one investment strategy that supports this split-brain reality, which is, in simple terms:

1. **Untouchable portfolio.** At a minimum, 90 percent is allocated for the low-risk, superconservative, rational, long-haul, retirement-thinking brain.
2. **Mad-money portfolio.** And the other 10 percent of your assets is specifically allocated for the hyperactive, high-risk, short-term-thinking brain, the fun-loving social animal with strong ego needs.

Just make darn sure you keep the two brains, the two personalities, the two portfolios, *very, very separate.*

VEGAS RULES, SET LIMITS—YOU LOSE, YOU STOP, PERIOD

Remember, this strategy will work as long as you're hard-ass about the asset split: One brain gets its protected 90 percent share, and the other only gets its 10 percent—*and you follow the ground rules with no exceptions. That is, if you lose your mad money, you stop, period.* And the mad one never gets to "steal" from the untouchable bank.

Play the two-portfolio strategy game by the rules, and both brains are likely to be happy with the arrangement. One brain is protected and safe. The other can play and have all the fun it wants with the separate mad-money portfolio (aware of the fact that it's okay to lose the money, since eventually you will lose some or all of your mad money). But you can never go back and touch your untouchable portfolio. Never. That's your protected retirement nest egg.

NEW SELF-DISCIPLINE PROTECTS "YOU" FROM THE "OTHER YOU"

And hopefully sooner rather than later, you'll finally discover for yourself how much money you're losing in the mad-money portfolio, and create a 100 percent untouchable portfolio of passive index funds!

In the end, however, it's very important to understand that a two-brain strategy *is not a real "lazy portfolio"—there's far too much trading involved.*

It is also important to understand that higher transaction and other costs will result in mad-money losses over time, as I discussed in the earlier chapters. Nevertheless, if you just cannot give up the itch to trade, then splitting your money into two portfolios will provide needed self-discipline—and that's why I've emphasized it here.

THE HOME STRETCH

Rounding the Final Turn
Heading for the Finish Line
and the Winner's Circle—
Tortoise Leads

Awaken the sleeping giant within you!

How? Think. Think with a positive mental attitude.

The starting point of all achievement is

definiteness of purpose with

a positive mental attitude.

—Napoleon Hill and W. Clement Stone,

Success Through a Positive Mental Attitude

EPILOGUE

The Ultimate Secret of Success for Millionaires and Lazy Investors

HOW ABOUT IT—DID YOU ENJOY A CUP OF YOUR FAVORITE COFFEE and a bagel, maybe tea and a muffin? Either way, I trust you had a chance to relax in a comfortable chair for a while, glance up at the sky, maybe listen to some music, and enjoy the day. That's also what lazy portfolios are designed to do— help make your financial life easier while you go about your day, doing what's really important.

Investing really is very simple stuff. You can do it yourself. If you've come this far with me, you now know all that you'll ever need to know about successful investing. Lazy portfolios are keep-it-simple, no-hassle, low-stress, time-saving, low-maintenance portfolios that work in the background on autopilot so you can get on with the business of everyday life.

THE REAL GOALS OF INVESTING (AND LIFE) AREN'T THINGS

Remember, the goal of investing isn't about collecting lots of tangible assets, stocks, bonds, cash, real estate, bank deposits, and other "things." For most of us investing is really about hard-to-describe intangibles—peace of mind, financial freedom, independence, and a whole bunch of other mushy stuff like smiles, hugs, kids, laughter, playing, an affectionate touch, music, love, and spirit.

When it's all working in harmony, something special happens, a magic that makes life truly worthwhile—that's a state of mind we call positive mental attitude, the secret energy in a lazy portfolio, the frosting on the cake.

LIVING WITH A POSITIVE MENTAL ATTITUDE, ONE DAY AT A TIME

True wealth is a state of mind. So is happiness. Actually, you'd have to say that *everything in life is a state of mind.* Grumpy people see a dark cloud over even the best of opportunities. And optimists invariably look for rainbows on the horizon, insisting that it's always darkest before dawn!

When I waver, my wife reminds me of her little story about two kids visiting a farm for the first time. When they go into the barn, one can't take the smell, starts complaining, and walks out. The other sees the manure pile and her eyes light up. She grabs a shovel and screams, "Oh wow! There's gotta be a pony in here somewhere," as she begins digging feverishly. And gets me digging, too, looking for the pony, the rainbow, the brighter side of life!

THE SECRET OF MILLIONAIRES, SURVIVORS, AND THE CLUELESS

Yes, winning, wealth, and everything else in life is a state of mind. We first learned about the power of our mental attitude years ago from Napoleon Hill's *Think & Grow Rich,* later reemphasized in his classic work coauthored with Clement Stone:

> After years spent studying successful men, the authors of *Success Through a Positive Mental Attitude* have come to the conclusion that a positive mental attitude is the one simple secret shared by them all.

The power of a positive mental attitude, *in bear markets as well as bull,* was driven home to me in an unusual way by a Special Forces instructor teaching survival skills. He told *FastCompany* magazine:

> If you have a guy with all the survival training in the world who has a negative attitude and a guy who doesn't have a clue but has a positive attitude, I guarantee you that the guy with a positive attitude is coming out of the woods alive. Simple as that.

The same applies in investing and wealth. There's no big mystery. The clueless one *(the laziest investor!)* with a positive mental attitude will win the money game. Chuck Carlson, the king of no-load stocks and a triathlete, echoes the message in *Eight $teps to $even Figures:* "Don't forget that most millionaires are often just like you . . . clueless when they started investing."

The truth is, success in virtually every area of life is that simple: Walk into any bookstore and you'll see many variations on the same simple message written over and over again in every nook and cranny and shelf—whether you're dealing with wealth, happiness, success, career, family, relationships, children, health, survival, investing, everything—*success is a state of mind.*

LAZY INVESTORS BECOME MILLIONAIRES USING PMA

And that's why *anyone* can become a millionaire, in spirit and in fact, when you have a positive mental attitude. The key is to live like a millionaire every step of the way *until you get there.*

As Napoleon Hill tells us over and over in *Think & Grow Rich,* "Whatever the mind can conceive and believe, it can achieve." Live with the spirit, the mind-set of a millionaire, until it's a fact. Quietly become what I call a "millionaire-in-training."

This reality came to me years ago from a wonderful teacher and mentor, Joseph Campbell, the man Bill Moyers made popular in their KCET series *The Power of Myth.* In one simple passage Campbell succinctly expresses the perfect state of mind of a millionaire-in-training:

> My life course is totally indifferent to money. As a result a lot of money has come in by doing what I feel I want to do from the inside. If you do that, you are doing things that attract money, because you are giving life and life responds in the way of its counterpart in hard coin. If you follow your bliss, you will always have your bliss, money or not. If you follow money, you may lose it, and you will have nothing.

This message is perhaps the single most important fact of life. You, too, can think and grow rich and become successful—*if you have a positive mental attitude!* And even if you don't become as rich as Buffett and Gates, you will be rich in spirit every step along the way.

MILLIONAIRE'S MIND-SET—POSITIVE MENTAL ATTITUDE TODAY

From the first dollar you invest at any age, you know that being a millionaire is more a mind-set than a bank account. Get into action: "Invest" your time and energy studying in this library. Then "spend" a lifetime making your dreams a reality—by living with a millionaire's mind-set!

Keep it simple, very simple.

Lazy investing works.

You deserve to enjoy what's really important in your life—today and every day! Lazy investing sets you free to live the dream, your dream, out there in the real world, where the best is yet to come!

The Complete Library for America's Laziest Investors

ALL OF THESE BOOKS HAVE A COMMON THEME—*HOW TO THINK LIKE a millionaire, today and every day, while you're slowly building that million-dollar nest egg*. Read them. Download this new positive mental attitude into your brain. Get the message and live by it every day for the rest of your life.

■ **The Four Pillars of Investing,** *William Bernstein*
"Since you cannot successfully time the market or select individual stocks," says Bernstein, "asset allocation should be the major focus of your investment strategy, because it is the only thing you can control." You "control" your risks by buying the whole market—by indexing. There's lots more of his work on his Web site, EfficientFrontier.com, in *SmartMoney* magazine, and in his book *The Intelligent Asset Allocator*.

■ **The Coffeehouse Investor,** *Bill Schultheis*

Here's our former Salomon Smith Barney broker turned financial adviser outlining the basics of successful investing. It's too darn simple. Bill narrows investing down to just three basic principles in building a successful portfolio: Save, diversify, and index. Do that and you'll come out a winner. Also check out Bill's Web site at CoffeehouseInvestor.com.

■ **It's Only Money,** *Scott Burns*

Burns has an incredible wealth of information on-line at DallasNews.com—probably enough for ten books. Log on to Burns's "It's Only Money" column and find out why he has such a huge national following. Most especially, check out all of his columns on the Couch Potato Portfolio's success over the years.

■ **FundAdvice.com,** *Paul Merriman*

Forbes magazine called Merriman's FundAdvice.com, the challenger among our laziest portfolios, one of "The Best of the Web" during the tough bear-market years from 2000 through 2002. The reason: lots of great educational content, plus model portfolios that work for conservative and aggressive investors.

The Brilliant Mind of the American Millionaire

■ **Ordinary People, Extraordinary Wealth,** *Ric Edelman*

Edelman discovered from interviews with five thousand millionaires that "they devote less than three hours a month to their personal finances. . . . You're not in a horse race, you're playing horseshoes. Therefore, you don't need to pick the winner . . . merely being close is good enough to win." Also see Edelman's other books, *The Truth About Money* and *Discover the Wealth Within You.*

■ Eight $teps to $even Figures, *Charles Carlson*

"Start Saving Now. . . . It's the most important of all. You can't get to the other seven steps without starting. Oftentimes it is the most difficult step. You may have to break old habits and start new ones. . . . Buy and hold . . . and hold . . . and hold . . . and hold . . . and hold. Millionaire investors never sell . . . buying and holding stocks makes you rich. . . . Buy with the idea that you cannot sell."

■ The Millionaire Mind, *Thomas Stanley*

"What do most millionaires tell me they learned? . . . They learned to: Think differently from the crowd. Much of this book has been designed around a central theme: It pays to be different." And one way to be very different is to master living like a millionaire *before* you have a million bucks, with the millionaire's mind-set that Stanley has captured so well.

■ The Millionaire Next Door, *Thomas Stanley and William Danko*

"Most people have it all wrong about wealth in America. Wealth is not the same as income. If you make a good income each year and spend it all, you are not getting wealthier. You are living high. Wealth is what you accumulate, not what you spend. . . . Wealth is more often the result of a lifestyle of hard work, perseverance, planning, and most of all, self-discipline."

■ Getting Rich in America, *Dwight Lee and Richard McKenzie*

"All you have to do is recognize the opportunities that abound around you and work to seize a share of those opportunities; develop a long-term perspective; work and study hard; be reasonably frugal and judicious in your purchases; get married and stay married; take care of yourself; accept prudent risks and invest wisely—but above all, be patient."

■ Millionaire, *Wayne Wagner and Al Winnikoff*

Note the subtitle: "The best explanation of how an index fund can turn your lunch money into a fortune." Wayne and Al offer a simple twelve-step program to get you to your million bucks, beginning with: "Buy solid investments in good index funds . . . steady, consistent, regular, and planned purchases in a slice of America are what will make you rich." Short, simple, and a quick read.

■ Retire Young, Retire Rich, *Robert Kiyosaki*

America has only 7 million millionaires among 283 million people. But they own more than 90 percent of America's wealth. If you sincerely want to retire young and rich, says the popular author of the *Rich Dad, Poor Dad* series, you must leverage other people's money: "Leverage simply means the ability to do more with less"—such as borrowing a million bucks to create net worth by building businesses and developing real estate.

Simple Secrets of America's Financial Giants

■ The Warren Buffett Way, *Robert Hagstrom*

A billionaire many times over because he discovered the simple magic of compounding. It's not much more complicated than that. And read Hagstrom's other books on the Sage of Omaha, including *The Warren Buffett Portfolio* and *The Essential Buffett.* Also, for a quick injection of Buffett's wisdom, get a copy of Simon Reynolds's *Thoughts of Chairman Buffett.*

■ Take on the Street, *Arthur Levitt*

Former Securities and Exchange chairman Levitt was one of the greatest friends the individual investor ever had, and fortunately he continues to advocate reform. Read especially his chapter "Seven Deadly Sins of Mutual Funds" for a real eye-opener on how funds are secretly taking advantage of investors. Disclosure is a big issue: "They don't want you to know a lot about what goes on behind the curtain at fund headquarters," because it will shock and anger you.

■ **Bogle on Mutual Funds,** *John Bogle*

Bogle tells us that this earlier book is the best description of his investment strategy. I say read them all, especially *Character Counts,* if you want to understand the Vanguard phenomenon and how its mutual ownership structure and low-cost indexing strategy have become the individual investor's best allies—and a huge thorn in the side of Wall Street and the rest of the fund industry, by challenging their ethical compromises.

■ **A Random Walk Down Wall Street,** *Burton Malkiel*

"Many people say that the individual investor has scarcely a chance today against Wall Street's pros," says Malkiel, a former Amex governor. "Nothing could be further from the truth. You can do it as well as the experts, perhaps even better. . . . The point is rather that a simple 'buy-and-hold' strategy (that is, buying a stock or group of stocks and holding on to them for a long period of time) typically makes as much or more money."

■ **How to Be Your Own Stockbroker,** *Charles Schwab*

This is my favorite Chuck Schwab book, an earlier one he wrote back in the mid-1980s in which he bluntly tells investors to "take all advice with a grain of salt. In the final analysis, if you're going to be an independent investor, the decision is yours." You are responsible. Also check out some of his more recent books: *You're Fifty, Now What?* and *Charles Schwab's Guide to Financial Independence: Simple Solutions for Busy People.*

■ **One Up on Wall Street,** *Peter Lynch*

Winners instinctively know what he means: "Rule number one, in my book, is: Stop listening to professionals. Twenty years in this business convinces me that any normal person using the customary 3 percent of the brain can pick stocks just as well, if not better, than the average Wall Street expert. . . . Think like an amateur. If you invest like an institution, you're doomed to perform like one, which in most cases isn't very well. If you're a surfer, a truck driver, a high school dropout, or an eccentric retiree, then you've got an edge already."

■ The Great Mutual Fund Trap, *Gary Gensler and Gregory Baer*

Investors are "trapped into believing that 'experts' can help you beat the market, whether actively-managed mutual funds or great stock-picking fund managers." Unfortunately, say Gensler and Baer, two former senior officers in the U.S. Treasury Department, every method used to pick winners has failed to beat the market. Indexing is the best solution for today's investors.

Planning Gurus Love Do-It-Yourself Investing

■ Get a Life: You Don't Need a Million to Retire Well, *Ralph Warner*

The message is loud and clear: "Instead of focusing almost exclusively on our finances, we should be thinking about the things that truly make a difference in our later years," says Warner, "our health, spiritual life, relationships with family and friends, and having a plate full of interesting things to do." Yes, there really are more important things in life than your portfolio.

■ The 9 Steps to Financial Freedom, *Suze Orman*

Trust yourself: "Whether you want to believe it or not— you and you alone have the best judgment when it comes to your money. You must do what makes you feel safe, sound, comfortable. You must trust yourself more than you trust others, and that inner voice will tell you when it is time to take action. You have more than it takes to manage your money on your own."

■ Making the Most of Your Money, *Jane Bryant Quinn*

Here's one of America's true classics. "Be your own guru," says Quinn; "most of us don't need professional planners."

Get it in your reference library, as a reminder that you can take charge of your own financial life: "Don't put off decisions for fear you're not making the best choice in every circumstance. Often, there isn't a 'best' choice. Any one of several will work."

Wealth Building and the Psychology of Money

■ Do What You Love, the Money Will Follow, *Marsha Sinetar*

Here's an easy read to start. "The individual usually will not identify what he really wants because he is aiming for what he thinks is possible, rather than what he genuinely desires. Thus, he limits his goal-setting. If he wants to be a contractor, let's say, he may feel he cannot achieve that goal, and will settle for being a carpenter instead." Never settle; do what you really love, starting now!

■ Don't Worry, Make Money, *Richard Carlson*

"Wealth consciousness suggests a complete absence of money worries: an awareness that there is always plenty of money to go around," says Dr. Carlson. "People who live with true abundance never worry about having enough, they know creating wealth and affluence is a function of their own mind-set."

■ Money and the Meaning of Life, *Jacob Needleman*

"In our time and culture, the battlefield of life is money. Instead of horses and chariots, guns and fortresses, there are banks, checkbooks, credit cards, mortgages, salaries, the IRS. But," Professor Needleman says, "the inner enemies remain the same now as they were in ancient India or feudal Japan: fear, self-deception, vanity, egoism, wishful thinking, tension, and violence." And unless you confront and understand them, they will sabotage your investing, and your life.

■ Investment Madness, *John Nofsinger*

Here's a keep-it-simple review of our mental saboteurs. Every investor in America should know them. They expose your issues with money. Dr. Nofsinger says the biggest one that gets in the way of our success is overconfidence. We want to prove something, so we trade too much, paying high commissions and taxes. Believing we have the ability to beat the market, we take big risks, incur big losses, then deny what's going on.

■ Mind Over Money, *John Schott, M.D.*

People regularly lose money in the market, "because every emotional drive associated with money gets played out in investing," says Dr. Schott. "And when these constellations of emotions intersect with the churning, manic mood gyrations of the market itself, the result can be financially dangerous." Fortunately there are ways to deal with emotions successfully.

■ Success Through a Positive Mental Attitude, *Napoleon Hill and W. Clement Stone*

In the final analysis, it always comes down to this—a positive mental attitude wins the game. Billionaire Andrew Carnegie taught young Napoleon Hill his famous "Science of Success," which was published as Hill's classic, *Think & Grow Rich.* Later Hill and W. Clement Stone coauthored *Success Through a Positive Mental Attitude,* urging us to "awaken the sleeping giant within you! How? Think. Think with a positive mental attitude. The starting point of all achievement is definiteness of purpose with positive mental attitude."

Index

About the Author

PAUL B. FARRELL, J.D., PH.D., IS A PERSONAL FINANCE AND INVEST-
ing columnist for CBS.MarketWatch.com. He is the author of
five books on investing, including *The Millionaire Code, The
Winning Portfolio,* and *Mutual Funds on the Net.*

Previously, Dr. Farrell was an investment banker with Morgan Stanley. He was also an executive vice president of the
Financial News Network, where he was in charge of producing
a thousand hours of live cable news; executive vice president
of Mercury Entertainment Corporation, a publicly held film
producer; and the associate editor of the *Los Angeles Herald
Examiner.*

Dr. Farrell has four degrees: Juris Doctor, master's in
regional planning, bachelor of architecture, and a doctorate
in psychology. He served in Korea with the United States
Marine Corps, as a staff sergeant and aviation radar-computer
technician. Today, Dr. Farrell lives on the Central Coast of California with his wife, Dorothy Boyce, a psychotherapist.